GRIDLOCK

RANDAL O'TOOLE

GRIDLOCK

WHY WE'RE STUCK IN TRAFFIC
AND WHAT TO DO ABOUT IT

CATO INSTITUTE
WASHINGTON, D.C.

Library of Congress Cataloging-in-Publication Data

O'Toole, Randall.
    Gridlock! : why we are stuck in traffic and what to do about it /
    Randall O'Toole.
        p. cm.
    Includes bibliographical references and index.
    ISBN 978-1-935308-23-2 (hardback: alk. paper)   1. Transportation—
United States.   2. Transportation and state—United States.
3. Automobile driving—Social aspects—United
States.   4. Transportation—Planning.   5. Traffic congestion—United
States.   I. Title.

    HE203.086 2010
    388.0973--dc22

                                                                    2009042023

Cover design by Jon Meyers.

Printed in the United States of America.

                          CATO INSTITUTE
                1000 Massachusetts Ave., N.W.
                     Washington, D.C. 20001
                          www.cato.org

Contents

Introduction

In 1811, the state of New York laid out much of Manhattan on a grid, with most streets meeting at right angles and blocks as narrow as 200 feet. One hundred and sixty years later, this grid became a source of apprehension among the city's traffic managers. Too many auto drivers ran yellow lights, only to block intersections because of standing or slow-moving vehicles in the next block. If enough drivers blocked cross traffic at enough intersections, traffic managers realized they could end up with a situation in which no one could move. Two city engineers, Sam Schwartz and Roy Cottam, called this fearsome possibility "gridlock."[1]

Urban freeways are very different from city street grids. Because freeways do not form a grid and lack intersections to block, by definition they cannot become gridlocked. Even so, the term gridlock is now commonly applied to all serious traffic congestion. The technical term for such traffic is "level of service F," with F clearly representing "flunk."[2]

Millions of commuters and other travelers suffer level of service F every weekday. According to the Texas Transportation Institute, congestion in American cities wasted 4.2 billion hours in 2007.[3] This figure is nearly five times as much as 25 years before.[4] The institute's numbers focus on commuters and don't even count the costs to businesses, such as the cost of operating more trucks to deliver products in congested areas than would be needed if roads were not congested.

Why do we put up with this? If our cell phones refused to put calls through because the network was busy, we would change carriers. If our high-speed internet service stopped working because too many other customers were using it, we would change internet providers.

One reason we accept congestion on highways is that the government has a monopoly on roads: we can't simply decide to use another highway provider's roads. Some of us can decide to ride transit instead of drive, but the government has a monopoly on most transit as well. Partly because of that monopoly, transit for most people simply does not work as well as driving, even on roads at level of service F.

Fifty years ago, Americans boasted of having "the best transportation system in the world."[5] Today, that system is breaking down. Average urban traffic speeds began declining in 1995 for the first time in our history.[6] Bridge collapses and closures generate worries about deteriorating infrastructure. The last real revolutions in transportation technologies—superhighways and jet aircraft—are more than 50 years old. Transportation funding is increasingly politicized, wasting tens of billions of dollars each year on highly visible but little-needed projects. All these problems are exacerbated by a powerful anti-mobility coalition that blames modern transportation for numerous social ills that can allegedly be cured only by reducing personal travel.

Planners and policy analysts have offered many proposals for dealing with this growing congestion: light rail, congestion pricing, compact cities, high-occupancy/toll lanes, high-speed rail, traffic signal coordination, and intelligent highways and vehicles, among others. Some of these proposals will do better than others at relieving congestion, and *Gridlock* will suggest how we can determine which work best.

The real problem, however, is not technical but institutional. The federal, state, and local government agencies that build and operate our transportation systems have become masters at spending large amounts of money. Yet when addressing problems like congestion, pollution, and safety, they are almost totally dysfunctional. In some cases, Congress has given the agencies so many different and conflicting goals that the simple idea of safe, efficient transportation is almost forgotten. In other cases, the agencies themselves have given up on fixing congestion or even decided that they want more congestion, and they are willfully increasing it in the name of a vague goal they call "livability."

Congestion is really just a symptom of this dysfunctional system. So *Gridlock*'s main focus will be on institutional questions. How did transportation agencies change from ones trying to relieve congestion to ones accepting or even promoting congestion? How valid is their view and how much is simply a result of perverse incentives designed into their budgets? How do we change them back? Should we try to reform the agencies or completely abolish them?

If I bring a prejudice to these questions, it is that transportation decisions are best made by individuals who pay the full costs of their choices—a prejudice justified by both theory and experience. My personal transportation preferences are for cycling and trains, but—unlike some—I don't expect taxpayers to subsidize those preferences any more than if I liked hot-air balloons or miniature submarines.

As an economist who believes in the benefits of free markets, I am tempted to simply argue that we should privatize our roads and transit systems. As an American with faith in the original intent of those who wrote the Constitution, I am also tempted to argue that we should at least abolish federal transportation programs and leave transportation to state and local governments. These are useful ideas and may happen someday.

But I am also a pragmatist who realizes that, except in times of dire emergency, political change tends to be incremental. This book will offer a variety of incremental changes at the federal, state, and local levels that will significantly improve our transportation systems without foreclosing the option for more drastic changes later, should such changes become necessary or feasible.

Any book like this runs the risk of rapidly becoming dated. Between the time I finish writing and the day this book reaches print, the House Transportation and Infrastructure Committee will present its proposal for the next reauthorization of federal transportation spending, the Obama administration will announce which states will receive grants for high-speed rail, and several states may decide to increase gasoline and/or other taxes for transportation. Yet many of the proposals this book make in chapters 10 and 11 will be as valid 20 years from now as they are today or would have been 20 years ago.

These proposals revolve around three simple concepts. First, most of the benefits of a transportation system go to those who use it, so they should be the ones to pay for it. A user-fee-driven transportation system is inherently fair and more likely to be efficient than one funded out of taxes because transportation providers will be forced to design systems to please the users, not systems aimed at capturing the largest share of tax dollars.

Second, when dealing with the social costs of transportation such as pollution, it is essential that we find the most cost-efficient way of reducing those costs. Given a choice between a project that can reduce greenhouse gas emissions at a cost of $10 a ton and one that reduces emissions at a cost of $10,000 a ton, choosing the latter means forgoing 999 tons of emission reductions for every ton abated.

Third, mobility advocates must support and promote new technologies that can revolutionize transportation, particularly personal mobility. These new technologies include various sorts of intelligent highways and intelligent vehicles that can reduce congestion and increase average travel speeds. Higher average speeds will, in turn, make more jobs and other opportunities accessible to more Americans, which will replicate the enormous economic benefits that have resulted from previous technological revolutions such as the automobile, superhighway, and commercial jet air service.

These simple ideas seem logical and reasonable. Yet they encounter extraordinary resistance from many of the officials who plan, run, and tax us to fund our transportation systems. As a result, the federal, state, and local governments spend close to $200 billion a year on transportation systems that are increasingly failing to do what most people think they should: provide mobility for people and freight to efficiently and safely move around the country. With the help of this book, I hope we can turn it around so that, 25 years from now, Americans will not have to face the same congestion we suffer today, much less congestion that is five times as bad.

1. Land of Mobility

The United States is the most mobile society in history. In 2006, the average American traveled 18,700 miles, equal to three-fourths of the way around the circumference of the earth.[1] That's more than twice as much travel as the average European and nearly three times as much as the average Japanese.[2] Our freight systems also moved 15,000 ton-miles of goods per person.[3] That's nearly four times the per capita movement of goods in Europe or Japan.[4]

We Americans aren't mobile because sinister oil companies or evil automobile manufacturers forced us to triple our per capita driving since 1950. Airlines did not twist our arms and force us to increase our personal air travel by nearly 40 times since 1950. We are not victims of bad urban design. We are mobile because mobility gives us access to better jobs, a wide array of low-cost consumer goods, broad social and recreational opportunities, and many other benefits.

The benefits of mobility are huge and undeniable. The most tangible benefit is to our personal incomes. Increased travel speeds allow people to reach more potential jobs in a given commute time. Research in France found that, for every 10 percent increase in travel speeds, the pool of workers available to employers increased by 15 percent. This gives employers access to more highly skilled workers, which in turn increases worker productivity by 3 percent.[5] Similarly, research in California has found that doubling the distance workers can commute to work increases productivity by 25 percent.[6]

Economists estimate that construction of new highways contributed to nearly one-third of the rapid economic growth the United States enjoyed in the 1950s and a quarter of the growth in the 1960s.[7] The growth wasn't generated by construction jobs; it came from the increased mobility offered by new roads. It may be no coincidence that our economic growth slowed as highway construction tapered off in the 1970s and 1980s.

Mobility also reduces our consumer costs and gives us access to a wider diversity of consumer goods. The typical grocery store in

1912 had 300 different products for sale.[8] Today, the average supermarket has more than 30,000 products, and many sell well over 50,000.[9] Moreover, the costs of groceries, clothing, and other goods, as a share of personal income, have typically fallen by more than 50 percent since 1930.[10]

Thanks to our mobility, most Americans enjoy much better housing than they did a century ago and better than most other people in the world today. Mobility not only increases the income available for housing; it allows us to reach areas where housing, and the land it requires, is more affordable.

The most intangible benefit of mobility may be the thing many Americans say they value most: freedom. Mobility allowed blacks to escape oppressive conditions in the South in the 1920s and 1930s. Mobility was a fundamental part of, and perhaps a necessary prerequisite for, the civil rights movement of the 1950s and 1960s. "I've always viewed automobiles as freedom rides," says *Washington Post* writer Warren Brown, because shared automobiles allowed blacks in Montgomery, Alabama, to boycott local bus service after Rosa Parks was arrested for refusing to give up her seat to a white man.[11] Mobility also played an important role in the women's rights movement of the 1960s and 1970s: as American families went from owning one car to two, more women joined the work force and demanded equal rights. "You wouldn't believe how owning their first car frees women," says University of Arizona transportation researcher Sandra Rosenbloom.[12]

No matter where you are in the United States, you owe almost everything you see around you to mobility. If you live in a major city, your access to food, clothing, and other goods imported from outside the city depends on mobility. If you live in a rural area, your access to the services enjoyed by urban dwellers, such as electrical power and communications lines that are installed and served by trucks, depends on mobility. If you spend your vacations hiking in the most remote wilderness areas, your ability to reach the trailheads depends on your mobility.[13]

One way to appreciate the advantages of the mobility we enjoy today is to look back at American mobility during the past two centuries. The following vignettes of 1800, 1850, 1900, 1950, and 2000 are based on the best available records from those years.

1800: Humans and Horsepower

Average travel speed: 3 miles per hour
Average mobility: 1,500 miles per year
Per capita GDP: $1,200[14]

Thirteen years after America's constitutional convention, land mobility had not significantly advanced beyond the mobility enjoyed by Eurasians a thousand years before. No new inventions had truly revolutionized land-based transportation technology since the development of the stirrup by the Chinese around the third century AD and its adoption in Europe about a thousand years before the American Revolution.[15]

Virtually no living person in 1800 had ever traveled faster than a horse could run. A top racehorse can carry a light rider faster than 40 miles per hour for short distances. But most riders rarely exceed 30 miles per hour, and average horseback riding speeds over any great distance are more like 3 to 4 miles per hour. Horses pulling wagons or coaches were even slower: Forget the high-speed stage-coaches of Hollywood movies; a 20-mile trip over rutted and rocky roads could take all day.[16]

In 1800, fewer than 6 percent of people in the 16 United States lived in cities or other clusters of 2,500 people or more, the Census Bureau's present-day definition of "urban."[17] America produced an average per capita gross domestic product (GDP) of about $1,200 a year (adjusted for inflation to 2007 dollars), a 0.7 percent annual increase from the estimated $625 per capita GDP produced in 1700.[18]

Most of the nation's 3 million rural residents were probably farmers, and most of them must have owned horses. Men were more mobile than women, but the average adults probably left their farms no more than twice a week. A three-hour roundtrip at three miles per hour, twice a week, is about 1,900 miles per year. Counting children, personal travel probably averaged around 1,500 miles per year. Whether on foot or horseback, average speeds were about three miles per hour.

The harbingers of the first transportation revolution had already appeared, however. John Fitch demonstrated the first steamboat in America before the members of the Constitutional Convention in 1787. By the next year, he was operating the nation's only commercial steamboat service between Philadelphia and Burlington, New Jersey, a distance of about 18 miles. However, he had gone out of business by 1800, and no new commercial steamboat operations would begin for several more years.

1850: The Canal, Steamboat, and Rail Revolutions

Average travel speed: 4 miles per hour
Average mobility: 1,600 miles per year
Per capita GDP: $1,900

Five new technologies revolutionized transportation between 1800 and 1850. The first, of course, was steamboats. By 1850, more than 300 steamboats were operating on the Delaware, Hudson, Ohio, Missouri, Mississippi, and other American rivers. Close to 200 more boats, many of them steam powered, plied the Great Lakes.[19] Steamboats did not travel much faster than horses, but they could move a lot of freight and people at a much lower cost.

The second revolution was canals. America's first obstacle to westward settlement was the Appalachian Mountains. Canals were the solution, and the Erie Canal, completed in 1825, was followed by the Chesapeake and Ohio Canal and several more. By 1850, America had built about 5,000 miles of canals, mostly in New York, Pennsylvania, and Maryland.

Third, various entrepreneurs or government agencies also built a number of roads across the mountains. These included many private toll roads as well as the National Road, a free road stretching from Maryland to Illinois. These roads constituted only a minor revolution, given that the only really new technology they used was Macadam pavement, developed in 1820.

By mid-century, canals and wagon roads were being eclipsed by the fourth revolution, railroads. In 1830, the nation's first steam locomotive ran on the Baltimore and Ohio Railroad, whose cornerstone had been laid in 1828 by Charles Carroll, the last living signer of the Declaration of Independence. By 1850, more than 9,000 miles of rail lines—whose trains typically averaged between 10 and 30 miles per hour—crossed the 30 American states.

The fifth revolution was the horse-powered streetcar. Operating on rails, "horsecars" gave patrons shelter from the elements and smooth rides on the otherwise unpaved or poorly paved city streets of the era. The first American horsecar began operating in New York City in 1832, and by 1850 they could be found in scores of cities.

The first four revolutions had a much bigger impact on American freight transport than on passenger travel. The Erie Canal, for example, reduced the cost of shipping from Buffalo to New York City by 90 to 95 percent, which in turn increased the volume of products shipped at least a hundredfold. The canal effectively gave any farmer or manufacturer within reach of the Great Lakes access to America's largest markets as well as possible foreign export.

For most Americans, however, a trip on a steamboat, canal, or steam train was a rare treat. In 1839, Ulysses Grant considered himself the "best traveled boy in Georgetown, Ohio," where he went to high school, because he had "been east to Wheeling, Virginia [about 240 miles], and north to the Western Reserve [about 240 miles], in Ohio, west to Louisville [about 140 miles], and south to Bourbon County, Kentucky [about 70 miles], besides having driven or ridden pretty much over the whole country within fifty miles of home."[20]

For the journey to his 1839 appointment at West Point, Grant started on horseback, then used steamboats, canals, trains, and stagecoaches. He was most impressed by the train. "I thought the perfection of rapid transit had been reached," he later wrote. "We travelled at least eighteen miles an hour, when at full speed, and made the whole distance averaging probably as much as twelve miles an hour. This seemed like annihilating space." Even as late as 1850, however, such a journey would have been considered unusual.

In 1848, the Boston and Albany Railroad redefined the idea of speed when it ran a special train the 26 miles between Boston and Lawrence, Massachusetts, in 26 minutes. Reporters cowered in fear on the floor of the passenger cars, as this was the first time in history any group of people had ever traveled a mile a minute and lived to tell about it.[21]

Most of the 85 percent of Americans who lived in rural areas probably traveled only a little more in 1850 than their parents or grandparents had in 1800. For the 15 percent who lived in cities, the horsecar was an improvement over walking. But the fare was more than most people could pay on a regular basis. For those people, moving from the country to the city was probably a step backwards in mobility, at least as measured in miles per year. Few city residents could afford to maintain a horse and stable, so walking or the horsecar were their only choices.

Per capita GDP had increased by about 0.85 percent per year from 1800, slightly faster than the preceding century. The opportunities for personal mobility were greatly improved, but other than people in the transportation business, only a few could regularly take advantage of those opportunities. Typical 18-year-olds leaving their east coast homes to travel west on the canals, railroads, or steamboats might find an adequate living farming, but they would rarely be able to return to visit the families they left behind.

1900: Railroads and Streetcars

Average travel speed: 8 miles per hour
Average mobility: 2,000 miles per year
Per capita GDP: $5,000

The steam railroads that had begun to replace steamboats, canals, and horse-drawn wagons in 1850 had nearly completed their revolution in American transportation by 1900. The nation's 45 states and three contiguous territories now had more than 21 times as many miles of rail routes as in 1850, for a total of 193,000 miles.[22] In 1893, the New York Central awed the nation by operating the Exposition Flyer 960 miles from New York to Chicago in just 20 hours, for an average speed of 48 miles per hour, including stops.[23]

The railroads created a demand for coal, high-quality steel, and heavy machinery, and at the same time provided the means to transport such materials around the country for use by other industries. As a result, America was beginning to produce as much as Europe despite having less than a quarter of Europe's population.

Still, as in 1850, this incredible transportation revolution had a much greater impact on freight transport than on passenger travel. Americans traveled a phenomenal 16 billion passenger miles by rail in 1900, but this amounted to just 210 miles for each of the 76 million residents. The main reason was the cost: rail fares averaged 2 cents a passenger mile, equal to about 50 cents today.[24] Since real incomes averaged only about one-seventh of what people earn today, this cost was prohibitive to most people.

More than 60 percent of Americans still lived in rural areas, and most of them traveled little more than their counterparts had in 1850. "Although most farm families made periodic trips into town or to relatives," writes historian Michael Berger (quoting a 1915 magazine article), "such journeys were often 'an experience to be classed with the hardest work.'"[25] As a result, rural life, especially for women, continued to be lonely and isolated. "No burden has ever set quite as heavily on farming and upon the farm family as has the curse of isolation and loneliness," observed a writer looking back from 1927.[26]

Other innovations had a greater effect on urban passenger travel. At this point, 30 million Americans lived in urban areas, and most of them had access to at least two new modes of transportation not available in 1850.

The first, velocipedes—two-wheel, human-powered machines, appeared in the United States in the 1860s but were impractical for most people. America's first real bicycle craze began with the introduction of the "safety bicycle," a chain-driven, rear-wheel-drive bike, in the 1880s. These bikes were physically very similar to the single-speed bicycles that have become popular among city residents today. Bikes were mainly used by young people, but even so they led to the first major movement for better rural roads since the railroads eclipsed roads in the 1840s.

The other urban transportation revolution was the development of the electric streetcar, which also occurred in the 1880s. This mode of transportation was so economical compared to horsecars, cable cars, and other forms of mass transportation that, by 1900, electric streetcars trundled around some 500 to 800 American cities at an average speed of about 11 miles per hour, counting stops.[27]

A few big cities, such as New York and Chicago, also had elevated rapid-transit lines. Separated from pedestrians, horses, and wagons, the Chicago El averaged 13 miles an hour, including stops.[28] Eleven to 13 miles an hour doesn't sound like much today, but it was a huge advance over three-miles-per-hour walking speeds.

Still, not everyone could afford to regularly ride the streetcars or elevated trains. In 1902, the earliest year for which data are available, streetcars made 5.8 billion passenger trips. Transit ridership grew at about 10 percent per year in the early 1900s, so ridership in 1900 was probably less than 5 billion. If a typical commuter took two trips a day 300 days a year, and no one rode transit except for commuting, transit would have carried about 8.3 million commuters. This suggests that less than a third of urbanites were regular transit riders, and the rest used it only occasionally.

The average bus transit trip today is a little under four miles long. In terms of speed and other service characteristics, the streetcars that dominated in 1900 were most like buses today, so transit trips probably averaged about four miles. For a regular commuter working six days a week, that amounted to 2,400 miles a year. Average urban travel for all urbanites combined must have been a little less, about 2,200 miles per year. Adding in the 210 miles of intercity rail travel (cited above) brings that total to a little over 2,400 miles a year. If rural travel was about the same as in 1850 plus the occasional train trip, total average travel was about 2,000 miles per year.

Those who could afford to do so—mainly families of white-collar workers—used streetcars for shopping as well as commuting. In 1900, most groceries were sold at public markets with individual stalls for produce, meat, coffee, and other products. The average public market might have between 500 and 1,000 different products for sale. People would take the streetcar to the market, select their groceries with the assistance of a clerk, then pay the vendors to deliver the food so they could ride the streetcar home without being laden with purchases.

The nation's first automobiles appeared a few years before 1900. By 1900, more than 250 companies claimed to be making motorcars.[29] Most, however, built just a few cars, so only about 8,000 cars were on American roads that year, or roughly one for every 1,000 people.[30] Thus the automobile was little more than a toy and not yet a major contributor to personal mobility.

The average increase in personal mobility since 1850 was small—perhaps a 20 percent increase in average distances traveled—and not evenly distributed. Still, it represented a major boon for those who could afford transit or intercity rail. A quadrupling of urban speeds meant people could access 16 times as many jobs and other resources. The railroads had far more than quadrupled intercity speeds. Mobility improvements for both freight and passengers directly or indirectly accounted for most of the 1.9 percent annual increase in per capita productivity since 1850, and that was twice the rate of the previous half-century.

1950: The Automobile Revolution

Average travel speed: 24 miles per hour
Average ground speed: 23 miles per hour
Average mobility: 6,900 miles per year
Per capita GDP: $12,000

Along with two world wars and a great depression, the years between 1900 and 1950 witnessed two transportation revolutions

Table 1.1
PASSENGER MILES AND AVERAGE SPEEDS BY MODE IN 1950

Mode	Passenger Miles (billions)	Passenger Miles Per Capita	Miles Per Hour
Auto	730	4,800	25
Truck	89	600	25
Intercity Rail	27	180	30
Commuter Rail	5	30	30
Other Transit	90	630	11
Intercity Bus	26	170	30
Domestic Air	8	50	200
Walking	60	400	3
Cycling	8	50	10
Total/Average	1,048	6,900	24

SOURCES: Auto and truck from *Highway Statistics Summary to 1995*, Table VM-201; intercity rail, commuter rail, and air from *Historical Statistics of the United States*, pp. 729, 769; intercity bus from *Historical Statistics*, p. 707; other transit from *2008 Public Transportation Fact Book*, Part 2, p. 1.

NOTE: Walking and cycling estimated. Auto occupancies assumed to average two per vehicle; truck occupancies one. Other transit average trip assumed to be 5.2 miles. Per capita numbers rounded.

that had a far bigger effect on personal mobility than any that had come before. Henry Ford's mass-produced automobile brought mobility to the masses. Commercial air service, used only by the wealthy and elite at this point, was nonetheless growing rapidly as well.

The 1920 census was the first to find more Americans living in cities than in rural areas. By 1950, about three out of five Americans lived in urban areas, so urban transportation was much more important than it had been a century or even 50 years before. Since 1900, America's rural population had grown by 18 percent, while its urban population more than tripled. Although the suburbs were growing, more than three-quarters of urban residents still lived in central cities.

The railroads, streetcars, and other public transit systems did yeoman service during the war. But by 1950, transit ridership had fallen by about 30 percent from its 1944 peak of about 900 miles per

13

capita. The prewar peak also briefly reached 900 miles per capita in 1920. By 1950, it was less than 630 miles per capita.

One disadvantage facing transit was the age of the streetcar fleet. "In 1947 most [Chicago] streetcars were close to forty years old," observes one historian, "and most elevated cars, made of wood, were between 45 and 50."[31] Replacing streetcars implied a commitment to replacing rails and other infrastructure as well. With labor costs much higher in 1950 than in 1900, and transit fares strictly regulated by local boards and commissions, reconstructing streetcar lines made no sense, so transit companies began converting to buses as fast as possible.

At the end of the war, the railroads were financially better off than transit companies, and many ordered shiny new passenger equipment even before the war ended. Yet intercity rail travel suffered an even greater decline than urban transit, plummeting a devastating 67 percent in just six short years after 1944.

Before the war, rail service peaked about 1920 with close to 250,000 rail miles across the country, carrying some 20,000 scheduled passenger trains each day. Yet the average American in 1920 traveled only about 450 miles per year by train. With huge troop movements and wartime restrictions on driving, per capita train travel reached nearly 650 miles per year in 1944.

However, by 1950 intercity rail travel had declined to just 180 miles per capita, less than it had been in 1900. Curiously, passenger fares had only grown from 2.0 cents per mile in 1900 to 2.6 cents per mile in 1950—meaning that, after adjusting for inflation, they declined from 50 cents to about 20 cents a mile in today's pennies. By comparison, intercity bus fares averaged just over a penny per passenger mile.[32]

The highest level of personal mobility ever achieved by American urban transit and intercity rail together was less than 1,600 miles per capita in 1944. Despite the Great Depression, per capita vehicle miles—not passenger miles—of driving exceeded that number by 1934, and passenger miles must have been at least double vehicle miles. (Auto occupancies are a function of family size, and family sizes in the 1930s were larger than today, when average auto occupancy is about 1.6.)

By 1950, Americans drove an average of 3,000 miles per year for every person in the country.[33] Assuming an average of two people per car and one person per truck, that works out to 4,800 passenger miles per capita—nearly three times as many as the most ever carried by transit and intercity rail. Americans spent an average of six cents a mile driving their cars, so intercity trains would have been less expensive for one or two people. But the convenience of a private automobile that would go when and where people wanted apparently outweighed the possible savings from taking the train.

The first automobiles were expensive, and when they began appearing in large numbers—the United States had well over a million, or more than one per hundred people, by 1913—they were seen as playthings for the rich. "Nothing has spread Socialistic feeling in this country more than the use of automobiles," warned Woodrow Wilson in 1906. "To the countryman they are a picture of arrogance of wealth with all its independence and carelessness."[34] But Thomas Edison, who perhaps could see a bit further ahead than politicians, was more optimistic. "In time the automobile will be the poor man's wagon," he said in 1904. "He will use it to haul his wood, convey his farm freight, get to and from the post office and for the family for church."[35]

Henry Ford—who considered himself a disciple of Edison's—proved Edison right when he introduced the moving assembly line in 1913. This allowed him to cut the price of cars in half even as he doubled worker pay. By 1922, the United States had one auto for every 10 people, and most of them were Fords. By 1950, auto numbers had increased to nearly 50 million, or one for every three people.[36]

The mass-produced automobile revolutionized every part of life. By effectively tripling ground transportation speeds, autos gave people access to nine times as many jobs and resources as people in 1900. Moreover, "auto mobility" extended across social classes. The streetcars of 1900 were used mainly by the middle class, while working-class commuters and families mostly walked. By 1950, the vast majority of both working- and middle-class American families owned at least one automobile. Homeownership rates had grown by nearly 20 percent since 1900 as automobiles brought single-family homes within reach of working-class urban families for the first time in history.[37] (Indeed, planning historian Peter Hall shows that much of the debate over "urban sprawl" is really a class debate, as middle- and upper-class residents resented the intrusion of working-class families, with their different values and tastes, into suburban enclaves.[38])

Replacing public markets, supermarkets catered to auto owners by providing free parking. With customers driving in from miles around, grocers could offer a diverse selection of some 5,000 different products for sale. Since the customers served themselves and carried their purchases home, the supermarkets could offer much lower prices than would be found at the few remaining public markets.

Postwar Americans found automobiles so useful that they devoted 9.8 percent of their personal incomes to driving, including buying cars, repairs, tires and other parts, fuel and oil, taxes, tolls, and insurance. As recently as 1948, that percentage had been just 7.4; the increase reflected the growth in auto ownership as wartime restrictions were lifted.[39]

Air travel was still fairly insignificant, but average speeds of 180 miles per hour made a big difference to those who used it.[40] Passengers paid 5.5 cents a mile, more than twice as much as for train travel. But the number of people using air travel probably remained small as much due to people's fear of flying as to the cost: as of 1950, more than 90 percent of Americans had never flown in a commercial airliner.[41]

While the amount of freight carried by rail peaked in 1944, by 1950 it had declined by only 20 percent and was destined to exceed wartime records in the 1960s. In 1950, American railroads carried more than 4,000 tons of freight per capita, more than twice as much as in 1900 and more than all other modes of shipping combined.[42]

Highways also carried more than 1,100 ton miles of freight per capita, exceeding shipping on inland waterways for the first time in 1950. Total domestic shipping per capita, including railroads, highways, inland waterways, pipelines, and air, exceeded 7,200 ton miles.[43] While complete data are not available for 1900, this is probably a tripling of per capita shipping since the beginning of the century.

Although the growth in shipping is impressive, this is the first half-century in which the growth in passenger travel exceeded the growth in freight. These increases in both passenger travel and freight shipments contributed to a 1.8 percent annual increase in per capita GDP since 1900. This was slightly less than the previous half-century, no doubt due to the dual world wars and the Great Depression.

2000: Superhighways and Jetliners

Average travel speed: 73 miles per hour
Average ground speed: 34 miles per hour
Average mobility: 18,000 miles per year
Per capita GDP: $35,000

Relative to the revolutions witnessed in the previous half-centuries, the only significant improvements in transportation technology since 1950 were fairly minor: First, the widespread construction of interstate highways and other limited-access freeways significantly increased personal travel speeds and reduced shipping costs. Second, commercial jet air service, approximately twice as fast as propeller-driven planes, also increased travel speeds. Finally, the railroads' replacement of steam locomotives with diesel-electrics, a transition that began before 1950, greatly reduced rail operating costs. Though not as spectacular as the changes of the previous century-and-a-half, these improvements had a huge impact on American travel habits.

America's population almost doubled between 1950 and 2000, and nearly all of the growth was in urban areas; where rural numbers had increased 8 percent, urban populations grew 130 percent. The 2000 census found that 79.9 percent of Americans lived in urban areas of 2,500 people or more. The big story was the explosion of the suburbs, which more than quadrupled in population since 1950, while the central cities only doubled.

As shown in Table 1.2, intercity rail and public transit (including commuter rail) had shrunk to insignificance. Intercity buses carried almost three times as many passenger miles as rail and urban transit combined, and the airlines carried two-and-one-half times as many as buses and rails combined. Americans lost much of their fear of flying: by 2000, 83 percent of Americans had flown in a commercial airplane, and some three-quarters of those had flown many times.[44] As a result, air travel increased by more than 66 times since 1950. Although airlines still accounted for only about 10 percent of passenger miles, their high speeds more than doubled average speeds: with air service, average speeds were 73 miles per hour, while ground speeds averaged 34 miles per hour.

The other big story for passenger transport was the 450 percent increase in driving. The near doubling of the nation's population and likely 20 percent decline in auto occupancies largely accounts

17

Table 1.2
PASSENGER MILES AND AVERAGE SPEEDS BY MODE IN 2000

Mode	Passenger Miles (billions)	Passenger Miles Per Capita	Miles Per Hour
Auto	4,024	14,300	35
Truck	206	700	35
Intercity Rail	6	20	35
Commuter Rail	9	30	30
Other Transit	38	130	20
Intercity Bus	160	600	40
Domestic Air	531	1,900	400
Walking	60	200	3
Cycling	30	100	10
Total/Average	5,060	18,000	73

SOURCES: Auto and truck from *Highway Statistics Summary to 1995*, Table VM-201; intercity rail, commuter rail, other transit, intercity bus, and air from *National Transportation Statistics*, Table 01-37.

NOTE: Walking and cycling estimated. Auto occupancies assumed to average 1.6 per vehicle; truck occupancies 1. Per capita numbers rounded off.

for this increase; even so it represents a near tripling in per capita auto mobility.

Although data are not available for 1950, in 1960 64 percent of American commuters drove to work, while 12 percent rode transit. By 2000, 87 percent used automobiles to get to work (including motorcycles and taxis), while only 5 percent rode transit.

Auto mobility continued to revolutionize day-to-day life. Within a fixed amount of travel time, increasing ground transportation speeds from less than 24 miles per hour in 1950 to 34 miles per hour in 2000 gave people access to twice as many jobs and resources.[45] One result was that homeownership rates grew another 20 percent since 1950. By 2000, two out of three American families owned their own homes. This statistic would have been closer to three out of four if some states, such as California, hadn't passed land-use legislation making housing unaffordable. Because of such restrictions, home-ownership rates grew by only 5 percent in California and actually declined in Oregon and Washington.[46]

The average supermarket now carried 30,000 different products. Many consumers were attracted to new retail formats such as Wal-Mart and other supercenters, which typically carried more than 100,000 different products, as well as warehouse stores, club whole-sale stores, and several other types of food sellers. None of these types of retail would be possible without automobiles.

One little-known benefit of auto mobility was its effect on rural lands. The automobile is often blamed for urban sprawl, which is a term used to demonize the greatly improved housing that working-class people could thus afford. But the effect of automobiles, trucks, and tractors on rural land was even more significant. Prior to 1920, American farmers dedicated as much as a third of their land to pasture for horses and other beasts of burden. After 1920, the substitution of motor for animal power allowed farmers to put those lands to more productive uses.

Between 1920 and 2003, farmers reduced pasture and grazing lands by 244 million acres. Almost all of this land was converted to forests, quite possibly the largest area of deforested land ever to be reforested. At the same time, despite complaints about urban sprawl, the number of acres of cropland remained constant.[47] Apparently, any conversions of croplands to urban uses were compensated by conversions of pasture to croplands. Since pasture is the least-valuable use of agricultural lands, these changes significantly increased overall farm productivity, while reforestation of former pastures increased biodiversity and watershed values.

The 2000 census found that all of America's urban areas of 2,500 people or more occupied less than 93 million acres, most of which would be urban even without the automobile. Thus, motor vehicles saved many more acres from "horsepasture sprawl" than they contributed to urban sprawl.

Americans were able to nearly triple personal auto travel since 1950 without increasing the share of personal incomes they devoted to driving. In fact, in 2000 that share was only 9.4 percent, down from 9.8 percent in 1950. Over the second half of the 20th century, auto costs averaged 9.3 percent and ranged from 8.1 to 10.1 percent of personal incomes.[48]

Changes in the relative costs of passenger travel accounted for some of the changes in travel habits. In 1950, airline fares were more than twice rail fares; however, Amtrak's average fare of 23.2 cents

19

per passenger mile in 2000 was nearly 60 percent greater than airfares of 14.6 cents a mile, while intercity buses charged an average of only 12.8 cents a mile.[49] Americans spent $794 billion driving, or 19.7 cents a passenger mile.[50] Public transit agencies attempted to be competitive by charging fares averaging 18.3 cents a passenger mile.[51]

Of course, these personal costs were supplemented by government subsidies to the airlines, highways, transit, and Amtrak. In 2000, total subsidies to airlines and airports averaged less than 0.1 cents per passenger mile, while highway subsidies averaged 0.8 cents per passenger mile (less if some of the subsidies are allocated to trucks).[52] Subsidies to Amtrak averaged more than 14 cents a mile, while subsidies to transit averaged 50 cents a mile.[53]

Airline subsidies were, for some reason, unusually low in 2000 and more typically averaged between one and two cents per passenger mile in previous and later years. Otherwise, these relative subsidies have changed only a little since 1971, when Amtrak took over private passenger trains and public agencies assumed ownership of most transit systems. Despite the huge subsidies to Amtrak and transit since 1971, intercity rail and public transit have grown increasingly insignificant to passenger transport.

Railroads continued to carry more freight than any other form of transportation, an average of 5,200 ton-miles per capita. Counting all methods of transport, total shipments were nearly 13,400 ton-miles for every American, nearly double that of 1950.[54]

The freight railroads benefited greatly from deregulation in 1980.[55] While railroads had carried close to 90 percent of freight in 1900 and more than 50 percent in 1950, by 1980, heavy regulation had driven their share of freight to around 30 percent.[56] Thanks to deregulation, rail's share recovered to 39 percent in 2000 and reached 40 percent in 2001.[57]

While the 92 percent growth in per capita freight shipments since 1950 made a big difference to Americans, the 160 percent growth in personal travel made an even bigger difference. Thanks to mobility, moving assembly lines, and electrification, per capita GDP grew by 2.2 percent per year from 1950 to 2000, faster than in any other half-century in American history.

What Makes America So Mobile?

These vignettes reveal important lessons about mobility. First, the transportation revolutions of the 19th century were much more important for their effects on shipping than on personal travel. By reducing the costs of moving freight, steamboats, canals, and railroads greatly increased American wealth and productivity. But they added little to the personal mobility of the average person. Even at their zenith, intercity rail plus urban transit moved Americans fewer miles per capita than the airlines, and barely 10 percent as many miles as autos do today.

Moreover, the improvements in personal mobility that did result from 19th-century technologies benefited mainly the upper and middle classes of society. Through the early part of the 20th century, a large share of Americans spent their entire lives without ever traveling more than 50 miles from where they were born, and for most working-class families, travel by train was a rare event.

The real revolutions in personal mobility had to wait for the mass-produced automobile and the jet airliner (especially when combined with airline deregulation). Not only did these technologies greatly increase passenger travel, they were affordable to almost every economic class. The 2000 census found, for example, that 93 percent of American households had access to at least one automobile.[58]

Driving today is so inexpensive that the main limiting factor for most Americans is not how much money they can afford to spend on travel, but how much time. Researchers have found that people, regardless of income, are willing to dedicate, on average, a little more than an hour a day to travel.[59] Since time is more limiting than dollar cost for most Americans, the wealthiest 20 percent of Americans drive only a few more miles per year than the poorest 20 percent.

This means the automobile is the most egalitarian form of mechanized travel ever developed. This point is so important that it is worth repeating: Not only is America the most mobile nation in history, this mobility is spread across a much broader range of economic and social classes than it is in any other nation.

This, in turn, means that lifestyle differences between white-collar and blue-collar families are much smaller than they were in earlier eras. In 1900, working-class, blue-collar families lived almost exclusively in rented multifamily housing. But the automobile allowed many of them to acquire single-family homes very similar to those owned by white-collar families. They drive on the same roads, shop at the same malls, and send their children to the same schools.

Table 1.3
PER CAPITA MILES TRAVELED IN THE UNITED STATES, EUROPE, AND JAPAN (2004) AND THE UNITED STATES (1944)

Mode	United States	Europe	Japan	United States in 1944
Auto	15,200	6,000	4,010	3,070
Rail	50	480	1,880	1,550
High-speed	10	100	400	0
Bus	480	680	350	200
Air	1,900	650	400	20
Total	17,630	7,840	6,640	4,840

SOURCES: 2004 U.S. and European Union data from *Panorama of Transport* (Brussels, BE: European Commission, 2007), p. 103; 2004 Japan data from "Summary of Transportation Statistics," Ministry of Land, Infrastructure and Transport, 2008, tinyurl.com/6x7rx6; 1944 data from *Historical Statistics of the United States: Colonial Times to 1970* (Washington: Census Bureau, 1975), pp. 729, 769; *Highway Statistics Summary to 1995* (Washington: Federal Highway Administration, 1996), Table VM-201.

NOTE: Numbers rounded to the nearest 10. Rail includes high-speed rail.

While the mobility revolutions of the 19th century exacerbated class differences in American society, the revolutions of the 20th century reduced them.

Among the many wealthy countries in the world, the United States far outpaces all the others in personal mobility. After America, the most mobile nation on earth appears to be Iceland, whose residents average some 11,000 miles a year. Next are Italy and France, whose residents travel about 10,000 miles per year. In Europe as a whole, the average is less than 8,000 miles per year, while in Japan, it is less than 7,000 (see Table 1.3).

America's greater mobility does not appear to be due to its low population density: Canada's density is much lower, yet the average Canadian travels only about two-thirds as many miles per year as the average American.[60] It does not appear to be due to income: the per capita GDPs of Norway, Switzerland, and Denmark are all as high as the United States, yet none enjoys much more than half the per capita travel of the United States.[61]

Average incomes in many European countries are lower than in the United States. The French and Germans produce about three-quarters the per capita GDP of Americans. But mobility and incomes are synergistic: higher incomes can lead to more mobility, but more mobility can also lead to higher incomes by giving employers access to more highly skilled workers. Thus, it may be just as accurate to say these countries have lower incomes because of their lower mobility as to say they have lower mobility because of their lower incomes.

One factor that seems to account for America's greater mobility is the difference in government attitudes towards various forms of transport. The United States has historically taxed autos and fuel in order to pay for highways. Individual states may charge additional sales taxes on automobiles, but at no higher rates than they charge for other dry goods. Congress and some state legislatures have occasionally diverted gas tax revenues from highways to transit and other programs, but those diversions have, since 1957, been matched or more than matched by general funds spent on roads.

In contrast, European nations, Japan, Canada, Australia, and New Zealand punitively tax automobiles and fuel. Thus, the taxes collected from highway users amount to significantly more than the nations spend on highways, roads, and streets and are higher than those collected on other goods. These high tax rates are a deliberate social policy aimed at discouraging driving.

In the United States, state and federal tax rates on gasoline average 39 cents per gallon.[62] In Canada, provincial and federal gasoline taxes average 93 cents per gallon (not counting the general service tax and provincial sales taxes that are applied to all goods).[63] Australia and New Zealand charge 80 to 90 cents per gallon, while Japan charges $1.25. European countries charge between $1.25 and $2.70 per gallon.[64]

Most of these nations also tax automobiles, especially imports, at rates that are significantly higher than other goods. In 1956, Congress dedicated a 10 percent tax on autos to highways but repealed that tax in 1971.[65]

French economist Rémy Prud'homme estimates that European road-use tax revenues on autos and fuel—over and above regular goods-and-service or value-added taxes—are nearly twice government spending on highways.[66] These taxes pose a major barrier to the mode of transportation that provides the greatest mobility in all of these countries.

A large share of these taxes is spent subsidizing urban transit and intercity rail. Yet the increased mobility provided by immense

23

subsidies to these modes does not come close to making up for the mobility restrictions from high auto and fuel taxes. In 2004, the average resident of the European Union travelled only 6,200 miles by auto, compared to more than 15,000 in the United States. The 1,200 miles that the average European travels by buses and trains hardly make up for the lost auto mobility.

Europe's per capita GDP in 2004 was about the same as the United States's in 1982. Thanks to anti-mobility taxes, however, European mobility is more than 50 years behind the United States: per capita auto, bus, and rail travel in 2004 were roughly the same as the United States averages in 1952. Given the relationship between mobility and incomes, this lack of mobility is likely a major reason why European incomes are lower.[67]

Japan is only slightly different. The Japanese travel by rail more than the people of any other country. Yet in 2000, the average Japanese travelled less than 1,900 miles by train, slightly less than the number of miles Americans flew. Only 400 miles of that was by high-speed rail.

The cases of Japan and Europe are clear: Even with heavy taxes on autos and gasoline and heavy subsidies for urban rail and high-speed intercity rail programs, railways contribute little to personal mobility. Very likely, only a small share of Europeans and Japanese frequently travel by rail, while everyone else must share the tax subsidies whether they use rail or not.

America has a clear choice. We can follow the European model by taxing and otherwise discouraging auto mobility while subsidizing passenger trains and other mass transportation. Or we can build a transportation system that relies on user fees without punitive taxation. The first choice means that everyone will subsidize transport systems used by only a small elite. The second choice means more mobility for everyone on a pay-as-you-go basis. Before making that choice, we need to clearly understand the benefits, costs, and trade-offs of each alternative.

2. Potholes in the Road

Personal mobility has played a key role in making America a wealthy nation with opportunities open to nearly everyone without regard to race, class, or sex. Yet America's future mobility faces a variety of threats, including congestion, infrastructure failures, a massive campaign to reduce auto driving, and a failure to adopt technological improvements that can make more effective use of our transportation system.

The Cost of Congestion

According to the Texas Transportation Institute's annual survey of urban mobility, congestion cost American commuters $78 billion in 2007. That's almost 10 times the cost in 1982, the earliest year for which data are available. Commuters wasted more than 4 billion hours sitting in traffic in 2005, nearly five times the number of hours of delay 25 years before. Drivers also burned nearly 3 billion gallons of fuel sitting in traffic, again more than five times the amount wasted in 1982.[1] In turn, this waste of fuel put more than 25 million tons of greenhouse gases into the atmosphere.

Congestion has grown, on average, 7 percent per year, and the cost of congestion has grown faster than 10 percent per year. The reason for this growth is simple: traffic on urban highways has increased 3 percent per year, while the number of lane-miles on those roads has grown at only 1.4 percent per year.[2] Congestion growth is like the proverbial frog in the pot of heated water. The difference between 3 percent and 1.4 percent does not seem like much after one year. But this difference accumulates exponentially, and after 20 years or so, it can become huge.

The Texas Transportation Institute has some of the best data available on congestion, yet it counts only the cost of congestion to personal travelers. If the impact of congestion on businesses was added, the total cost might have to be doubled. Manufacturers who rely on "just-in-time" deliveries of parts and raw materials, retailers

25

who require frequent deliveries of groceries and other goods, contractors who need construction materials, utility companies that must maintain power and telecommunications lines, and large businesses such as hospitals that require outside supplies all are adversely affected by congestion.

A recent survey of businesses in the Portland, Oregon, area found that congestion increased their costs in several important ways. First, businesses that had already given up on shipping during the afternoon rush hours were finding that opportunities for making deliveries in the morning were closing as well. As congestion grows, the morning and evening rush hour peaks merge, leaving no daylight hours available for effective movements of goods.[3]

This delivery crunch in turn forces businesses to increase their warehouse space and inventories so they can deal with uncertainties in deliveries. Businesses also have to spend more to ship the same volume of goods. Congestion might force a shipper who once could meet delivery schedules with 10 trucks and crews to buy several more trucks and hire more crews to make the same volume of deliveries.

People's short-term response to congestion is to shift travel to different times, different routes, or—in a few cases—different modes. But the longer-term response is to shift locations of home, work, or other destinations. Many forces were responsible for the rapid suburbanization of America after World War II, but one of them was the desire to get away from congested roads. Jobs followed the population, so that by 2000, metropolitan areas had more jobs in the suburbs than in the central cities.[4]

As a result, although rush-hour congestion more than quadrupled in the 20 years after 1980, travel times to work increased only slightly. American workers spent an average of 21.7 minutes getting to work in 1980, and 25.5 minutes in 2000, about an 18 percent increase.[5] This increase was due more to a longer commute than to congestion: between 1983 and 2001, average auto commute distances rose by 36 percent, from 8.9 to 12.1 miles.[6] This indicates that commuting speeds increased despite congestion, as jobs migrated to less congested and more affordable parts of urban areas.

As chapter 1 showed, the trend to faster travel and commute speeds was strong throughout most of the 20th century. This trend may have ended, however. Surveys by the Federal Highway Administration found that average commuter speeds before 1995 were growing by 1.3 percent per year. After 1995, however, commute speeds declined by 1.4 percent per year.[7] To the extent that increasing travel speeds were responsible for much of the growth in incomes and other benefits in the 20th century, a permanent reversal of this trend could seriously harm our economic future.

The Infrastructure Panic

The 2007 collapse of the I-35W bridge in Minneapolis led to a great hue and cry about the need to repair the nation's infrastructure. Soon after the bridge's failure, groups such as the American Society of Civil Engineers presented their lists of trillions of dollars worth of projects that are supposedly needed to bring infrastructure up to modern standards.[8]

The nation's media dutifully generated a crisis atmosphere by showing videos and photos of crumbling concrete and rusty steel bridges. "Nearly 30 percent of bridges in the U.S. are structurally deficient or functionally obsolete," CBS News breathlessly reported. "You heard that right: one-third of the bridges in the U.S. should have a sign that says, 'Use at your own risk.'"[9]

Many politicians were quick to jump on this bandwagon. Minnesota Congressman James Oberstar quickly offered proposals to raise gas taxes anywhere from 5 to 40 cents per gallon in order to replace and repair bridges.[10] As chair of the House Transportation Committee, he promised a gathering of steel company lobbyists that the next federal transportation bill would spend $550 billion over six years (up from $285 billion in the previous bill). "We're talking about a lot of steel," he emphasized.[11]

Barack Obama latched onto this issue in his presidential campaign, promising to dedicate $60 billion to rebuilding national transportation infrastructure. When the economy tanked in September, Obama and various members of Congress started talking up an infrastructure bill aimed at stimulating the economy. With great fanfare, Congress passed this stimulus bill in February 2009.

All this publicity and debate no doubt led most Americans to believe we are suffering some sort of infrastructure crisis and that the stimulus bill went far towards solving that crisis. Both of these statements are flat-out wrong. The crisis was entirely fabricated by special interest groups. Fully aware of that, Congress dedicated less than 20 percent of the $787 billion stimulus bill to infrastructure—

and much of that will go to new construction, not repair or replacement of existing infrastructure.

The first clue that the infrastructure crisis was phony is the National Transportation Safety Board's report on the Minneapolis bridge collapse. The bridge failed, the report found, because of a design or construction flaw: certain parts were one-half inch thinner than they should have been. The board was unable to determine whether the designers had specified the wrong parts or the builders had substituted cheaper parts to save money, but it was clear about one thing: No amount of bridge maintenance would have detected or fixed the problem.[12]

What about the "one-third of the bridges in the United States" being risky to drive upon? That was based on Department of Transportation reports that 12.1 percent of roadway bridges are *structurally deficient* and 13.3 percent are *functionally obsolete*.[13] Note that CBS News generously rounded up the total—25.4 percent—to "almost 30 percent," which it immediately inflated to "one third" (which, of course, is 33.3 percent).

At most, however, the real number was 12.1 percent (meaning CBS News was merely 175 percent too high). The 13.3 percent of bridges that are "functionally obsolete" are not in any danger of falling; they merely have narrow lanes, inadequate overhead clearances, overly sharp on- and off-ramps, or other outdated design features. These bridges pose no risk to auto drivers unless the drivers themselves behave recklessly.[14]

The 12.1 percent "structurally deficient" bridges have suffered enough deterioration or damage that their load-carrying abilities are lower than when they were built. But that still doesn't mean they are about to fall down. Though they may be closed to heavy loads, the most serious problem is that they cost more to maintain than other bridges.[15]

A close look at the data reveals that more than 90 percent of structurally deficient bridges are local, not state or federal, and more than 80 percent are rural.[16] The average structurally deficient bridge is also less than three-fourths the size of the average bridge in good condition.[17] In other words, we are not talking about the George Washington or Golden Gate bridges; the vast majority are small rural bridges that get little use. Moreover, far from being a growing crisis, recent investments have reduced the number of structurally deficient bridges by nearly 50 percent since 1990.[18]

Bridge collapses due to poor maintenance are rare, and none have taken place in the United States in the last 20 years. Of 20 notable bridge collapses in the last 50 years, nearly half were caused by collisions with ships or barges, motor vehicles that caught fire, or—in one case—an airplane. Three resulted from earthquakes or a tornado, two—including the Minneapolis bridge—resulted from design or construction flaws, and one was overloaded when someone drove a 90-ton vehicle on a bridge rated to hold 17.5 tons.

Between 1960 and 1990, just four bridge collapses were blamed on maintenance issues. The 1967 collapse of the Silver Bridge across the Ohio River at Point Pleasant, West Virginia, led to radical changes in bridge maintenance and inspection procedures, yet the collapse itself was due more to design flaws than lack of maintenance. The 1928 bridge was an unusual design known as a chain suspension bridge. A notable flaw in the design was that a failure of any component would lead to a catastrophic failure of the entire bridge.[19]

The bridge had been inspected and found structurally safe just two years before the collapse. After the accident, the National Transportation Safety Board found that corrosion had led to a minute crack in one of the thousands of pieces holding the bridge up. The corrosion, the board concluded, was inaccessible to visual inspection and could not have been detected by then-available inspection methods without disassembling the part. The collapse, which killed 46 people, led to an increase in the frequency and intensity of bridge inspections. But, perhaps more important, it led to the closure of the only other chain suspension bridges in existence and to requirements that future bridges be designed with built-in redundancies so that, if one part fails, other parts will still bear the load.[20]

Despite stepped-up inspections, three more bridge collapses in the 1980s were blamed on maintenance failures. Connecticut's Mianus River Bridge failed in 1983, killing three people. Analysis showed that openings for draining water had been paved over a few years before. Collected water led to corrosion that should have been detected by bridge inspectors. But Connecticut had only 12 inspectors responsible for 3,425 bridges. Better maintenance procedures and inspections could have prevented the collapse.[21]

The collapse of a New York Thruway (I-90) bridge over Schoharie Creek, which killed 10 people, was also blamed on poor maintenance. A 1955 flood had removed rip-rap protecting the bridge supports, and that rip-rap was never replaced. A second flood in 1987 undermined the unprotected pillars.[22] Finally, in 1989, a US 51 highway bridge in Tennessee killed eight when it collapsed into the Hatchie River. Investigators determined that timber supports for the bridge, placed in dry ground in 1936, had rotted after the river changed course and saturated the posts; they blamed the state for failing to follow the recommendations of its own inspectors to correct the problem.[23]

All of these accidents led the National Transportation Safety Board to order more intensive inspections and maintenance. The United States has more than 600,000 highway bridges, and the fact that four failed due to maintenance problems in the last 50 years—and none in the last 20 years—hardly suggests that the nation has some sort of infrastructure crisis.

Mary Peters, the secretary of transportation under George W. Bush, tried to introduce some calm into the debate by pointing out that transportation infrastructure problems, to the extent that they exist, are largely a matter of misplaced priorities. Legislators, she noted, prefer "ribbons over brooms," that is, they prefer to fund capital projects (and the opportunity to cut ribbons when projects open) over maintenance. Moreover, the increasing trend has been to spend gas taxes and other highway user fees on transit and other nonhighway projects. No new taxes are needed to repair structurally deficient bridges, Peters argued; instead, the existing funds should simply be spent more responsibly.[24]

For example, the Sellwood Bridge, which crosses the Willamette River in Portland, Oregon, is structurally deficient and has been closed to trucks and buses since 2001. Both Multnomah County, which owns the bridge, and Metro, the agency that allocates federal and state transportation funds throughout the region, say they have no money to replace the bridge. Yet Metro is spending hundreds of millions of dollars on new streetcar lines, light-rail lines, and a light-rail bridge across the Willamette River. All of these lines put together will carry fewer people than the Sellwood Bridge. The only thing Metro has promised about the Sellwood Bridge is that if it does replace it, the new bridge will have no more capacity to carry cars than the existing one, as if Portland travel has not grown since the bridge opened in 1925.[25]

After all of the hullabaloo about crumbling bridges, Congress did not specifically allocate a single dollar of the 2009 stimulus bill to bridge repair. It did dedicate $27.5 billion to highways. Most of this will go to metropolitan areas and cash-strapped states that are not likely to share much with the rural counties that own most of the nation's structurally deficient bridges. At the same time, virtually all of the $8 billion that Congress allocated for high-speed rail, more than 80 percent of the $8.4 billion that Congress allocated for urban transit, and much of the $1.3 billion that Congress allocated to Amtrak will go for new construction, not for infrastructure repair.

Significantly, Portland plans to use none of its share of federal stimulus funds on the Sellwood Bridge, instead dedicating well over 40 percent of the funds to transit.[26] Portland's congressional delegation also earmarked $81.6 million of the 2009 Omnibus Appropriations Act for light rail and another $45 million for streetcars, but none for the Sellwood Bridge.[27]

This pattern is being repeated in cities across the country. Cincinnati, Milwaukee, Tucson, and Washington, D.C., all want to use stimulus funds to build new streetcar lines—which will stimulate the economy about as well as digging holes and filling them up.[28] With the possible exception of Tucson, each of these cities has plenty of crumbling infrastructure, but they are electing to spend stimulus money on ribbons, not brooms.

The Sellwood Bridge shows that the nation does have structurally deficient bridges and other infrastructure that need replacement or repair. However, the infrastructure crisis has been heavily overblown, and the real problem is a misallocation of resources, not a shortage of funds. The Minneapolis bridge collapse was used by special interest groups seeking to raise taxes for increased spending on projects that often, like downtown streetcars, are a needless waste of funds.

Impeding Mobility

While the infrastructure debate diverted attention from the nation's costly congestion problems, a bigger barrier to any solution to congestion comes from an anti-mobility coalition that blames America's mobility for all sorts of problems, real and imaginary. According to anti-auto dogma, automobiles have made Americans fat and lazy, contributed to the destruction of millions of acres of valuable farmland and open space, and polluted the skies, and they are a major cause of global warming. The only solution they see is

31

to reduce mobility by reducing per capita driving, and congestion is one of the tools they use to achieve that goal.

"Congestion is our friend," says Florida urban planner Dom Nozzi. "Communities with free-flowing traffic and big roads fuel sprawl [and] environmental destruction," he argues, while "congestion is a powerful disincentive for sprawl."[29] Although few planners are as outspoken about their preference for congestion as Nozzi, the policies they implement reveal that they would prefer that streets and highways be more congested and more dangerous.

Take, for example, the question of one-way versus two-way streets. In the 1950s, traffic engineers found that converting streets in congested downtowns from two-way to one-way operation greatly increased the capacity of those streets to handle traffic. Traffic on one-way streets experienced fewer turn delays, and traffic signals could be more easily coordinated to allow smooth traffic flows. One study found that converting two-way streets to one-way led to a 19 percent increase in traffic at 37 percent higher average speeds—not because the maximum speed limit on the one-way streets was greater than on two-way streets, but because drivers experienced 60 percent fewer stops. To top it off, accidents decreased 38 percent.[30] Pedestrian safety on one-way streets was so much greater than on two-way streets that one major study called one-way streets "the most effective urban counter-measure" to pedestrian accidents.[31] Several studies also found that, because of increased traffic flows, businesses on one-way streets were able to attract more customers than on two-way streets.[32] A survey of merchant associations across the country found that 90 percent favored one-way streets.[33]

Despite the proven benefits of one-way streets, many urban planners in recent decades have urged cities to convert one-way streets back to two-way operation. Such conversions had predictable results. A 1986 conversion in Denver increased accidents by 37 percent.[34] A 1993 conversion in Indianapolis increased accidents by 33 percent.[35] A 1996 conversion in Lubbock, Texas, reduced traffic flows by 12 percent but led to 25 percent more accidents causing 34 percent more property damage.[36] Undaunted by these results, numerous other cities, from San Jose to St. Petersburg, have converted one-way streets to two-way operation.

Converting one-way streets to two-way is just one of a broad array of practices euphemistically known as *traffic calming*. Contrary to the soothing name, the goal of traffic calming is to increase congestion or otherwise discourage auto driving. The government of Great Britain has proposed installing traffic calming measures to reduce driving speeds to 15 miles per hour on major roads through several towns specifically to discourage people from driving.[37]

Traffic calming measures include reducing the number of lanes of auto traffic, narrowing lane widths, installing speed humps, and adding median strips or other barriers. One favorite technique is to close a right-turn lane by installing a curb extension or bump out. This forces right-turning vehicles to stay in the main lane of traffic and effectively slows down the entire traffic flow.

Besides increasing congestion, traffic calming delays emergency service vehicles. An analysis by a deputy fire chief in Austin found that such delays would lead to many more deaths than the number of pedestrians that might be saved by slower, "calmer" traffic.[38]

Planners often claim that two-way conversions and other traffic calming measures make streets more "pedestrian friendly" or produce some other immeasurable benefit. Planners in Albuquerque advised, "The slowed and more congested auto travel which is projected to accompany the conversion [of one-way to two-way streets] promotes a positive ambiance of urban activity and vibrancy."[39] Planners apparently believe that "ambiance" will be undisturbed by the increased pedestrian accidents, the exhaust from cars stuck in traffic, or the number of stores boarded up because fewer people can get to those businesses.

Mobility versus Accessibility

One of the most aggressive traffic calming programs in the nation is conducted in Portland, Oregon, which also pioneered modern light-rail and streetcar construction. The region likes to think of its visionary plans as "the template for America."[40] City and regional planners have made clear their goal is to discourage driving, and to meet that goal, they will make congestion as bad as possible. They are willing, they say, to allow traffic to increase to level of service F on nearly every freeway and arterial in the region before they will do anything to relieve congestion.[41]

The region's population has increased by more than 70 percent since the last major new highway opened in 1983. The time the average Portland-area commuter wastes in congestion has nearly tripled since then.[42] When a local business group persuaded Rep. David Wu (D-OR) to secure federal dollars to increase the capacity of one of the region's most congested highways, the funds were rejected by Metro, Portland's regional planning agency.[43]

As noted, the 84-year-old Sellwood Bridge, 1 of 10 bridges crossing Portland's Willamette River, is so decrepit that safety engineers have closed it to trucks and buses. Planners say the region lacks the $100 million needed to replace the bridge, but they are moving ahead with plans to spend as much or more on a nearby light-rail bridge that will carry far fewer people.[44] When Bechtel offered to replace the Sellwood Bridge with a toll bridge, planners rejected the proposal.[45] While planners dither about replacing it, they have officially ruled out the possibility of building a new bridge that has more highway lanes than the existing one.[46]

The Oregon Transportation Commission shares this attitude. In 2000, the state highway division closed a number of structurally deficient bridges to heavy trucks. To replace these bridges, the legislature approved the sale of nearly $2 billion in bonds, to be repaid out of highway user fees.[47] Although the plan included replacement of many bridges on the congested I-5 corridor between Portland and Eugene, the Transportation Commission decided to provide no increases in capacity. "We can't build our way out of congestion," argued then-commission chair Henry Hewitt, implying that the state shouldn't even try.[48]

Portland planners say they are less interested in "how quickly we commute from Point A to Point B" and more interested in "linking land-use and transportation policies."[49] They are proud of the fact that the region's per capita driving has increased by only one-half percent per year since 1982, compared with the national average of 1.7 percent per year.[50] Yet congestion and high housing prices caused by Portland's urban-growth boundary have pushed much of the region's growth beyond Metro's authority. Thanks to those high housing prices, Vancouver, Washington, directly across the Columbia River from Portland, has grown far faster than Portland. In 1990, Vancouver had 10 percent as many people as Portland; by 2000, it was 27 percent larger.[51]

Portland's anti-mobility policies have also boosted growth in Salem, Oregon's state capital located less than 50 miles from downtown Portland. In the 1990s, Salem experienced a population boom, allowing it to overtake Eugene as Oregon's second-largest city. This led Salem's per capita driving to grow by 2.5 percent per year.[52] Much of this driving was people commuting to Portland, but of course Metro didn't count the rapid growth of miles driven outside of Portland's urban-growth boundary.

Even if congestion has suppressed some of the region's auto travel, the light-rail and streetcar lines the region has built have not provided an adequate substitute for the loss in auto mobility. From 1980 to 1982, before Portland began building its first light-rail line, the region's bus system carried 9.8 percent of commuters to work.[53] By 2007, after the region had spent more than $2 billion building nearly 50 miles of rail lines, transit carried just 6.5 percent of commuters to work.[54] The Portland area's vaunted light-rail and streetcar system carries less than 0.9 percent of mechanized passenger travel in the region.[55]

According to planners, this loss in mobility is all part of the plan. "Why go anywhere?" asks University of California (Berkeley) planning professor Robert Cervero. Cervero advocates *accessibility* rather than mobility; that is, that neighborhoods be designed so that stores, jobs, and other destinations are more often within walking distance or are at least fewer miles apart so that people don't have to drive as far to get to them. This means higher-density "compact cities" and mixed-use developments combining housing with shops, offices, and other uses.[56]

Portland planners have followed Cervero's philosophy with a vengeance. Metro drew an urban-growth boundary around the region in 1979. Although the region's population has grown by 60 percent since then, Metro has made only small additions to the boundary and then placed so many obstacles to development that virtually no new housing has been built in those additions.[57]

Metro's motto is "grow up, not out," which often means replacing single-family homes with four- and five-story apartment buildings or high-rise condos. Planners in Portland and its suburbs have enticed developers to build dozens of *transit-oriented developments*, meaning high-density, mixed-use projects, near rail stations. Portland's population is expected to grow by 300,000 people—nearly 55 percent—by 2035. When he was still a city commissioner, Portland's Mayor Sam Adams announced that he favored housing all of these new residents in transit-oriented developments "within one-quarter mile of all existing and to-be-planned streetcar and light-rail transit stops."[58]

Yet Portland's transit-oriented developments are proven failures, argues John Charles, president of Oregon's Cascade Policy Institute. Despite the region's high housing costs, the developments require huge subsidies to entice residents and businesses. Moreover, the developments are not particularly transit oriented. Though they may be near rail stations, they require extensive parking and, when they lack such parking, remain largely vacant.[59] Surveys have found that people living in these developments do not use transit significantly more than people in other Portland neighborhoods.[60] Similar results have been found with transit-oriented developments in other cities.[61]

Advocates of transit-oriented developments point to studies showing that people who live in dense neighborhoods with lots of transit service ride transit more and drive less than people in low-density suburbs.[62] But such studies suffer from a self-selection bias: that is, people who want to ride transit more tend to locate in transit-friendly neighborhoods. That does not mean that building more transit-friendly neighborhoods will lead to more transit ridership. It certainly doesn't seem to be working in Portland, where—as noted above—transit's share of travel has declined over the past 25 years.

To the extent that anything is working in Portland, another self-selection process may be at work. Portland's high housing costs have forced families with children to move to distant suburbs such as Vancouver and Salem. Portland's school district has been closing schools every year and now educates fewer children than it did 80 years ago, when Portland's population was half its current level.[63] The remaining households tend to be singles and childless couples, who tend to drive less than families with children. At least some people are not driving less because of Portland's plans; they were merely pushed out of the immediate vicinity.

Stuck in the 1950s

Perhaps the most fundamental reason for America's growing congestion problem is one that is rarely mentioned: our surface transportation network is based on technologies that are more than half a century old. The vehicles we drive may incorporate the latest in microprocessor technologies, but these do little to relieve congestion. The highways we drive on are based on designs and standards developed in the 1950s. While the interstate highway system was an incredible advance in its time, it is simply not capable of providing the mobility Americans demand today, much less in the coming decades.

Research has shown that worker productivities increase with increasing commuting speeds.[64] People seem to have an "ideal travel-time budget"; increased speeds make more potential jobs accessible without exceeding their travel-time budget.[65] Employers, in turn, have access to a more highly skilled work force, and people can more easily find the optimal jobs for their capabilities.

Faster travel times increase social productivity in other ways as well. Deliveries of raw materials and finished products cost less. Retail outlets serve larger consumer markets, leading to increased competition, a greater diversity of goods for sale, and lower prices. Emergency response vehicles can reach more areas within the critical time periods needed to save lives.

From the 1830s, when the first steam and street railways were built in the United States, to the early 1990s, when the interstate highway system was completed, the average speed of urban travel steadily increased. This gain in speed greatly contributed to the growth in personal incomes and the middle-class.

As previously noted, however, commute speeds declined after 1995. The drop can be attributed to the failure of transportation departments to build new roads in response to increasing demand. But the lack of any major technological breakthroughs in urban transport is equally responsible.

Though often sold to voters as modern, rail transit is fundamentally based on 1890s technology. As with automobiles, light-rail cars may be filled with microprocessors, but they still trundle along at an average of about 20 miles per hour. Rail transit fails to relieve congestion because, when the time needed to get to and from stations plus waiting for trains is added in, rail transit is far slower than driving for most people. Similarly, the 110-mile-per-hour high-speed trains that President Obama wants to build are no faster than trains that operated in many parts of the United States in the 1930s. And while other forms of mass transit may use more modern technology, any form of mass transit is a step backwards from the direct, door-to-door convenience and flexibility offered by the automobile.

True improvements in surface transportation will be those that focus on personal transportation systems. The problem is that major institutional barriers prevent the adoption of these improvements. One such barrier is the government's near-monopoly on highways, which allows little competitive pressure to make any improvements. Chapter 9 will discuss this issue in greater detail.

3. A Fork in the Road

Two different visions compete for America's transportation future. Since 1991, they have clashed whenever Congress has reauthorized federal surface transportation programs. Congress' choice of visions in the next reauthorization, most likely in 2010 or 2011, will have a profound influence on the American economy, environment, and lifestyles for many years to come.

The first vision—I would call it the anti-mobility vision but its advocates call it *smart growth*—is based on the premise that Americans need to drive less to reduce congestion, energy consumption, and environmental impacts. To reduce driving, the vision calls for spending more money on urban transit, intercity rail, and bike/ pedestrian facilities. The vision also calls for reducing the average size of lots for single-family homes and increasing the percentage of people who live in multifamily housing or mixed-use developments, both of which are supposed to reduce driving. In short, this vision calls for huge changes in American lifestyles.

The second vision—call it *efficiency*—is based on the premise that the resources available for transportation improvements are scarce and should be used as effectively as possible. This vision relies on user fees rather than taxes to pay for transportation. Transportation decisions are made by setting goals (sometimes called performance standards) and ranking transportation projects according to their ability to meet those goals. Goals could include congestion relief, energy savings, pollution reduction, and safety. Reducing driving is not a goal but merely one possible means to attaining some of the other goals. The projects that achieve the goals at the lowest cost are selected.

Every six years, Congress reauthorizes federal surface transportation funding, most of which comes from gasoline taxes and other taxes on autos, trucks, and tires. Through 1990, some variation of efficiency was the dominant vision. Though the term *smart growth* was not coined until 1996, Congress made a radical shift in 1991 that soon evolved into the smart-growth vision.

Although smart-growth advocates like to portray themselves as underdogs, smart growth has not only been the dominant vision in federal legislation since 1991, it or some variation dominates transportation planning in many states and urban areas, particularly on the Pacific Coast, and in some cases has been the dominant paradigm since the 1970s. Advocates of efficiency argue that these decades of experience demonstrate that smart growth hasn't worked and urge Congress to return to the efficiency vision.

The recent economic crisis provides new arguments for both sides. Smart-growth advocates say that increased spending on rail transit projects and intercity rail will provide an economic stimulus to help the nation recover. Efficiency advocates say that, now more than ever, the nation needs to invest its limited resources wisely to improve productivity and minimize waste.

Smart-Growth Advocates

The term *smart growth* was coined in 1996 by then-Governor Parris Glendening of Maryland. As one of his staff members later admitted, choosing the name was "one of the Glendening Administration's smartest strategies," because anyone who questioned smart growth could be (and usually was) immediately accused of favoring "dumb growth."[1] But the basic concepts behind smart growth were originally formulated in about 1989 by 1000 Friends of Oregon and the Surface Transportation Policy Project. These concepts in turn were based on ideas that had been brewing among urban planners for many years.

Up until 1989, Oregon's land-use planning rules, which are among the strictest in the nation, were founded on the notion that growth should take place in concentric rings around cities. Development was strictly limited outside of the urban-growth boundaries that defined those rings: in more than 95 percent of the state, landowners could not build a house on their own land unless they owned 80 acres and actually earned (depending on soil productivity) $40,000 to $80,000 a year farming those acres.[2]

To accommodate population growth, planners originally promised to regularly expand the urban-growth boundaries. But in a highly influential 1989 study called *Land Use, Transportation, Air Quality,* or LUTRAQ, 1000 Friends argued that low-density suburban development required too much driving. As an alternative, 1000

Friends proposed that urban areas should "grow up, not out," and they encouraged the state to stop or slow expansion of the urban-growth boundaries so that people would live in higher densities. LUTRAQ claimed this would lead people to drive less and ride transit, walk, or bicycle more.[3]

Meanwhile, the Surface Transportation Policy Project was founded in 1989 to promote alternatives to driving at the national level. In 1991, STPP influenced Congress to dramatically change the direction of federal surface transportation policy. Among other things, the 1991 Intermodal Surface Transportation Efficiency Act encouraged metropolitan areas to divert their share of federal gas taxes that would otherwise be spent on highways to transit instead. In combination with the Clean Air Act Amendments of 1990, the Intermodal Surface Transportation Efficiency Act presumed that new highways led to more air pollution and discouraged, and in some cases forbade, cities with poor air quality from using federal funds to build new roads.

During the mid-1990s, the Environmental Protection Agency, working hand-in-hand with STPP, set up two programs aimed at funding grassroots support for smart growth and reductions in auto driving. Starting in 1995, EPA's "Transportation Partners" program gave more than $6 million to STPP (which alone received nearly $1 million) and other groups whose goal was "to reduce the growth in Vehicle Miles Traveled throughout the U.S."[4] Because of controversy over the political use of these funds, EPA terminated the Transportation Partners program in 1999.

By then, however, EPA had created a new program called the "Smart Growth Network," through which it continued to give money to groups like STPP. Among other things, EPA designed two web sites, smartgrowth.org and transact.org (for "transportation action network"), which it then turned over to smart-growth groups. Transact.org is now the official web site of STPP, while smartgrowth.org is maintained (with continued EPA support) by a nonprofit group called the Sustainable Communities Network, of which STPP is a member. The amounts of money EPA distributed to smart-growth lobbying groups are small compared with the billions the federal government spends on transportation each year but had a major impact on the budgets of these supposedly grassroots groups.

In 1998, Congress reauthorized federal transportation funding with the Transportation Efficiency Act for the 21st Century. At the instigation of Oregon Senator Ron Wyden, this law contained a new program called "Transportation and Community and System Preservation Pilot Programs," under which the Department of Transportation would give grants to local governments to do LUTRAQ-like studies promoting smart growth. Local governments were encouraged to share the funds with nonprofit partners, thus transferring millions in federal funds to smart-growth lobby groups from Washington state to New Jersey.

For example, the Lane County Council of Governments, in Eugene, Oregon, received a $600,000 grant to promote "livability" in Oregon's Willamette Valley. The council shared much of this money with the Willamette Valley Livability Project, a group created by 1000 Friends of Oregon. Among other things, the money was spent on an eight-page newspaper insert delivered to 450,000 Oregon households promoting even stricter land-use regulation and higher urban densities.[5]

While "livability" proponents are the "Baptists" of the smart-growth coalition, the most important "bootleggers" are the rail transit industry.[6] Transit agencies spend about $9 billion a year building or reconstructing rail transit lines, about half of which comes from the federal government.

To keep that money flowing, engineering firms such as Parsons Brinckerhoff, construction companies such as Kiewit Rail Group, and railcar manufacturers such as Siemens Transportation freely dispense campaign contributions to politicians and ballot measures supporting new rail transit lines. All of these companies are also members of the American Public Transportation Association, whose $22 million annual budget greatly exceeds the combined annual budgets of the various highway lobby groups.

Efficiency Advocates

Because smart-growth advocates are ends-oriented, they assume—at least for rhetorical purposes—that their process-oriented critics are as well and accuse them of being tools of the highway lobby. In fact, very little remains of a highway lobby today. Auto manufacturers and oil companies spend little money or effort trying to influence transportation policy except as it affects them directly in the form of taxes or regulation.

Highway builders were once the majority partner of the highway lobby. Now most of them can make as much if not more money building rail transit. Thus they can build rail lines, which do little to relieve congestion, and enjoy the added bonus of demands to build something else—either more rails or highways—to relieve the congestion. Not surprisingly, the American Road Builders Association, once the biggest group in the highway lobby, changed its name to the American Road and Transportation Builders Association and today is just as enthused about building rail as highways.

The transit lobby—represented by the American Public Transportation Association—has an annual budget of about $22 million per year. The two main groups left in the highway lobby—the American Highway Users Alliance and The Road Information Program—together have budgets of less than $2 million per year.[7]

The leading efficiency advocates are not part of any highway lobby but are fiscally conservative think tanks. The Reason Foundation's Galvin Mobility Project issues a steady stream of reports about the most cost-effective solutions to congestion. It is largely funded by Robert Galvin, former chief executive officer of Motorola—hardly a member of the highway lobby.

Other think tanks that actively promote cost-effective transportation solutions include the Heritage Foundation, Cato Institute, and American Enterprise Institute. State-based think tanks that are most active in this area include the Cascade Policy Institute, Georgia Public Policy Foundation, Grassroot Institute, Independence Institute, John Locke Foundation, and Washington Policy Center. Other advocates of efficiency include various taxpayer groups such as the Taxpayers League of Minnesota and state chapters of Americans for Prosperity. None of these groups are particularly committed to autos or highways; their analysts just want an efficient transportation system.

The Smart-Growth Vision

The smart-growth vision for America is, in a word, Europe—or at least Europe as seen through the eyes of American tourists. Smart-growth advocates seek to rebuild American cities into compact places with dense populations (so that people won't need to travel as far), mixed-use developments (so people can walk to the store), and lots of rail transit both in and between the cities (so people can take transit instead of drive).

Smart-growth advocates say they are not against driving. But they fiercely resist any increases in highway capacities and instead propose that existing roads be modified to slow traffic and reduce capacities. For example, one-way streets can move 20 to 50 percent more traffic than two-way streets and experience 10 to 50 percent fewer accidents. Yet, as one way of discouraging driving, smart-growth planners in many cities are converting one-way streets to two-way even though postconversion records show the result is more congestion and accidents.[8]

As previous chapters have noted, the smart-growth vision of rail transit is extremely expensive. But smart growth has other costs as well. By creating artificial land shortages, it makes housing unnecessarily expensive. By increasing congestion, it wastes people's time. All of which also increase the costs to businesses, creating an unfriendly business environment.

The Efficiency Vision

Efficiency advocates do not focus on a mode such as roads or rail but on finding the most efficient or cost-efficient transport solutions. Efficiency and cost-efficiency are two different things. *Efficiency* can be calculated only when all benefits and costs can be measured in dollars. A program or plan is efficient if all of the individual components or projects in the plan have benefits that are greater than their costs. If funding is limited, then only the projects with the greatest benefit-cost ratios should be funded.

Cost-efficiency is calculated when some of the benefits cannot easily be measured in dollars. Those benefits might include such things as hours of congestion relief or tons of greenhouse gases abated. These benefits are estimated for each candidate project along with the dollar costs. The projects are then ranked in terms of dollars per hour of congestion relief, dollars per ton of greenhouse gases abated, and so forth. Only the projects with the highest rankings (lowest cost per unit of benefit) should be considered.

Efficiency calculations go hand in hand with projects that can be paid for out of user fees. If users are willing to pay for the full costs of building, maintaining, and operating a transportation facility, then that facility is efficient by definition. The weakening connection between transportation policy and user fees means that policymakers and planners have little incentive to worry about efficiency.

Cost-efficient transportation planning includes the following steps:

1. Developing performance measures, such as congestion, fatalities, energy consumption, pollution, and greenhouse gas emissions. Each performance measure must be an end result, not a means to an end. For example, "reducing per capita driving" is not a legitimate performance measure because it is merely a means to some other end, such as reducing pollution, and there may be less costly ways to achieve that end.
2. Collecting data regarding those measures.
3. Designing a transportation model that can estimate the effects of various transportation projects on each of the performance measures.
4. Making a list of all possible transportation projects.
5. Estimating the cost of each project and its effects on the performance measures.
6. Ranking the projects by cost per unit of each performance measure; for example, dollars per hour of congestion relief, dollars per BTUs of energy saved, etc.

At this point, planners can develop alternatives based on each performance measure: a congestion-relief alternative, a safety alternative, an energy-saving alternative, and so forth. Each alternative should include the projects with the lowest cost per unit of that performance measure's output up to the total available funds.

Some transportation projects may score well (that is, have a low cost per unit of each performance measure) for all performance measures, but others may require trade offs between, say, safety and pollution reduction. Based on the results, planners can design a preferred alternative that cost effectively achieves all of the goals. As chapter 8 shows, this system is known to planners as the *rational planning process*. But most urban planners today have abandoned it in favor of the smart-growth vision.

Efficiency advocates have no preconceived notions about what the resulting plans should look like. In general, however, the following is likely:

- Operational improvements such as traffic signal coordination and freeway ramp metering tend to be the most effective investments by any performance measure.

- Adding variable-priced tolling—tolls that increase with traffic so as to prevent congestion—to any highway project will increase that project's efficiency.
- For projects requiring new construction, the best highway projects are more cost-efficient than other modes, though many highway projects are far from efficient.
- Within any transit corridor, new bus service tends to be more cost-efficient than any form of rail transit. Buses operating on congestion-priced highways can be faster and far more cost-effective than rails.
- New rail construction is spectacularly inefficient compared with bus and highway alternatives in the same corridor.
- While trains running on the tracks of an existing freight railroad are more efficient than new rail construction, hardly any rail will be as efficient as buses.
- Ferries tend not to be cost-efficient because the dollar, energy, and pollution costs of operating ferryboats are very high.

Efficiency advocates are skeptical about the need to raise gas taxes or to use any other taxes to support transportation. They contend that existing gas taxes, or other user fees such as tolls, are sufficient to maintain existing roads and urge that new highways be built with tolls. However, recognizing the defects in gas taxes, many efficiency advocates are looking at vehicle-mile fees to replace such taxes—but only as user fees, not to raise money for transit or other nonhighway programs.

Results of Smart Growth

At least a dozen major urban areas have wholeheartedly embraced the smart-growth vision. In the 1970s, Boston; Honolulu; Portland, Oregon; Sacramento; San Diego; and the San Francisco Bay Area all began adopting plans that were or would become smart growth. By the 1990s, Baltimore, Denver, Minneapolis-St. Paul, Salt Lake City, and Seattle had joined the smart-growth community.

Most of these regions have imposed strict urban-growth boundaries to increase population densities, spent billions of dollars building rail transit systems, and used coercive zoning and subsidies to build mixed-use, transit-oriented developments near rail stations. Despite a steady stream of press releases extolling the virtues of planning in some of these cities, the actual results have been poor.

Table 3.1
DRIVING AND TRANSIT TRENDS IN SMART-GROWTH URBAN AREAS
(PERCENT)

Urbanized Area	Per Capita Driving (1982–2005)	Per Capita Transit (1982–2005)	Change in Transit's Share from 1982
Baltimore	68.4	18.6	−28.8
Boston	58.1	62.9	2.9
Denver–Boulder	36.1	20.1	−11.5
Honolulu	30.7	−38.4	−50.0
Minneapolis–St. Paul	63.8	−5.2	−41.6
Portland, OR	17.6	35.3	14.6
Sacramento	1.7	−30.6	−31.5
Salt Lake City	46.2	85.1	26.1
San Diego	39.8	34.3	−3.9
San Francisco–Oakland	32.4	8.6	−17.2
San Jose	29.5	−22.4	−39.7
Seattle	38.0	10.2	−19.7
Average of above	38.5	14.9	−16.7
Average of 85 urban areas	52.5	−5.7	−37.1

SOURCE: David Schrank and Tim Lomax, *The 2007 Urban Mobility Report* (College Station, TX: Texas Transportation Institute, 2007), spreadsheet "complete data."

NOTE: Since 1982, driving has grown faster than transit in 9 out of 12 urban areas that have emphasized smart-growth policies over the past decade or more.

Table 3.1 shows that the major urban areas which have adopted smart growth are only marginally different from the average of the 85 major urban areas included in the Texas Transportation Institute's database. The growth in per capita driving in the smart-growth areas is slightly lower and growth in per capita transit usage slightly greater. But only three of the dozen smart-growth urban areas have seen transit usage grow faster than driving (and Salt Lake City's numbers are tainted by the recent revelation that the region's transit authority systematically overestimated light-rail ridership by about 20 percent[9]).

Even if smart growth could ensure that transit usage would grow faster than driving, the results might still be virtually meaningless

47

because transit starts out carrying such a small proportion of travel. Transit carries a little more than 10 percent of travel in the New York urban area; 4 to 5 percent in the Honolulu, San Francisco-Oakland, and Washington urban areas; 3 to 4 percent in Boston and Chicago; and 2 to 3 percent in Philadelphia, Portland, and Seattle. Everywhere else, it is less than 2 percent.

If transit carries 2 percent of travel in your urban area, and smart-growth policies lead transit to grow at 2 percent per year while driving grows at only 1 percent per year, after 100 years transit will still be carrying only 5 percent of travel.[10] This is an example of what University of California (Irvine) economist Charles Lave called "the Law of Large Proportions," which he defined as "the biggest components matter most."[11] In this case, it means that, since automobiles are by far the dominant form of travel, small improvements in automobile fuel economy or toxic emissions will have a bigger effect on energy consumption or clean air than big changes in public transit.

Smart growth's fundamental flaw is faith in what planners call the "land-use transportation connection." "Transportation affects land use and land use affects transportation," say planners.[12] No doubt, transportation technology affects land use. The development of horsecars, streetcars, and the automobile each gave more people access to lower-cost land. This allowed higher rates of homeownership and increased the lot sizes of single-family residences. Changing transportation technologies also changed the way we shop, recreate, and socialize.

Smart-growth planners, however, think we can go back to the time when people drove less and rode streetcars more simply by mandating higher rates of multifamily housing or small residential lots. In fact, the evidence is that the effects of land-use on transportation choices are weak at best. As University of Southern California planning professor Genevieve Giuliano observes, "Land use policies appear to have little impact on travel outcomes."[13]

Census data, for example, reveal that the population densities of urban areas range widely, from about 1,000 to 7,000 people per square mile. Yet the percentage of people who drive to work in nearly 90 percent of these areas ranges only narrowly from 89 percent in the densest areas to 98 percent in some of the least-dense areas. If it takes a sevenfold increase in densities to get 9 percent of people out of their cars, then the density increases that any urban area can realistically achieve are not going to have a worthwhile effect on travel choices.

The share of commuters driving to work is lower than 89 percent in about 11 percent of urban areas. But this has nothing to do with density: the lowest rate of auto commuting is in the Ithaca, NY, urban area, whose population density is only 1,800 people per square mile. Instead, two factors explain low rates of auto commuting: age structure and job concentrations. Nearly all of the urban areas with low rates of auto commuting fall into one of two categories. Most are, like Ithaca, college towns with large numbers of young people. Age structure, however, is beyond the control of urban planners.

The second category of urban areas with low rates of auto commuting is older regions like New York and Chicago that have very high job concentrations in the urban center. These cities are closest to what planners call the *monocentric model* of a city, that is, a city with most jobs located downtown. Most urban areas, especially ones that have experienced most of their growth since about 1900, do not come close to this model.

Today, urban planners rely on a *polycentric* model, calling for the creation of regional and town centers in which jobs can be concentrated. They hope that this will create a jobs-housing balance in which individual suburbs and neighborhoods have about the same number of workers and jobs so that no one will have to commute far to work.

The first problem with this idea is that there is no guarantee that people will both live and work in the same neighborhood or suburb. In fact, some evidence shows that people would rather live some distance away from work so they can keep their work and family lives separate.[14] So it is not surprising that University of California planning professor Robert Cervero found that jobs and housing in many San Francisco Bay Area communities "are nearly perfectly balanced, yet fewer than a third of their workers reside locally, and even smaller shares of residents work locally."[15]

The second problem is that even the polycentric model does not fit modern urban areas. Economist William T. Bogart has shown that, in a typical American urban area, no more than 30 to 40 percent of jobs are located in downtowns and suburban centers.[16] This means the land-use and transportation plans that focus on providing transit to regional centers will serve less than half the commuters in their regions. For example, Denver has built or is planning nearly 150 miles of rail transit lines, yet after all the lines are built, Denver planners project that only 26 percent of the region's jobs will be within one-half mile of a rail station.[17]

In short, if smart-growth planners really wanted to reduce driving, they would mandate that all or a high percentage of jobs in an urban area move downtown. However, it is much harder for planners to impose mandates on large and politically powerful employers than on individual homebuyers. The result is that smart growth's connection between land use and transportation is more rhetoric than reality. "If the aim is to reduce environmental damage generated by automobiles, the effective remedy is to directly price and regulate autos and their use, not land use," concludes USC's Giuliano.[18]

Despite the evidence that urban densities have little influence on driving, the California legislature passed a law in 2008 requiring the state's urban areas to become denser, with the expectation that this will reduce greenhouse gas emissions.[19] Historically, residential zoning has specified the maximum housing densities allowed in any particular zone: no more than eight homes per acre, four homes per acre, etc. Developers and homebuyers were free to build at lower densities if they wanted. The new California law follows the smart-growth practice of cities like Portland in requiring *minimum* housing densities.[20] This means that new developments will be significantly denser than homebuyers might prefer in order to increase the density of California urban areas as a whole.

Thanks to several decades of growth-management planning, California already has some of the densest urban areas in the nation. The 2000 census found that, at 4,000 people per square mile, the average density of California urban areas was two-thirds greater than the national average of 2,400 people per square mile. New York was the only state with denser urban areas, at 4,200 people per square mile; but outside of New York City, New York urban areas had fewer than 2,100 people per square mile.

If urban densities have a large influence on per capita driving, then California should have one of the lowest rates of per capita driving in the nation. In fact, at more than 9,000 miles per person in 2000, California is just slightly below the national average of 9,770 miles per person. Eleven states, most of which have much lower urban densities than California, have lower rates of per capita driving.

Numerous analysts have looked at the relationship between density and driving and found it to be very weak. "Density matters, but not much," reported transportation planner Paul Schimek after reviewing National Personal Transportation Survey data. "The effect of density is so small that even a relatively large-scale shift to urban densities would have a negligible impact on total vehicle travel." In particular, he found that a 50-percent increase in 1990 urban residential densities would reduce driving by less than 3 percent.[21] Another study found that increasing residential densities from about 3,000 to 25,000 people per square mile would reduce driving by only 11 to 25 percent.[22] On the basis of this and similar studies, Department of Transportation analyst Don Pickrell concluded that claims that increased densities would reduce driving were "spurious"; factors such as income and household size were much more important to people's driving habits than residential densities.[23]

The California law attempts to overcome these problems by focusing on reducing the distance people travel to work. However, as USC planning professor Genevieve Giuliano observes, "commuting considerations play a limited role in residential-location choices." Instead, the desire for better schools and other neighborhood amenities may encourage people to live far from work. In addition, multiworker households may not be able to locate close to the jobs of all workers. For these reasons, "development density must increase dramatically if we want to induce significant changes in mode shares and trip lengths," which, she suggests, is probably not "possible in the United States."[24]

My own calculations use census and Department of Transportation data to compare the effects of changes in urban population densities on per capita driving. I found that the correlation between changes in urban densities and changes in driving is very low. To the extent that any correlation exists, the data indicate a 100 percent increase in urban densities is associated with an average decline in per capita driving of just 3.4 percent.[25] This means that densities would have to roughly quadruple to reduce per capita driving by just 10 percent.

The new California law also gives urban areas an incentive to plan "transit-priority projects," meaning transit-oriented developments. But we have already seen that these aren't particularly effective at reducing driving either.

Nor is multifamily housing more energy-efficient than single-family housing: According to the Department of Energy, single-family detached homes use less energy per square foot than any other form of housing.[26] To truly save energy using smart-growth principles, Americans will have to accept not only smaller yards, but smaller homes. In fact, just as making cars that are more energy-efficient makes more sense than trying to get more people to ride transit, efforts to make new and existing single-family homes more energy efficient will do more to save energy and reduce greenhouse gas emissions than trying to get more people to live in denser housing.

If the results of smart growth have been modest, the costs are high. First is the cost to taxpayers of rail transit and other smart-growth schemes. Since 1992, American taxpayers have spent more than $130 billion (in 2007 dollars) constructing rail transit lines, mostly in cities with smart-growth agendas. Taxpayers also subsidize many of the transit-oriented developments built near rail transit stations. Portland, Oregon, for example, has spent close to $2 billion subsidizing real-estate developments on light-rail and streetcar lines.

Second is the cost of congestion. While most American cities are congested, the smart-growth policy of deliberately spending transportation dollars on projects that do little to reduce congestion instead of ones that can have a significant effect on congestion makes congestion a particularly bitter pill to swallow in smart-growth cities.

A third cost is the loss of mobility. To the extent that any reductions in driving result from congestion and not better accessibility, the benefits of that lost mobility disappear.

The fourth and possibly most important cost is the effect on housing prices of land-use restrictions aimed at creating more compact urban areas. Smart growth is one form of *growth-management planning*, which attempts to dictate either the rate or location of population growth. Close to 20 states practice some form of growth management, and housing in those states tends to be much more expensive than in states that do not.

There are several reasons why this is so. In the most common forms of growth management, rural areas are placed off limits to development through large-lot zoning or other restrictions, while growth is concentrated in politically prescribed urban areas. Such restrictions inevitably create an artificial land shortage which drives up the cost of housing and any other form of development.

The secondary effect of growth management is even more serious. If a city imposes severe planning restrictions on developers in an area with no growth management, the developers can simply take their developments outside the city line. Given a competition for tax dollars, cities and counties will tend to keep development costs low through speedy permitting processes.

In contrast, growth management allows cities to conspire to prevent development from taking place outside of prescribed lines. When developers have nowhere else to go, cities are free to impose lengthy permitting processes with high development fees and onerous planning requirements. This cartelization of development can have a significant effect on housing prices.

For example, in 2002, California homebuilders compared housing prices in San Jose (which has practiced growth management since the early 1970s) with those in Dallas (which does not practice growth management). The study found that land shortages caused by San Jose's political growth boundary added about $200,000 to the cost of a bare lot. San Jose's permitting process added another $90,000 to the cost of each home, and impact fees added yet another $24,000. In addition, mainly because of high housing prices, the labor costs of building a home in San Jose were $43,000 more than in Dallas.[27]

Housing prices in some cities are greater than in others because of differences in income: people in wealthier cities tend to buy bigger or higher-quality homes. Before 1970, the median cost of housing throughout most of America was about two times median family incomes. The major exception was Hawaii, which had passed a growth-management law in 1961 and whose median housing cost three times median family incomes.

Today, median homes still cost about two times median family incomes in states and urban areas that do not practice growth management. But areas with growth management have seen median prices soar to as much as 11 times median family incomes. This makes single-family housing unaffordable to all but the wealthiest people and fulfills smart-growth goals of increasing the percentage of people living in multifamily housing.

In most cases, the year when price-to-income ratios began to rise above two closely follows the year when those states or urban areas began growth-management planning. Furthermore, the correspondence between urban areas that practiced growth management and urban areas that suffered a major housing bubble in the 2000s is almost one-to-one. Housing prices in California, Florida, and other smart-growth states doubled and then crashed; prices in Texas, Georgia, and other non-smart-growth states did not dramatically rise or fall.[28]

As a result of the "planning tax" imposed by smart-growth planning, 2006 homebuyers in smart-growth states paid more than $200 billion more for their homes than they would have in the absence of smart growth.[29] Some of this amount was recouped by home sellers in the form of windfall profits resulting from land-use restrictions. But a large share of the added cost of new homes was simply a deadweight loss to society: neither homebuilders nor the state or local governments making the rules benefited from the extra charges paid by homebuyers. In the San Jose case cited earlier, for example, the $90,000 permitting cost is due to the lengthy periods required to obtain a permit (and the risk that it will never be granted), while the $43,000 labor cost is absorbed by the higher cost of housing workers must pay.

Smart growth's goal of suppressing mobility is questionable at best. The effectiveness of smart-growth practices in accomplishing that goal is limited. Yet smart growth imposes high costs on the people who live in cities and states that practice it.

Results of Efficiency

While an increasing number of urban areas are adopting the smart-growth vision, chapter 8 will show that few have rigorously followed the efficiency model. Yet plenty of anecdotal evidence shows that this model can work. At the national level, technical changes to automobiles have led to huge improvements in energy, safety, and pollution. At the regional level, some urban areas have proven that, contrary to popular belief, cities can build their way out of congestion if investments are focused on the right projects. At the local level, many analyses have shown that some transportation investments can be hundreds of times more cost-effective in reducing congestion and other social costs than other projects, yet many plans focus on the least cost-effective projects.

In 1970, the skies of American cities were dark with pollution, the average vehicle (including trucks) went only 12 miles per gallon of fuel, and nearly 50 people died for every billion miles driven. Today, automotive air pollution is negligible, the average vehicle goes 17 miles per gallon, and fewer than 15 people die for every billion miles driven.[30]

These gains weren't achieved by encouraging people to drive less. Despite efforts by the Environmental Protection Agency and some cities to reduce driving, Americans now drive nearly three times as many miles as in 1970.[31] Instead, all of these improvements have come from better cars and better highways. Moreover, fatalities, pollution, and per-mile energy consumption are steadily declining as new cars are cleaner, safer, and more energy efficient than cars made just the year before.

Urban congestion has two causes. First, new highway construction has not kept up with driving. Between 1980 and 2006, the amount of driving on urban freeways increased by 188 percent, but the number of lane-miles of urban freeway increased by only 77 percent.[32] This is partly because a significant share of gas taxes and other user fees has been diverted to nonhighway uses. In 2006, for example, less than $94 billion of the $116 billion collected from highway users was spent on highways.[33]

The second reason for congestion is that gas taxes, the main source of highway revenues, do not accurately price roads. The cost of providing roads to meet peak-period demand is much greater than the cost to meet average demand. Airlines, hotels, phone companies, and many other businesses charge users more during peak periods, but highways paid for by gas taxes cost the same to use anytime of the day.

"We can't build our way out of congestion," highway opponents claim, "because new roads simply lead to more driving." That would be like Ford saying, "We can't build enough Mustangs to keep up with the demand, so let's build Edsels instead." Only the government would think that we shouldn't build infrastructure that people use and instead should invest in infrastructure that people don't use.

In fact, many cities have shown that they can build enough highways to meet the demand for driving. In 1984, for example, San Jose voters agreed to build several new freeways and expand existing freeways.[34] Between 1989, when the new roads were first opened to travel, and 1993, the amount of time travelers had to waste in traffic declined by nearly 30 percent.[35] After 1995, however, the region started spending most of its transportation funds on rail transit instead of roads. Because those rail lines moved far fewer people than the roads, congestion again grew.[36]

Cities have also achieved significant results with projects aimed at cost-effectively reducing congestion and other transportation problems. In 2003, San Jose coordinated traffic signals at 223 intersections for a cost of about $500,000. This reduced travel times in those corridors by 16 percent and saved 471,000 gallons of gasoline per year, which in turn significantly reduced air pollution.[37]

The fuel savings translates to a reduction of 4,200 tons of greenhouse gas emissions per year. If the $500,000 cost were amortized over 10 years, the cost would average $7 per ton of abated greenhouse gas emissions. In fact, since motorists saved $942,000 per year (at $2 per gallon), signal coordination actually saved more than $200 per ton of greenhouse gas emissions abated. By comparison, many rail transit projects produce more greenhouse gases than they save, and the ones that do reduce greenhouse gases do so at a cost of thousands of dollars per ton.[38]

This is not to say that no rail transit project makes sense or that all highway improvements are worthwhile. Many highway proposals are far from efficient, and somewhere in the United States may be an efficient rail transit project. But funding of any transportation projects should only follow rigorous analysis and consideration of a full range of alternatives, something that is lacking from today's transportation planning.

4. Lies My Transit Agency Told Me

In 1964, private transit companies served the vast majority of American cities. These companies operated profitable, if declining, businesses in the face of increasing auto ownership. Perhaps their biggest handicap was that they were considered public utilities and thus had to seek permission from state or local governments for every route change, fare increase, or any other innovation they cared to make.

One thing unified the industry: virtually every private transit operator in the nation agreed that buses were less expensive, more flexible, and safer to operate than streetcars or other forms of rail transit. By 1964, almost all of the remaining operators of rail transit were public agencies that could tap taxpayers to cover the higher costs of rails.

Congress effectively nationalized the transit industry when it passed the Urban Mass Transit Act of 1964, promising federal capital grants to any public agencies that took over private transit companies. Within a decade, the private transit industry was virtually wiped out, replaced almost completely by tax-subsidized public agencies.

Today, these transit agencies have become insatiable parasites on American productivity, eagerly gulping tens of billions of tax dollars a year into their collective maws. Far from responsibly using scarce tax dollars to provide a necessary urban service, these agencies deliberately choose high-cost solutions to transportation problems, thereby making our transportation networks less efficient and (by taking money from more effective programs) more congested. Far from promoting mobility, these high-cost solutions contributed to a 26 percent decline in per capita transit ridership since 1964 and an 11 percent decline since 1980.[1]

The moral and economic bankruptcy of the public transit model is illustrated by a financial gimmick many transit agencies used in the 1990s and early 2000s to boost their capital budgets. Transit agencies pay no taxes, so they sold their buses, railcars, and other capital equipment to banks and other investors and then leased them back. The banks reduced their taxes by depreciating the value of the equipment. For every $100 million in capital, the banks saved about $6 million in taxes, which they split with the transit agencies. Effectively, the transit agencies would get $3 million in "free" money for every $100 million they spent—but that $3 million would cost taxpayers $6 million.[2]

Transit agencies supposedly work in the public interest. But for government agencies to create tax shelters costing taxpayers millions, without any democratic process approving the expense, is certainly not in the public interest. Fortunately, the Internal Revenue Service put a stop to this practice with new rules in 2004, but not before dozens of transit agencies took advantage of this tax loophole.[3]

Examples of transit agency waste abound, but none is clearer—and more controversial—than rail transit. As it happens, I have been a rail fan at least since I was five years old and rode the *Western Star* from Grand Forks, North Dakota, to Portland, Oregon. Many people love trains, but I've carried my obsession with passenger trains far beyond most. I helped restore the nation's second-most-powerful operating steam locomotive and once owned five full-sized passenger cars to run with that locomotive. I have taken dozens of coast-to-coast trips on American and Canadian passenger trains. Trains are always my preferred method of travel when I'm in other countries. My home and office are decorated with old rail memorabilia, including posters, china, paperweights, linens, and blankets. Yes, I also have a model railroad.

In short, if rail transit made sense, I would be first in line to support it. But the fact that I am a rail fan does not mean I think the government should force other taxpayers to subsidize my hobby.

Outside of a few hyper-dense places such as Tokyo and Hong Kong, rail transit is a luxury for the few whose costs are shared by everyone. Commuter trains and subways may be necessary to keep Manhattan going, but that doesn't mean that everyone else in the nation should have to subsidize them. Outside of New York City, rail transit has an insignificant effect on local American economies. The main beneficiaries of new rail transit projects are the contractors who design and build them, not the people who eventually ride them.

The most important kinds of rail transit include the following:

- *Heavy rail*, including both subways and elevated trains that always use their own exclusive right of way;
- *Light rail*, meaning vehicles usually powered by overhead wires that sometimes run in the streets and sometimes in their own exclusive right of way;
- *Streetcars*, meaning vehicles that are smaller than light-rail cars and almost always operate in the streets;
- *Commuter rail*, which may be powered by electric or diesel locomotives and usually uses tracks shared with or once used by freight trains.

A handful of cities also have monorails, automated people movers, inclined planes, and a few other variations. But none of these are unimportant relative to heavy rail, light rail, streetcars, and commuter rail, because none move a substantial number of people and few cities are looking to build more of those kinds of transit. Incidentally, the terms "heavy" and "light" rail refer to the passenger loads, not the weight of the cars or rails. Heavy-rail trains can be much longer than light rail, so they can carry more people.

Basic rail transit technology dates back to the 19th century. The first commuter trains served Boston suburbs in 1838. The first successful electric streetcar opened in Montgomery, Alabama, in 1886. Chicago opened the first electric-powered elevated train in 1895, while New York opened the first electric heavy-rail subway line in 1904.[4] Electric-powered commuter trains date to 1906. Like modern automobiles, modern railcars may have lots of computer circuits under their skirts, but the basic technology of electric motors turning steel wheels on steel rails remains unchanged.

Cities' frustration with autos and highways using 1950s-technology is evident as they turn to 1886–1906 technology instead. This interest in rail transit is based partly on a nostalgic view of the past, partly on pork, and partly, as chapter 7 will show, on incentives in the federal budget.

Six Reasons Cities Should Not Build Rail

1. Cost

The most important thing to understand about rails is that they are really expensive. I mean really, *really* expensive. The Government

Accountability Office has shown, for example, that buses can provide service as fast and frequently as light rail at a lower operating cost and for about 2 percent of the capital cost.[5] Outside of a few very dense places such as Manhattan, Tokyo, and Hong Kong, there is nothing trains can do that buses cannot do faster, better, more flexibly, and for a lot less money.

The typical light-rail project being planned or built today costs $20 million per track mile ($40 million per double-tracked mile). The least expensive is about $15 million per mile, and the most expensive—one being planned in Seattle—is expected to cost more than $100 million per mile.[6] Heavy rail typically costs at least twice as much as light rail: A plan to extend the Washington Metrorail system 23.1 miles toward Dulles Airport is currently expected to cost $5.2 billion, or $225 million per mile.[7] Commuter-rail costs depend on the condition of existing track but typically run $5 to $10 million per mile. A new commuter-rail line in Portland, Oregon, for example, cost about $8 million per mile.[8]

Complicated freeway interchanges can be expensive, but the average cost of a complete freeway is typically much lower than rail. The Fort Bend Tollway Authority recently completed a 6.2-mile, four-lane freeway on the outskirts of Houston, complete with interchanges and various over- and underpasses, for $60 million, or about $2.4 million per lane mile.[9] The Colorado Department of Transportation recently widened Interstate 25 through the heart of Denver, which required numerous overpasses, at a cost of $19 million per lane mile.[10] Counting urban and suburban areas together, the average cost is less than $10 million per lane mile.

Rail advocates love to claim that a rail line can move as many people as several freeway lanes, but capacity (which is discussed in more detail below) counts for much less than actual use. Only one American rail system—New York City subways—carries more (just 20 percent more) passenger miles per track mile than the average mile of New York City–area freeway lane. In 2007, the average track mile of light and commuter rail carried less than 15 percent as many passenger miles as the average freeway lane mile in urban areas with rail transit. Outside of New York, the average heavy rail mile carried only 70 percent as many passenger miles as the average urban freeway lane mile.[11]

In comparing rail and highway productivities, rail supporters often use a double standard: comparing *full* railcars with the *average* occupancy of commuter automobiles.[12] In fact, like automobiles, the average transit vehicle carries far fewer people than its capacity. Most rail cars and buses carried less than one-sixth of their capacity in 2007.[13] Even sport utility vehicles (SUVs) do better than that.

2. Overruns

The people who run bus transit systems normally have to look ahead no more than a year to predict such things as ridership trends, fuel costs, tax revenues, and other factors relating to their business. Rail projects generally take more than a decade to plan, design, and build. Transit managers are ill-equipped to predict construction costs a decade into the future.

The truth is, of course, that no one can predict what is going to happen a decade from now. But rail transit projects are notorious for far exceeding the budgets originally approved. In 2002, Danish planning professor Bent Flyvbjerg found that, after adjusting for inflation, the average North American rail project cost more than 40 percent above its projected cost when approved, while highway projects went only 8 percent over their projected costs.[14] Two studies of more recent rail projects, one published in 2006 and one in 2008, found that they, too, averaged 40 percent over budget.[15]

The most recent projects, both completed and in the planning stages, reveal that rail planners still have not learned from their mistakes.

- In 1998, Phoenix proposed to build a 13-mile light-rail line for $390 million, or $30 million per mile.[16] Completed in 2008, the final cost of the 19.6-mile line was $1.41 billion, or $72 million per mile.[17]
- In 2000, Charlotte, North Carolina, estimated that a light-rail line would cost $331 million.[18] The final cost turned out to be $427 million.[19]
- In 2004, the first, 12-mile leg of the Dulles rail project was projected to cost $1.5 billion.[20] Today the projected cost has increased by nearly 100 percent to $3.0 billion.[21]
- In 2004, Denver's Regional Transit District persuaded voters to support a $4.7 billion rail transit system. The latest estimate is that this system will cost $7.9 billion, or 68 percent more than the 2004 estimate.[22]

61

Part of the problem, as noted, is that people can't predict what the weather is going to be a week from now, much less what the economy is going to be like a decade from now. This in itself should caution transportation planners against trying to plan projects that take more than a decade to complete.

Flyvbjerg, however, believes persistent underestimates of rail construction costs result from "strategic misrepresentation, that is, lying."[23] Planners deliberately lowball estimates in order to gain project approval. Once the project is approved, they develop more realistic estimates, add expensive bells and whistles, and respond to political pressures to lengthen the originally proposed project. Having approved the original project, funders become "invested" in the idea and rubber stamp cost increases with little hesitation.

Many of the original estimates are made by engineering and consulting firms such as Parsons Brinckerhoff (now known simply as PB). These companies must know that, if a project is funded, they are likely to get some of the contracts for engineering and building the lines. Thus they have an incentive to develop projections that will gain approval, both by underestimating the costs and overestimating the benefits.

In one blatant example of strategic misrepresentation, PB compared a proposal to bring rail transit to Madison, Wisconsin, with simple improvements in bus service. To its dismay, the company found that bus improvements alone attracted more riders than bus improvements combined with rail transit. Later, PB admitted that it crippled the bus alternative, making it appear that rail transit was needed to boost transit ridership.[24] When the government agency that hired PB presented the results to the public, it never mentioned the bus alternative at all, making it appear that rail transit was the only way to attract people to transit.[25]

In a further example of strategic misrepresentation, many transit agencies maintain that they always build rail lines "on budget." After adjusting for inflation, Denver's Southwest light-rail line cost 28 percent more than its original estimate.[26] The city's Southeast light-rail line went 59 percent over its original estimate.[27] Yet Denver's Regional Transit District insisted that it built both projects "on budget."[28] What it meant was that it built both projects for the final budgeted costs, not the lower costs projected when originally approved.

Since rail transit projects have a continuing history of going, on average, 40 percent over budget, Flyvbjerg believes that transportation planners and funders should routinely add at least 40 percent to all cost projections. This presumes, of course, that planners and funders actually care about how much of the public's money they are wasting. In fact, rail advocates often seem to believe that rail lines should be built no matter what the cost.

3. Rehabilitation

Because rail transit projects are so expensive, transit agencies generally go heavily into debt to fund them. Much of this debt is in the form of bonds that must be repaid within 30 years. But the costs don't end when the bonds are paid off: rail lines must be completely replaced, rebuilt, or rehabilitated about every 30 years. Except for the right-of-way, everything—cars, tracks, roadbed, stations, electrical facilities—must be replaced or upgraded.

The first Washington, D.C., Metrorail line opened for business in 1976. In 2002, just 26 years later, the Washington Metropolitan Area Transportation Authority estimated that it needed $12.2 billion—roughly the cost of constructing the original system—to rehabilitate the system.[29] It has not found any of this money, so the system suffers frequent breakdowns and service delays.[30]

Rail transit systems in Chicago, San Francisco, Boston, and New York also face fiscal crises. The Chicago Transit Authority is "on the verge of collapse" as it needs $16 billion it doesn't have to rehabilitate its tracks and trains.[31] Similarly, the San Francisco BART system faces a $5.8 billion shortfall to replace worn-out equipment.[32] Boston borrowed $5 billion to restore its rail lines and now more than a quarter of its operating budget goes to repay this debt, which is "crushing" the system.[33]

According to one New York transit advocate, New York's Metropolitan Transportation Authority "is in deep doo-doo" because it doesn't have the money it needs to rehabilitate its system.[34] It is already spending $1.5 billion per year—an amount that is expected to reach $2 billion by 2010—repaying debts incurred by past rehabilitation efforts.[35] It says it needs $30 billion for rehabilitation over the next 10 years, of which it has only $13 billion.[36] As a result, it may need to cut subway, commuter rail, and bus service.[37]

The projected costs of rehabilitating the Washington, Chicago, San Francisco, and New York heavy-rail systems all average more than

$100 million per route mile of rail. Pittsburgh recently rehabilitated streetcar lines to light-rail standards for $32 million per mile.[38] The first modern light-rail lines, including those in Buffalo, Portland, Sacramento, and San Diego, will reach their 30th birthdays in the next decade, and their rehabilitation will cost similar amounts. Few, if any, of these agencies know how they are going to finance this cost.

Because such rehabilitation does not increase the productive capacity of a transit system, but merely maintains it at as-built levels, it should properly be considered a maintenance cost. But the Federal Transit Administration allows transit agencies to count rehabilitation as a capital cost. The significance is that when rail advocates claim, as they often do, that rail lines cost less to operate and maintain than buses, they are ignoring these long-term maintenance costs.

The same agencies that cannot afford to maintain their existing systems are nonetheless embarking on expensive expansion programs. New York's MTA is spending $16.8 billion building an eight-mile Second Avenue Subway. Washington's Metro, of course, is spending $5.2 billion building the Dulles rail extension. San Francisco's BART is preparing to spend more than $6 billion building a line to San Jose. Chicago is extending several of its commuter-rail lines. This complete disconnect between planning and budgetary reality has become typical of rail-transit agencies.

Ironically, the anti-highway "fix-it-first" mantra makes perfect sense when applied to rail transit. Rail transit fares do not come close to paying the operating costs, much less the costs of line rehabilitation or new rail construction. If transit agencies cannot afford to maintain their existing lines, it makes no sense for them to build new ones.

Moreover, not a single place in the country "needs" a new rail line. As will be shown below, new rail won't relieve congestion, reduce energy consumption, or abate greenhouse gas emissions. Rail is simply a luxury that most places can't really afford. So the new mantra should be: When user fees can pay for it, build it now. When they can't, fix it first.

4. Ridership

"Middle-class automobile owners won't ride a bus," rail advocates claim, as if this somehow justifies spending billions of dollars to get a few snooty people out of their automobiles. In fact, transit ridership is more sensitive to frequency and speed than to whether the vehicles run on rubber tires or steel wheels. "When quantifiable service characteristics such as travel time and cost are equal," say researchers, "there is no evident preference for rail travel over bus."[39]

The real problem is what happens to overall transit system ridership when agencies facing cost overruns, stiff mortgage payments, or high rehabilitation costs must choose between keeping the trains running and maintaining their bus systems. Having built rail, too many agencies have been forced to cut bus service, thereby leading transit ridership to drop or, at best, stagnate.

In the late 1970s, Atlanta began building a heavy-rail system. By 1985, it had 25 route miles, and ridership had grown to 155 million trips per year. Since then, the Atlanta urban area population has doubled, rail miles have also doubled, yet ridership continues to hover around 155 million. In 2007, it reached 158 million. While rail ridership has grown, that growth has been at the expense of bus ridership.[40]

In the early 1980s, Los Angeles had a policy of maintaining low bus fares, and between 1982 and 1985, ridership grew by more than a third. Then it decided to build rail transit lines, which suffered huge cost overruns. In response, the Los Angeles Metropolitan Transportation Authority raised bus fares and cut back on service, leading to a 17 percent drop in bus ridership by 1995. The NAACP sued, arguing that the agency was cutting service to minority neighborhoods in order to finance rail lines to white middle-class neighborhoods. The court ordered the MTA to restore bus service, forcing it to curtail its rail plans.[41] Today, bus ridership has rebounded and far exceeds its 1985, prerail level. Meanwhile, rail ridership remains stagnant, carrying fewer riders each year than the bus system lost between 1985 and 1995.

When St. Louis opened its first light-rail line in 1993, it was hailed as a great success because system ridership, which had shrunk by nearly 40 percent in the previous decade, started growing again. But when St. Louis opened a second line in 2001, doubling the length of the rail system, rail ridership remained flat and bus ridership declined. By 2007, total system ridership was no greater than it had been in 1998.

San Jose opened its first light-rail line in 1988 and quickly added to the system. At first things seemed to go well, but when the Valley

Transportation Authority's tax revenues declined in the recession of 2001, it was forced to choose between defaulting on its bonds or making severe cuts to its rail and bus service.[42] It cut service by 20 percent, and by 2005 it had lost more than a third of its transit riders. Today, ridership remains less than it was in 1990.

Unable to both maintain its aging rail system and provide decent bus service, Chicago lost more than a quarter of its transit riders between 1985 and 1995. Ridership has recovered somewhat since then, but still remains 18 percent below its 1985 peak. Similarly, Philadelphia transit ridership peaked in 1984, fell by 32 percent by 1998, and since has recovered to 84 percent of its 1984 peak.

As of 2003, about half the urban areas with rail transit saw ridership declines starting in the mid-1980s. The remaining areas enjoyed increases in ridership, but at rates slower than increases in driving and, in most cases, slower than the population growth.[43]

Many areas with bus-only transit systems did far better. From 1983 to 2003, ridership on bus transit systems in Austin, Charlotte, Houston, Las Vegas, Louisville, and Raleigh-Durham all grew faster than auto driving. The 2000 census revealed that the number of commuters taking transit to work in urban areas with rail transit collectively declined, while the number in bus-only urban areas increased.[44]

Part of the problem is that many transit agencies rely on sales taxes, which are particularly volatile during economic recessions. Property taxes are more stable than sales taxes, so transit systems subsidized out of the former are less likely to suffer cuts—such as those required in San Jose when sales tax revenues declined in 2001.

Another, more helpful, solution is to operate a low-cost bus system that does not require selling bonds or other borrowing. When tax revenues decline, agencies cannot simply stop paying their creditors. If half of a transit agency's revenues go to debt service, then any cuts made when revenues fall have to be twice as great than if the agency had no debt.

5. Land Use

Buses are flexible and can easily be rerouted when travel patterns change. Rail lines take years to build, and once built can only be rerouted after great time and effort. While bus systems can respond to rider demand, rail systems must generate their own demand.

This leads transit agencies to promote intrusive land-use regulation that discourages low-density development away from their rail lines and mandates and/or subsidizes high-density developments close to rail stations.

Welcome to what Portland researcher John Charles calls the mythical world of *transit-oriented development*.[45] Instead of customizing transit systems to serve American cities as they exist today, transit agencies want to rebuild the cities to suit the kind of transit service the agencies want to provide. There are many problems with this aspiration, not least of which is the fact that transit carries less than 5 percent of travel in all American urban areas except New York (where it carries about 10 percent of travel), and it seems absurd to design cities around such little-used transportation systems.

A bigger problem is that such social engineering violates basic American freedoms in several ways. Families should be able to choose the form of housing they want, not have their choices manipulated by transit agencies and planners seeking to reduce the share of people living in single-family homes and increase the share living in apartments or condos. Property owners should be able to use their property as they want, provided they don't harm others, and not have their choices limited by onerous land-use restrictions.

An even bigger problem is that, as noted in the previous chapter, land-use policies have, at best, marginal effects on people's transportation choices. Transportation technologies clearly influence land uses: Cities built before 1890, when most people walked for most of their travel, were much denser than cities built between 1890 and 1930, when streetcars were popular; those cities, in turn, were denser than cities built after World War II, when autos were dominant. But this process is not reversible: building cities to preauto or prestreetcar designs will not lead people to significantly reduce their driving.

According to Robert Cervero, a long-time enthusiast of transit-oriented development, such developments do increase transit ridership, but this is "due to residential self-selection—i.e., a life-style preference for transit-oriented living."[46] In other words, people who prefer transit over driving choose to live in such areas, but that doesn't mean that the urban design has influenced their travel habits. This market is limited: surveys suggest more than four out of five Americans would prefer a home with a yard to living near shops, transit, or jobs.[47] Once that demand is met, cities like Portland and

Denver have had to resort to huge subsidies to entice developers to build more high-density developments, and the evidence indicates that the people who live in those developments drive just as much as people elsewhere.

If the market for such developments were strong, then developers would build to profit from that market. But a study by University of California planning professors John Landis and Robert Cervero found that, 25 years after the opening of San Francisco BART lines, population densities actually decreased closer to BART stations. "Population has grown faster away from BART than near it," they say, concluding that "the land use benefits [and by "benefits" they mean increased population densities] of investments in rail are not automatic."[48]

The same thing happened in Portland, Oregon. When it opened its first light-rail line in 1986, it immediately zoned all the land near rail stations for high-density, transit-oriented developments. Ten years later, not a single such development had been built. So the city decided to subsidize such developments. It sold public land to developers at below-market prices. It waived property taxes on high-density housing for 10 years. And it used tax-increment financing to provide additional subsidies and support to developers.

Tax-increment financing is a popular financial tool cities use to promote redevelopment. Invented in California in the 1950s, it is now legal in every state but Arizona. To use it, planners draw a line around a district to be redeveloped. The property taxes currently being collected in that district continue to go to schools, fire, police, and other urban services. But all new or incremental taxes, whether taxes on new developments or taxes assessed because existing developments increase in value, are kept by the city to subsidize new development.

City planners typically estimate the stream of income that will come from incremental taxes and then sell bonds that can be repaid by that income. The bonds are then used to pay for infrastructure, to buy land and resell it to developers at discounted prices, and sometimes to provide direct grants to the developers.

City officials act as if these taxes are free money. "The developments pay for themselves," they say. In fact, new developments need fire and police protection just as much as anywhere else. If children live in these developments, they will go to schools. But the funds to pay for those schools, fire, police, and other urban services must come from other taxpayers, who will either have to pay more taxes or accept a reduced level of urban services as their taxes are spread out to cover people whose taxes aren't paying for those services.

Since 1996, the city of Portland has drawn five urban-renewal districts along the routes of existing or planned light-rail lines and used four preexisting districts along those lines to promote transit-oriented developments. The total subsidies offered in these districts amount to well over $1.5 billion, not counting the tens of millions of property tax waivers offered to high-density residences.[49] The total subsidies to transit-oriented developments are close to the total capital costs of the rail lines themselves, on which Portland has spent more than $2 billion (in 2008 dollars, including projects currently under construction) since 1980. If the goal of transit-oriented developments is to increase transit ridership, that subsidy should be added to the cost of rail transit. Many other cities, including Denver, Minneapolis, and San Jose, have similarly used tax-increment financing to support transit-oriented developments.[50]

Not surprisingly, since 1996, developers have built dozens of transit-oriented developments. Yet, as John Charles points out, the developments aren't really transit-oriented. They only work if they have lots of parking places. Projects with limited parking either never get built or have very high vacancy rates. Mixed-use projects with limited parking to serve the retail shops end up with vacant shops.[51] Most important, studies show that households in these developments are just as prone to drive, and just as unlikely to ride transit, as similar households elsewhere.[52] Similar results have been found in other cities that subsidized transit-oriented developments.[53]

Perhaps the biggest problem with land-use policies aimed at promoting transit ridership is their effects on housing prices. With the strong support of transit agencies, Portland and other cities have drawn urban-growth boundaries around their regions. These create artificial land shortages, which in turn make housing more expensive and force more people to live in multifamily housing that requires less land. To a large degree, the housing bubble that led to the 2008 financial meltdown resulted from such land-use policies: states with such policies, such as California and Florida, suffered from severe bubbles, while states without land-use restrictions, such as Georgia and Texas, had virtually no bubbles.[54] Urban and transit planners should not be proud of themselves for making housing unaffordable and destroying the American dream of homeownership.

6. *Capacity*

Rail transit is often described as "high-capacity transit." Yet its capacity really isn't that high. Some idea of the limits of rail capacity can be seen by the way Washington, D.C., Metro dealt with the huge crowds expected on the day of Barack Obama's inauguration: Metro turned off the escalators going into key stations out of a fear that the escalators would deliver people into the stations faster than the trains could carry them away.[55] Apparently, escalators can move more people per hour than eight-car subway trains.

Heavy-rail lines—subways and elevateds—are the highest capacity form of transit available. If people jam in as tightly as they do in Tokyo—which most Americans would find unacceptable—the "crush capacity" of a heavy-rail car is about 180 people. An eight-car heavy-rail train can therefore carry about 1,440 people. If rail systems can manage to move one train every minute—and only a few American rail lines can support such traffic—the line can move 86,400 people per hour. This is where rail advocates are able to claim that a rail line can move as many people as several freeway lanes. As table 4.1 shows, the capacities of other forms of rail transit are much lower. If heavy-rail lines have the highest capacities, commuter rail and light rail are really only moderate-capacity transit and street-cars are low-capacity transit.

An important question is this: who really needs high-capacity transit? People looking at the thousands of cars driving down a freeway at rush hour often think, "If only we had a rail line, all those people could ride." But the reality is that the people in each of those cars have different origins and different destinations. They may all be in this freeway corridor now, but a rail line will only serve a tiny number of them because most do not both live and work near a rail station.

What cities really need is *flexible-capacity transit*: transit capable of moving large numbers of people where needed but economically moving small numbers where demand is lower, such as in suburban areas. Rail transit, with its very high fixed costs, cannot qualify. Rail-transit agencies try to provide flexible capacities by having buses

Table 4.1
TRANSPORTATION CAPACITIES (PEOPLE PER HOUR)

Heavy Rail	86,400
Commuter Rail	15,000
Light Rail (4-car trains)	18,000
Light Rail (2-car trains)	9,000
Streetcar	2,800
Exclusive Bus Lane	56,000
Buses on HOV/HOT Lane	9,000
Suburban Buses	200
Autos on Freeway Lane	8,000
Autos on Arterial Lane	4,000

NOTE: These capacities are rarely if ever achieved in practice, but they show what alternative transportation systems can do. Commuter rail assumes eight-car trains with 120 seats and 40 standees moving every five minutes. Streetcar assumes cars with 40 seats and 100 standees moving every three minutes. Suburban buses presume frequencies of four buses per hour. Autos presume four people per car with 2,000 cars per hour on freeway lanes and 1,000 per hour on arterials. See text for calculations of subway, light rail, and other buses.

feed into rail stations, but transit agencies know that they lose riders every time they ask people to change vehicles.

Buses can provide true flexible-capacity transit. They can run on city streets in the suburbs where demand is low, move to high-occupancy vehicle (HOV) or high-occupancy/toll (HOT) lanes where demand is higher, and if demand warrants, use exclusive bus lanes. While the capacity of exclusive bus lanes may not be quite as high as heavy rail, buses, unlike the trains, can easily start from different origins and diverge to different destinations, allowing more people to make their transit journeys without transfers.

This means that light rail and commuter rail really make no sense anywhere. Cities that need low-, moderate-, or high-capacity transit can meet those needs with buses. Only areas that need ultra-high-capacity transit might need to consider heavy rail, and outside of New York City, no place in the United States truly needs such high capacities.

Six Wrong Reasons to Build Rail

Despite the fact that rail transit loses trainloads full of money and fails to attract significantly more riders than improvements in bus service, rail advocates argue that cities should build rail lines for other reasons. Here are six popular, but wrong, reasons for building new rail lines.

1. Economic Development

Rail advocates say that rail transit stimulates economic development. They often point to a streetcar line built in downtown Portland, Oregon, that supposedly stimulated $1.5 billion worth of new development. In fact, much of that development was subsidized with hundreds of millions of dollars of tax-increment financing, tax waivers, and other support to developers. Some of the developments would have been built without the streetcar or subsidies. Others would have been built with the subsidies but without the streetcar. It isn't likely that the streetcar alone would have led to any developments without the subsidies.

Does any rail transit stimulate new development? In the mid-1990s, the Federal Transit Administration asked this question of Robert Cervero, who as previously noted is a strong proponent of transit-oriented developments, and Samuel Seskin, who works for Parsons Brinckerhoff, the consulting firm that has had a hand in almost every major rail transit project since the first New York City subway was built. If anyone could find support for the idea that rail transit stimulates economic development, these two would.

Yet Cervero and Seskin found that "urban rail transit investments rarely 'create' new growth." At best, rail transit may "redistribute growth that would have taken place without the investment." "The greatest land-use changes," they add, "have occurred downtown."[56]

In other words, rail transit is a "zero-sum game" that may benefit some property owners at the expense of others. The main property owners who benefit are those who own land downtown, mainly because most rail systems are hub-and-spoke systems that focus on downtown. This explains some of the political calculus behind rail: Downtown property owners benefit a lot, so they lobby for rail. Other property owners each lose a little, so they have little incentive to lobby against it.

Many planners and city officials take for granted that anything that improves downtown is a good thing. But, other than generating campaign contributions from downtown property owners, why is it so important to improve downtown? Downtowns "are relics of a time past," says Joel Garreau in his book, *Edge City*.[57] The conventional image of a city as a place with a high-density downtown surrounded by lower-density housing "is only one way to think of a city," adds Garreau. "In fact, it is only the nineteenth-century version."[58] Before 1820, people did not build downtowns because they didn't have industries that concentrated jobs, and they lacked the technology to build taller, denser structures. After 1920, the automobile, electrical power, and telephones made downtowns unnecessary.

If rail transit does not stimulate new development but merely, at best, transfers it from one part of an urban area to another, then rail planners gain the power of creating winners and losers among a city's property owners. Giving government officials such power is never a good idea, as all it can do is lead to corruption. Portland-area newspapers, for example, call the coalition of elected officials, rail contractors, and transit-oriented developers who support Portland's transport policies the "light-rail mafia."[59]

2. People Won't Ride Buses

Rail advocates claim that buses won't entice middle-class auto drivers out of their cars. But what is so important about getting snobs to ride transit? Improvements in bus service can attract as many new transit riders as rail construction—and at a far lower cost.

A recent survey found that the median income of Washington, D.C., Metrorail riders was 47 percent higher than Metrobus riders, and that 98 percent of rail riders owned an automobile, compared with only 80 percent of bus riders.[60] For those who want to get middle-class commuters out of their cars, this is a Pyrrhic victory, considering that (as will be shown in chapter 6) the fossil-fuel-generated electricity used to power the Metrorail system emits more carbon dioxide (CO_2) per passenger mile than the average SUV. Meanwhile, "beleaguered bus" riders face repeated service cuts so that the transit agency can keep the train system running.[61]

In the late 1990s, the San Francisco Bay Area Metropolitan Transportation Commission—which spends two-thirds of the region's transportation funds on transit systems that carry only 4 percent of the region's passenger travel—was considering how to spend more money on transit.[62] One possible project was an extension of BART trains to San Jose, a line so expensive that taxpayers would spend nearly $100 every time someone took BART instead of driving. Another project was improved bus service in Richmond, a city with a heavy population of low-income minorities. Bus improvements, planners estimated, would attract Richmond residents out of their cars at a cost of just 75 cents per trip.[63]

Needless to say, the commission decided to support the rail line and not the bus improvements. In the commission's judgment, spending $100 to attract one high-tech worker, who probably drives a relatively pollution-free automobile, onto a train was more important than spending the same $100 to attract 133 low-income workers, who are more likely to drive older, more polluting cars, onto buses.

The calculation may actually be more cynical than that. Middle-class employees are more likely to vote and have more political power than low-income workers. Getting those voters to support the idea of transit as a daily necessity, rather than something used only by those who can't afford their own cars, may be a part of the rail agenda. As the late Paul Weyrich, a strong rail supporter, wrote, "It is well to target the poor, the unemployed, and minorities, but if the transit project is designed only to serve them, middle class voters will be turned off."[64]

In short, the real goal is not to get people out of their cars. After all, since most transit subsidies are paid by auto drivers, getting everyone out of their cars and onto transit would make transit too expensive to operate. Instead, the goal is to get enough people out of their cars to create a feeling of transit dependency so that voters will support increased transit funding.

3. Rails Avoid Congestion

Rail advocates say that rail cars won't be slowed by congestion. Thus, they can offer people a real choice: drive in traffic or avoid congestion by taking the train. And note that buses cannot avoid the congestion.

First, the obvious question is why a relatively tiny number of people deserve a heavily subsidized transit system which allows them to avoid congestion, while everyone else who is paying the subsidy has to sit in traffic. Second, the premise that buses can't avoid congestion is simply wrong.

Most major urban freeway systems have high-occupancy vehicle (HOV) lanes or their more recent variant, high-occupancy/toll

Table 4.2
COMPARISON OF ALTERNATIVES FOR DENVER'S EAST CORRIDOR
(MILLIONS)

Alternative	Capital Cost	Operating Cost	Annualized Cost	Hours Saved Per Year	Cost Per Hour Saved*
New I-70 Lanes	$305	$15.6	$40.1	18.36	$2.18
New HOV Lanes	337	14.9	42.0	12.57	3.34
Diesel Rail	374	33.7	63.4	8.91	7.12
Electric Rail	571	29.2	75.1	9.09	8.26

*Cost per hour saved is in mere dollars.

SOURCE: Kimley-Horn & Associates, *East Corridor Major Investment Study Final Report* (Denver, CO: DRCOG, 1997), pp. 37–39.

(HOT) lanes, which are open to low-occupancy vehicles that pay a toll. HOT lane tolls are adjusted—sometimes as frequently as every 10 minutes—to ensure that the lanes never become congested. An urban area with a complete network of HOV or HOT lanes as a part of every freeway would allow buses to avoid congestion throughout the region.

Such HOV or HOT lanes cost less to build than rail lines, and the congestion relief they provide benefits everyone, not just the few who ride rail transit. Transit riders benefit because buses traveling at freeway speeds go faster than light rail (which averages about 20 miles per hour) or heavy-rail or commuter-rail trains (which generally average no more than 40 miles per hour). The other drivers using HOV or HOT lanes benefit because they also avoid congestion. People who don't use the lanes also benefit: HOT lanes built parallel to a freeway in southern California draw a third of the traffic off the freeway.

Table 4.2 gives the results of an analysis of alternative transportation improvements in a corridor between downtown Denver and Denver International Airport. The study showed that rail transit cost more to build and more to operate and did less to relieve congestion than new freeway or HOV lanes. Nonetheless, planners picked rail transit, and—supposedly to save money on operating costs—they picked electric rail even though the added capital costs of electric rail equal 127 years of the operational savings from diesel rail. Since the study was completed, the projected cost of rail transit in the east corridor has nearly tripled, while the projected cost of bus rapid transit on HOV lanes in another Denver corridor increased only 12 percent.[65]

With an appropriately designed highway system, buses can not only avoid congestion as well as trains, they can do so at a far lower cost and be put into service almost immediately instead of after a decade of planning and construction.

4. Political Equity

Rail advocates will sometimes say, "Let's build one line and see how it works." The construction of one line then creates momentum for additional lines. A major part of that momentum stems from every urban community's desire for a share of federal rail dollars, no matter how poorly rail might actually serve that community.

Suburbs in the Denver area agreed to support their Regional Transit District's multibillion-dollar rail plan on the condition that all of the rail lines be built at once. Suburban officials realized that the plan would probably suffer major cost overruns (as proved to be the case) and that whatever line was last on the schedule would probably never be built. In response to the cost overruns, the transit agency proposed to build just four of the six planned lines—a proposal that was naturally rejected by officials from the suburbs whose lines would be left out.[66]

Rail advocates have applied the equity argument to neighborhoods as well as cities. San Francisco wants to spend a whopping $1.4 billion on a 1.7-mile transit tunnel as a part of a project to extend light rail to the Bayshore neighborhood.[67] According to the Federal Transit Administration, Bayshore transit ridership is already very high, but one of the main reasons for building this line is "to achieve a goal of equity with other communities currently served by rail."[68]

Operating subsidies to San Francisco bus riders average $1.50 per trip, while subsidies to rail riders are $1.90 per trip. Light rail also has much higher capital costs. By the Federal Transit Administration's reasoning, if one neighborhood is served by a ridiculously expensive transit line, equity demands that every other neighborhood get equally expensive service. In fact, the real equity problem is how to reduce the subsidies that some taxpayers have to pay to allow others to ride transit.

5. It Works in Europe

American tourists visit Europe and ride the London subway, the Paris metro, or trams in Italy, and come home wishing the United States had a similar transit system. The easy answer is that the United States isn't Europe: our population densities are lower, and our incomes are higher, so fewer people are likely ride transit even in dense areas.

The real answer is that Europe isn't Europe either, at least not the Europe that American tourists fantasize about. There is no doubt that Europe has a lot more rail transit than the United States. As of 2007, at least 150 European urban areas had some form of rail transit, compared with 30 in the United States.[69] Europe spends several times as much money subsidizing these rail lines as the United States spends on transit.[70]

These rail lines may be convenient for tourists, but the average European rarely uses them. In 2004, the average American traveled 87 miles on rail transit; the average European just 101 miles.[71] This difference hardly commends Europe as an example of successful rail transit. Moreover, the share of European travel on rail transit declined from 1.4 percent in 1980 to 1.1 percent in 2000. Meanwhile, the share of European travel using automobiles increased from 76.4 to 78.3 percent.[72]

6. Protecting the Environment

Many people take it for granted that rail transit has lower environmental impacts than driving and that investing more money in rail transit will be good for the environment. The late University of California economist Charles Lave questioned this as long ago as 1979. "The received wisdom on this topic is easily stated," he wrote. "1. It is self-evident that public transportation is vastly more energy-efficient than automobiles; 2. It is self-evident that investing money to improve transit facilities will attract many more passengers." Unfortunately, he continues, "both of these 'self-evident' premises turn out to be false."[73]

As chapter 6 will show in detail, transit uses just about as much energy and emits just about as much pollution, per passenger mile, as automobiles. To the extent that rail transit might save any energy at all, the cost of getting a few people to ride trains and drive less is huge.

People who sincerely want to save energy and reduce pollution, Lave pointed out, would do better to focus on making automobiles more environmentally friendly, not on trying to get people to ride transit instead of drive. This is "necessarily so" due to what he called the "Law of Large Proportions," meaning "the biggest components matter most."[74] In other words, Americans travel 60 times as many passenger miles in urban areas by automobile as by transit, so a small investment in reducing the environmental effects of autos will go much further than a large investment in transit.

Why Rail?

If rail transit is so expensive and ineffective, why do cities want to build more? And why do voters support it? As chapter 7 will show, the answer to the first question is that incentives in federal funding encourage cities to choose high-cost forms of transit.

When voters support rail transit, it is partly nostalgia for a time that never existed, when anyone could take a convenient, affordable train or streetcar wherever they wanted to go. Partly, it is innumeracy: in an era when the federal government counts spending in the trillions of dollars, few are fazed by proposals to spend billions of dollars of other people's money. And partly, it is the successful efforts of narrow special-interest groups in persuading people that 19th-century trains are somehow technologically, environmentally, and morally superior to 20th-century automobiles and buses. Yet voter support is tenuous. Prior to 2000, voters rejected the vast majority of rail proposals that were placed on ballots. In general, measures passed only when faced with little organized opposition. Opponents could defeat rail if they raised at least $1 for every $100 spent by pro-rail campaigns.[75] Many transit agencies responded to defeat by bringing measures back to the voters again and again: Phoenix voters rejected rail three times before approving it in 2002. Marin County voters rejected it twice before approving it in 2008. Similar repeated votes took place in Denver, Salt Lake City, San Jose, and elsewhere.

In 2000, the calculus changed when transit agencies became much more aggressive in lobbying the public. Such lobbying by public agencies is technically illegal in most states, but transit agencies got around it by not specifically mentioning the ballot measures.

The Utah Transit Authority pioneered the technique for a ballot measure for raising sales taxes to pay for light rail. For several months before the November 2000 election, the transit agency ran frequent television advertisements showing an empty freeway and stating that light rail removed enough cars from the road to fill the freeway the entire 78 miles from Ogden to Provo. "Even if you don't use it, you use it," concluded the ad. Although Salt Lake City voters had previously rejected light rail, these ads more than doubled the resources devoted to promoting rail, and the measure passed.

The Utah Transit Authority gleefully reported its results to other transit agencies which were quick to follow suit. Denver's Regional Transit District is forbidden from lobbying the public but only after measures are placed on the ballot. In August 2004, just days before a $4.7 billion rail measure was formally put on the ballot, the district spent close to $1 million mailing a six-page, four-color "informational" brochure claiming that rail transit would reduce congestion, pollution, and otherwise improve the region's quality of life.

Operating with modest budgets, rail critics in Austin, Texas, were able to defeat a rail ballot measure in 2000. But in 2004, Capital Metro, Austin's transit agency, spent $2 million on television and other advertising supporting rail transit, leading opponents to simply give up.[76] In 2008, Albuquerque's transit agency spent tax money supporting a rail ballot measure for that city.[77]

Democracy is not perfect. When government projects require taxing some people to benefit others, those who expect to reap hundreds of millions or billions of dollars—primarily, in this case, rail contractors and real estate developers—will be willing to spend millions to gain the project's approval. With millions spent on one side and thousands on the other, voters get a very one-sided view of the project. Such election results should not be interpreted to mean that voters want rail transit but that they want congestion relief, reduced air pollution, and the other things that rail proponents falsely claim rail will provide.

The Transit Model Is Broken

The average American transit agency gets only a third of its operating funds, and none of its capital funds, from fares. This means transit officials are less interested in increasing transit ridership than they are in persuading appropriators and taxpayers to give them more money. Increased ridership is actually a burden on transit systems: even though transit vehicles are, on average, only one-sixth full, they tend to be fullest during rush hour, when new riders are most likely to use transit.

Although transit officials love to describe their programs as "sustainable," in fact, automobiles and highways are far more financially sustainable than most current transit agencies. Today's rail transit systems work only because few people use them and everyone else subsidizes them. Because rail transit costs at least four times as much, per passenger mile, as driving, if everyone rode the transit services offered today instead of automobiles, then cities would go bankrupt trying to keep the transit systems running.

Yet transit does not have to be expensive, and it does not even have to be subsidized. The United States has several completely unsubsidized transit systems that work very well. One is the Atlantic City Jitney Association, whose members own identical 13-passenger buses. Each bus is operated by its owner on routes scheduled by the association. Rides are $1.50 each and cover all major attractions in the city. Unlike most publicly owned transit systems, the jitneys operate 24 hours a day, 7 days a week, and receive absolutely no subsidies from any government agency.[78] Such jitney service is illegal in most other American cities because it would compete against the government's monopoly transit agency.

Another unsubsidized transit system is the *públicos*, or public cars, of San Juan, Puerto Rico. Like the Atlantic City jitneys, *públicos* are independently owned and operated buses that typically seat 17 passengers. At least six different companies operate *públicos*, similar to the multiple taxi companies that coordinate operator-owned taxis in Washington, D.C., and some other American cities. The *públicos* provide both urban and intercity service. Fares vary depending on the length of the ride, but in 2007 they averaged less than a dollar. Although *públicos* compete against a public bus system and a recently built heavy-rail line (whose cost rose from a projected $1.0 billion to $2.2 billion), the *públicos* carry more riders each year than the public buses and trains combined.[79]

A third unsubsidized transit operation is the NY Waterway ferries, which connect 10 different points in New Jersey with Midtown, Wall Street, and the World Finance Center in Manhattan. Founded in 1986 by Arthur Imperatore, who co-owned a New Jersey trucking company, NY Waterway offers a service that none of the many transit agencies in the New York metropolitan area thought to provide.[80] Passengers arriving in New York City can take NY Waterway buses to and from various points in Manhattan at no extra charge. Although the company accepted a subsidy from the Federal Emergency Management Agency in 2001 to temporarily replace subway service between New Jersey and the World Trade Center after 9/11, it is otherwise funded entirely out of fares.[81] The company carried 4.8 million passengers in 2007, collecting $33 million in revenues against $21 million in operating expenses.[82] Like many other private companies, NY Waterway is imperiled by the recent financial crisis, but that doesn't mean private transit can't work.

Public transit agencies encourage people to believe that, if the taxes that subsidize them disappeared tomorrow, people without cars would lack any mobility. In fact, these examples show that private forms of transit would quickly spring up to take the place of government transit. Such private transit would, in many ways, be superior to the government transit. It would be more likely to offer door-to-door service, operate during more hours of the day, and provide more limited or nonstop services to popular destinations.

Private transit fares might be higher than subsidized transit fares, but if people believe that low-income and other people without access to automobiles deserve subsidies, government can directly subsidize them in the form of *transportation stamps*. Similar to food stamps, such transportation stamps could be redeemed for any public conveyance: taxis, buses, rail, Amtrak, or airlines. The redeemers would exchange the stamps for cash through the issuing government agency. Subsidies to transportation users, rather than providers, would create a competitive atmosphere and lead to efficient innovations that would benefit all transit users.

5. The Next Boondoggle

In February 2009, as Congress debated the $787 billion stimulus package, President Obama sent word to key senators that he wanted the package to include $8 billion for high-speed trains. High-speed rail, he said, would be his "signature issue" in the stimulus program.[1] Later that month, Obama's 2010 budget proposed to spend an additional $1 billion per year for five years on high-speed rail.[2]

In April, Obama presented his national high-speed rail "vision" to the public. Under the plan, about 8,500 route-miles of high-speed trains would connect key cities in 33 states along the eastern and Gulf Coast seaboards, in the Midwest, Texas-Oklahoma-Arkansas, California, and the Pacific Northwest.[3]

No doubt President Obama sees himself following in the footsteps of President Eisenhower, whose interstate highway system is the largest and one of the most successful public works project in history. Just as Eisenhower borrowed his "plan" from an existing proposal developed years before by the Bureau of Public Roads, Obama's high-speed rail network is identical to one proposed by the Federal Railroad Administration in 2005.[4]

But two key differences separate interstate highways and high-speed rail. First, President Eisenhower had a pretty good idea of how much the interstates would cost and how the government would pay for them. By 1955, the Bureau of Public Roads had well-developed cost estimates and knew how much revenue from gas taxes would be needed to pay for the system. Even though those estimates were undermined by a combination of inflation and the later addition of more route-miles to the system, the system was built on a pay-as-you-go basis out of the gas taxes and other user fees collected from the people who drove on the interstates. By comparison, Obama has no financial plan for high-speed rail, no cost estimates for his 8,500-mile system, no source of funds, and no expectation that passenger fares will cover all of the operating costs, much less any of the capital costs.

Table 5.1
OBAMA-FRA HIGH-SPEED RAIL CORRIDORS

Corridor	End-Point Cities	Miles	Top Speed
California	Sacramento-San Diego	692	
Empire	New York-Albany-Buffalo	439	125
Florida	Tampa-Orlando-Miami	356	120
Gulf Coast	Houston-New Orleans-Atlanta-Mobile	1,022	110
South Central	San Antonio-Little Rock-Tulsa	994	
Keystone	Philadelphia-Pittsburgh	349	110
Midwest	Minneapolis-Chicago-St. Louis, Detroit-Chicago-Cleveland-	1,920	110
	Cincinnati, St. Louis-Kansas City	283	90
	Indianapolis-Louisville	111	79
New England	Portland-Boston-Montreal	489	110
Northeast	Boston-Washington, D.C.	456	150
Pacific Northwest	Eugene-Vancouver	466	110
Southeast	Washington, D.C.-Atlanta-Macon, Richmond-Hampton Roads	874	110

SOURCE: Federal Railroad Administration, "High-Speed Rail Corridor Designations," (Washington, Department of Transportation, 2005), tinyurl.com/6s94zd.

NOTE: The FRA plan does not specify a top speed for the California corridor, but California wants to build a line with speeds as high as 220 miles per hour.

The second key difference is that the interstates are heavily used by almost all Americans, while only a small elite will use high-speed rail. In 2007, the average American traveled 4,000 miles and shipped 2,000 ton-miles of freight over the interstates.[5] Since interstate highways serve all major cities in all 50 states, the majority of Americans will likely travel over an interstate at least once if not several times a week. By comparison, total annual use of Obama's rail program will not likely amount to much more than 100 miles per person. And considering the premium fares charged to ride high-speed rail, most users will likely be wealthy and white-collar workers whose employers pay the fare.

As shown in Table 5.1, the Obama–Federal Railroad Administration plan could more accurately be titled "moderate-speed rail." For the most part, it calls for trains running no faster than 110 miles per hour. This is hardly innovative: Starting in the 1930s, several American railroads, including the Milwaukee Road, Santa Fe, and Pennsylvania, regularly operated passenger trains at top speeds of more than 100 miles per hour. The Milwaukee Hiawatha, for example, routinely reached 110 miles per hour on its route from Chicago to Minneapolis.[6] These fast trains did nothing to stop the decline of passenger trains after World War II.

Amtrak today runs trains at top speeds of 100 miles per hour or more in several corridors. Trains reach 150 miles per hour between New York and Boston, 135 miles per hour between New York and Washington, and 110 miles per hour between New York and Albany, Philadelphia and Harrisburg, and Chicago and Detroit. Between Los Angeles and San Diego, Amtrak trains reach 90 miles per hour. On other routes, Amtrak trains are limited to at most 79 miles per hour.[7] Of course, top speeds are far greater than average speeds; the average speed in the Boston-to-Washington corridor is less than 85 miles per hour; averages in the 110-mile-per-hour corridors range from 55 to 65 miles per hour.

Rail advocates point to much higher speeds attained by trains in other nations as evidence that the United States is behind the times. A train between Beijing and Tianjin, China, reaches speeds of nearly 220 miles per hour.[8] Starting in 2011, Japan plans to operate trains as fast as 200 miles per hour.[9] Trains in France go faster than 185 miles per hour, while trains in Germany and Britain are nearly that fast.[10]

High-speed rail aficionados do not even consider 110-mile-per-hour trains to be true high-speed rail. The California legislature defined *high-speed rail* as lines with a top speed of greater than 125 miles per hour. "The reason for the 125 miles per hour threshold," says the California Senate Transportation Committee, "is that existing passenger rail equipment can operate at this speed if the appropriate signaling technology is installed and the right-of-way meets a variety of design and safety standards."[11]

Obama has two reasons for focusing on moderate- instead of true high-speed rail. First, as Amtrak's president Joseph Boardman told Illinois legislators in May 2009, a complete network of true high-speed rail lines would be "prohibitively expensive."[12] Obama's plan calls for running 110-mile-per-hour passenger trains on existing tracks shared with freight trains. For safety reasons, faster trains would require the construction of an entirely new rail system. It is much less expensive to upgrade existing tracks to support 110-mile-per-hour trains than to build brand-new tracks.

Second, Obama has a hidden agenda: giving federal aid to private freight railroads. Obama hopes that upgrading freight lines to run faster passenger trains will also allow the railroads to increase their freight speeds and capacities, thus capturing traffic from truckers. Historically, the freight railroads have received very little federal aid: Only 18,700 of 260,000 miles of rail lines built in the United States received federal subsidies.[13] At least some congressional Democrats see federal aid to railroads as a means of reregulating the industry, which was deregulated in 1979. For example, if a railroad wants to close an unprofitable branch line, the federal government can use past aid to the railroad to justify a mandate that the line be kept open.[14]

Even upgrading the 8,500 miles in Obama's plan to moderate-speed rail standards will cost far more than the $13 billion Obama has proposed to spend over the next five years. In 2004, the Midwest High-Speed Rail Initiative—a consortium of state transportation departments—estimated that it would cost about $7.7 billion, or $2.4 million per mile, to upgrade about 3,150 miles of track to the FRA speed standards and purchase trains to run on that track.[15] Increases in construction and materials costs since 2004 would probably boost this total to nearly $13 billion, or an average of about $4.1 million per mile.[16] At that price, the entire 8,500-mile Obama-FRA system would cost about $35 billion. Rather than build the entire system, Obama's plan really just invites states to apply for funds for portions of the system.

Complicating the issue, however, is California. In November 2008, 52 percent of California voters agreed that the state should sell nearly $10 billion worth of bonds to start construction on a 220-mile-per-hour high-speed rail line from San Francisco to Los Angeles. The California High-Speed Rail Authority estimates the total cost of this line will be about $33 billion.[17] Many observers believe that is a drastic underestimate.[18] Future extensions to Sacramento and San Diego will be at least another $12 billion, and California is counting on the federal government to pay half the total.[19] This would bring the cost of the Obama-FRA plan for true high-speed rail in California and moderate-speed rail elsewhere to around $80 billion.

Since the projected cost of California's 400-mile plan to link San Francisco and Los Angeles is more than the total cost of the rest of the Obama-FRA plan combined, the California High-Speed Rail Authority believes it has "every right to think we would receive the lion's share of the" $8 billion Congress has approved for high-speed rail.[20] Like building the tallest skyscraper in the world, high-speed rail is really about ego, and politicians are not known for keeping their egos in check. If California does receive a significant share of federal funds, elected officials from other states will certainly ask, "Why is it prohibitively expensive for us to have high-speed rail, but not California?" Given the cost estimates for the California plan, building the entire 8,500-mile Obama-FRA network to true high-speed rail standards would cost roughly $500 billion.[21]

The costs are not likely to stop there. The 8,500-mile FRA network reaches only 33 states. Arizona, Colorado, Nevada, and Tennessee are among the fast-growing states left out of the network, and every excluded state is represented by senators and representatives who will wonder why their constituents have to pay for rail lines that only serve other states. Even in the 33 states in the plan, routes are discontinuous, with no high-speed links between Dallas and Houston, New York and Chicago, or Jacksonville and Orlando. Furthermore, once high-speed rail reaches places like Kansas City, Madison, and Tulsa, local transit advocates will demand federal funding for local rail transit lines so high-speed rail travelers won't have to sully themselves by riding buses or taxis to their final destinations.

Given these estimates and expectations, the total capital cost of a national high-speed rail network, along with associated local transit, could well end up reaching nearly $1 trillion, or about twice the inflation-adjusted cost of the interstate highway system. Operating the system will cost billions more each year. In an age where trillions are the new billions, some people might think this is reasonable.

In fact, high-speed rail is yesterday's fantasy. Modern airliners go much faster than the fastest trains yet do not require expensive infrastructure along their entire routes. America needs high-speed rail like it needs a giant hole in the middle of California. And that's just what high-speed rail will be: a giant black hole sucking in hundreds of billions of dollars and producing negligible benefits.

To fully understand how poorly high-speed rail will work in the United States, it is important to look at existing high-speed rail projects elsewhere. Rail advocates claim Japanese and European trains are great successes, yet Japanese and European cities are denser than those in the United States and spaced closer together. This makes them much more suitable for high-speed rail, which is most competitive with air travel on shorter routes. This means that high-speed rail is not likely to perform as well in the United States as it does in those countries.

Bullet Trains to Bankruptcy

Probably no country in the world is better suited to high-speed rail than Japan. From greater Tokyo, the world's largest and one of the world's densest metropolitan areas, rail lines travel north, east, and southeast to chains of other large, dense cities typically located about 25 to 50 miles apart from one another. In 1960, these rail lines carried conventional trains at conventional speeds. But when Tokyo was selected to host the 1964 Olympics, the Japanese government decided to show off its technical prowess by building the world's first high-speed rail line, the 130-mile-per-hour *Shinkansen*, or bullet trains.

As of 1949, most rail lines in Japan were owned by the Japanese National Railways, a government-owned corporation. Though nationalized, JNR was not subsidized and had earned a profit or at least broken even every year since its creation. It was helped by the fact that, in 1949, railroads were practically the only mechanized way of getting around Japan, accounting for more than 92 percent of all passenger travel, with most of the rest being by bus.

By 1960, when construction began on the Shinkansen, autos still accounted for just 5 percent of Japanese travel, while rails carried 77 percent. The bullet trains impressed many Americans and Europeans who went home to promote similar trains in their countries. They were impressed for good reason: the first bullet train between Tokyo and Osaka proved highly profitable and has carried more people than all other high-speed rail trains in the world combined.

Once this line was built, however, Japanese politicians demanded bullet trains to their own cities and prefectures. The second line, from Osaka to Hakata, roughly broke even. All lines built since then have lost money.[22] For example, when Kakuei Tanaka (later convicted of accepting a bribe) was prime minister, he made sure that a high-speed rail line was built into the prefecture he represented, though the line, says the University of Arizona's Louis Hayes, "served very few passengers."[23] These and other politically driven losses drove the Japanese National Railways into the red for the first time in its history in 1964, the year the Osaka line opened, and it was never again in the black.[24] JNR responded by raising passenger fares, but this only pushed more people off the trains and into automobiles.

Despite—or perhaps because of—the bullet trains, auto travel surpassed rail travel in 1977. Between 1965 and 2005, per capita driving increased by more than 900 percent, while per capita rail travel increased by a meager 19 percent.[25]

By 1987, expansion of bullet-train service and other below-cost operations had swelled JNR's debt to more than $350 billion.[26] (By comparison, General Motors' debt in early 2009 was $35 billion.[27]) This led to a financial crisis that significantly contributed to the nation's economic woes of the last two decades. The government was forced to absorb JNR's debt and privatize the railways. The government sold the first three Shinkansen lines—which cost more than ¥4 trillion to build before adjusting for inflation—to the private railroads for less than ¥16 billion.[28] More recent lines have been built at government expense and leased to the railway companies at rates that will never recover the construction costs.[29] The 2008 subsidy to new construction was ¥307 billion, or almost $30 billion.[30]

Instead of riding trains, many Japanese today are buying "light motor vehicles," tiny cars with engines smaller than 660 cubic centimeters. (For comparison, the engine in the Smart Fortwo car is 1,000 cubic centimeters.) The popularity of these cars has nearly doubled since 1990, and they alone now transport two-and-one-half times as many passenger miles as the high-speed trains.

As of 2007, rail's share of Japanese passenger travel has declined to 29 percent, which may still be more than in any other country in the world; the average Japanese travels about 1,950 miles per year by train, which is definitely more than any other country. But only about 20 percent of these miles, or 400 miles per person, is by high-speed rail.[31] Autos, including light motor vehicles, carry 60 percent. The remainder is about equally divided between bus and domestic air.

After adjusting for inflation, Japan has spent about the same amount of money per capita on high-speed rail as the United States spent on the interstate highway system.[32] Yet the returns to Japan's mobility are far smaller: the average American travels 10 times as many miles on the interstates as the average Japanese travels by high-speed rail. The interstates also carry 2,000 ton-miles of freight per capita, while high-speed rail carries virtually none.

The Japanese government's historic emphasis on using rail lines for passengers has had a detrimental effect on rail freight operations. Freight trains carry only about 4 percent of Japanese freight. Highways carry 60 percent, and coastal shipping carries 36 percent.

High-Speed Rail in Europe

Europe's experience with high-speed rail is even more instructive. Europe's land mass is, unlike Japan's, similar to the United States. No doubt inspired by the Shinkansen, Italy introduced the high-speed train to Europe in 1978 with its 160-mile-per-hour *Direttissima* between Rome and Florence. France followed with the Paris-Lyon *train à grande vitesse* (TGV) of the same speed in 1981. Germany and other countries followed a few years later.

Since then, France has been the European leader of the high-speed rail movement. French trains now carry 54 percent of Europe's high-speed rail passenger-miles, followed by Germany at 26 percent, and Italy at 10 percent. More than half of all rail travel in France is on high-speed trains, but in the EU-25 (the 25 countries that were members of the European Union in 2004), nearly four out of five rail passengers still travel at conventional speeds. The average resident of France travels about 400 miles per year on high-speed trains. Sweden and Germany see about 150 miles of high-speed rail travel per capita, and Italy about 80. No other country is more than 50. In the EU-25 as a whole, the average is about 100 miles per year.[33]

Today's French rail lines operate as fast as 185 miles per hour and extend into Belgium, Germany, Italy, and—through the English Channel tunnel—Great Britain. Other European nations with some form of high-speed rail include Austria, Finland, Norway, Portugal, Russia, Spain, and Sweden, though most of these trains run only in the 125–135 mile-per-hour range.

When operating at high speeds, the French TGVs run on dedicated tracks. But TGV trains also operate on conventional tracks at normal speeds. In fact, while TGV trains may be seen throughout France, they only operate at high speeds between Paris and a few other cities, including Marseille, Le Mans, St. Pierre Des Corps, London, and Brussels. Similarly, Germany's high-speed intercity express (ICE) trains operate at their highest speeds only on selected routes, such as Berlin-Hamburg and Munich-Augsburg, and run at lower or conventional speeds on other routes.

While convenient for tourists who want to travel Europe without renting a car, high-speed rail has done little to change European travel habits. In 1980, intercity rail accounted for 8.2 percent of passenger travel in the EU-15 (the 15 countries that were members of the European Union as of 2000). By 2000, that number had declined to 6.3 percent. Auto driving gained almost exactly the same market share that rails lost in this time period, growing from 76.4 to 78.3 percent. But the real challenge to high-speed rail has come from low-cost airlines. Thanks to deregulation of European airlines, domestic air travel increased from 2.5 percent of travel in 1980 to 5.8 percent in 2000. Intercity buses and urban transit both lost shares.[34]

Rail has continued to lose importance since 2000. In the EU-25, rail's share of travel declined from 6.2 percent in 2000 to 5.8 percent in 2004, while air's share increased from 7.7 to 8.0 percent and autos' from 75.5 to 76.0 percent.[35] Advocates might argue that high-speed rail has slowed the decline of rail's importance in passenger travel, but that provides little justification for building it in the United States, where Amtrak carries only 0.1 percent of travel.

Because of the prominence of high-speed rail in France and Germany, rail has a higher share of passenger travel in those countries than in the rest of Europe. But the automobile's share of travel in both France and Germany is also higher than in the rest of Europe. The average resident of France travels 7,600 miles per year by auto, a rate exceeded in Europe only by Italy (by just 100 miles per year) and Luxembourg (which is deceptive because nonresidents are responsible for a large percentage of travel).[36] Rail's higher share in France and Germany comes at the expense of bus travel, not auto driving.

Rail's declining importance in Europe has come about despite onerous taxes on driving and huge subsidies to rail transportation. Much of the revenue from those taxes is effectively used to subsidize rail. "Rail is heavily subsidized," says French economist Rémy Prud'-Homme, adding that taxpayers "pay about half the total cost of providing the service." For 2002, Prud'Homme estimated that rail

Table 5.2
PASSENGER TRAVEL MIX (PERCENT, 2004)

Mode	EU-25	United States	Japan
Air	8.3	10.8	6.3
Auto	76.3	86.2	57.5
Bus	8.6	2.7	6.5
Rail	5.8	0.3	29.3
Water	0.8	0.0	0.3

SOURCE: *Panorama of Transport* (Brussels, BE: European Commission, 2007), p. 103.

NOTE: "Auto" includes motorcycles; "bus" includes both intercity and urban buses; "rail" includes both intercity and urban rail.

service in the EU-15 received about 68 billion euros—or about $100 billion—of subsidies each year.[37]

Nor has the introduction of new high-speed rail service helped relieve highway congestion. "Not a single high-speed track built to date has had any perceptible impact on the road traffic carried by parallel motorways," says Ari Vatanen, a member of the European Parliament in his summary of a 2005 conference on European transport.[38] However, the introduction of subsidized high-speed rail has caused some airlines to end service paralleling rail routes.[39]

Europe's passenger travel mix is similar to that of the United States (see Table 5.2). The big difference is that European intercity rail carries a 5.8 percent share of the travel market compared with Amtrak's 0.1 percent. The massive subsidies Europe pours into high-speed rail may not even explain this difference, given that the European percentage is steadily declining despite those subsidies. Instead, the answer may be that Europe's lower incomes and high taxes on autos and fuel have simply slowed the growth of driving. European planners predict that rail and bus's combined share will continue to decline between now and 2030.[40]

However, as in Japan, Europe's emphasis on using rails to move passengers has had a profound effect on the movement of freight. While a little more than one-fourth of American freight goes on the highway and more than a third goes by rail, nearly three-fourths of European freight goes on the road, and just a sixth goes by rail (see Table 5.3). Moreover, rail's share of freight movement is declining

Table 5.3
FREIGHT TRAVEL MIX (PERCENT, 2004)

Mode	EU-25	United States	Japan
Air	0.1	0.4	0.2
Highway	72.5	28.2	59.9
Rail	16.5	37.9	4.0
Pipeline	5.5	20.6	0.0
Waterway	5.4	12.9	35.9

SOURCES: *National Transportation Statistics* (Washington: Bureau of Transportation Statistics, 2008), Table 1-46b; *Panorama of Transport* (Brussels: European Commission, 2007), p. 69.

NOTE: "Water" includes domestic shipping only.

in Europe—it was 22 percent in 1980—but increased in the United States from 27 percent in 1980 to 40 percent in 2006.[41]

Rail's poor performance at carrying freight in both Japan and Europe suggests that Obama's hope of getting both people and freight off the highways and onto trains may a pipedream: a country or region can apparently use its rail system for passengers or freight, but not both. The fact that American freight railroads are profitable while European passenger lines are not suggests that freight, not passengers, is the highest and best use of a modern railroad in most places. Spending tens of billions of dollars per year on passenger rail might get a small percentage of cars off the road—but one possible consequence is to greatly increase the number of trucks on the road.

California Dreaming

Three places likely to apply for some of the $8 billion in stimulus funds are California, Florida, and the Midwest. The California proposal comes closest to the high-speed lines in Japan and Europe. Just the first stage of the California plan would be the largest state-sponsored "megaproject" in American history. Danish planning professor and megaproject expert Bent Flyvbjerg observes that such programs almost invariably suffer from *optimism bias*, in which proponents deceive themselves by overestimating benefits or underestimating costs, and *strategic misrepresentation*, in which proponents deceive the public by selectively presenting or distorting facts to

93

make the projects appear more valuable than they really are.[42] The California plan includes many examples of both.

The California legislature created a high-speed rail authority in 1996. That authority published an environmental impact statement in 2005 and what it called a business plan in 2008. The business plan projects that constructing the line from San Francisco to Los Angeles and to Anaheim will cost $33 to $34 billion, or about $70 million per mile.[43]

Flyvbjerg argues that people evaluating megaprojects should routinely increase the cost estimates by the proportion by which similar projects have gone over their originally projected budgets.[44] No high-speed rail line has ever been built from scratch in the United States, so we do not have a good idea of whether the authority's cost projection is realistic. But historically, urban passenger rail projects have, on average, gone 40 percent over their projected costs.

Although the authority projects a cost of $33 to $34 billion, it asked California voters to approve the sale of only $9 billion worth of bonds for high-speed rail. The authority expects the federal government to cover half the costs and local governments to cover 6 to 9 percent. The authority hopes that private investors will be willing to put up the remaining $6.5 to $7.5 billion.[45]

In exchange, the private investors will get to operate the trains and keep all of the profits.[46] This is a "public-private partnership" in the sense that the public puts up most of the money and the private partners get all of the operating profits. Of course, the private investors risk losing their share of the capital cost, but once built, if the rail lines end up losing money, the state will likely feel obligated to cover the operating losses.

To attract private investors, the authority projects that the San Francisco-to-Anaheim line will carry 22.6 to 31.6 million trips in 2020, depending on the fares that are charged.[47] This is extraordinarily optimistic considering that Amtrak's Boston-to-Washington corridor carried just 10 million passengers in 2007.[48] On one hand, California is proposing to run its trains at somewhat higher speeds than Amtrak. On the other hand, the Northeast corridor has more people spaced more closely together than the California corridor is projected to have in 2020.

Spacing is important because high-speed rail works best over distances of about 200 to 250 miles. For shorter distances, rail is not

94

competitive with the automobile, and over longer distances it is not competitive with air service. New York to Washington is 228 miles; New York to Boston is 215 miles. But Los Angeles to San Francisco is more than 400 miles, with no New York City–like intervening concentrations of population to generate ridership.

Flyvbjerg notes that American passenger rail planners typically overestimate ridership by an average 100 percent.[49] An independent review of the California authority's business plan calls the ridership projections "the most unrealistic projections produced for a major transport project anywhere in the world." One of the authors of this report, Joseph Vranich, is a former Amtrak employee who was president of the High Speed Rail Association in the early 1990s and is the author of a 1993 book about high-speed rail.[50] Despite his general support for high-speed trains, he is highly skeptical of the California plan. "Having reviewed countless rail plans over many years," Vranich says, "I have found the Authority's work to be the poorest I have ever seen."[51]

The rail authority's claims that it can attract two to three times as many riders as the Northeast corridor trains, and its expectation that it can attract investors to put up billions of dollars on the basis of those projections, are clear examples of optimism bias. If no private investors are willing to take the risk, the authority is likely to simply proceed with its plans in the expectation that state and federal taxpayers will make up the difference.

The rail authority emphasizes that, at planned speeds as high as 220 miles per hour, its trains will offer shorter trip times than air service between downtown Los Angeles and downtown San Francisco. Air service suffers in this comparison because of the time required to get from airports to downtowns. This, however, is a strategic misrepresentation because it assumes that everyone wants to go from downtown to downtown. In fact, there are far more jobs and residents near the major airports—LAX, Burbank, Orange County, San Francisco, Oakland, and San Jose—than in or near downtown Los Angeles and San Francisco. Thus, the time advantage provided by the train will benefit only a minority of people.

The authority claims that high-speed trains will produce huge benefits in the form of congestion relief, energy savings, and pollution reduction.[52] Yet the authority's own environmental impact statement (EIS) reveals that the congestion benefits will be negligible.

According to the EIS, high-speed rail will take an average of just 3.8 percent of cars off the California highways that parallel the rail routes.[53] Moreover, what little congestion relief high-speed rail provides will be short lived. Between 1996 and 2006, traffic on rural California freeways grew by 1.9 percent per year.[54] That means that California will spend more than 10 years planning and building high-speed rail, and just two years after it opens for business, congestion will likely return to previous levels.

While high-speed rail does little to reduce highway traffic, it is projected to decimate California's in-state airline service. The EIS projects that, under its high-end rail ridership projections, in-state air travel will decline by two-thirds.[55] The EIS says that the rail service will have only minor effects on connecting air travel—people flying in and out of California and connecting to or from local in-state destinations—but the airlines may not consider such service to be economically viable after losing two-thirds of their local customers.

The EIS is more optimistic about energy savings. It projects that the energy saved from operating high-speed rail will repay the energy cost of construction in just five years.[56] The EIS's energy analysis is flawed, however, by an assumption that autos and airplanes will be as energy intensive in the future as they are today.[57] In fact, if auto makers are able to meet the fuel-economy targets announced by President Obama in May 2009, and if American auto buyers continue to replace the nation's auto fleet at historic rates, the average cars and light trucks on the road in 2020 will be almost 25 percent more energy efficient than they are today, and by 2030, they will be 38 percent more fuel-efficient. If fuel prices significantly increase, those projections may end up being conservative.

Airplane manufacturers are also responding to high fuel prices by making planes more energy efficient. Since 1980, the energy efficiency of air travel has increased, on average, 2 percent per year.[58] Boeing promises that its 787 plane will be 20 percent more fuel efficient than comparable planes today.[59] Jet engine makers have set a goal of doubling fuel efficiency by 2020.[60]

If autos and airplanes become, over the life of the high-speed rail project, an average of 30 percent more fuel-efficient than they are today, then the payback period for high-speed rail rises to 30 years. This payback period also crucially depends on high-speed rail attracting the authority's optimistic estimate of riders. If ridership is lower, the payback period will be longer. Since rail lines require expensive (and energy-intensive) reconstruction and rehabilitation about every 30 years, high-speed rail is likely to save no energy at all.

Steven Polzin, of the University of South Florida's Center for Urban Transportation Research, points out that autos and buses have relatively short life cycles, so they can readily adapt to the need to save energy or reduce pollution. Rail systems "may be far more difficult or expensive to upgrade to newer, more efficient technologies," Polzin adds.[61] In other words, the American auto fleet completely turns over every 18 years, and the airline fleet turns over every 21 years, so both can quickly become more fuel-efficient; builders of rail lines, however, are stuck for at least three to four decades with whatever technology they select.

California's EIS projections of other environmental benefits of high-speed rail are similarly problematic. The EIS estimates, for example, that rail will reduce California transportation-related air pollution, relative to the no-build alternative, by 0.7 percent (for particulates) to 1.5 percent (for nitrogen oxides), with other pollutants in between. Unlike energy, this does take into account improvements in pollution control technology. The EIS reports, for example, that in 1997, cars, planes, trains, and electric utilities emitted more than 9,700 metric tons of carbon monoxide. By 2020, under the no-build alternative, the EIS projects this will decline to 3,101 metric tons. High-speed rail will reduce carbon monoxide emissions still further to 3,074 metric tons.

Note that modest improvements in relatively low-cost pollution technologies are projected to reduce carbon monoxide pollution by nearly 70 percent despite growth in population and travel. By comparison, at a cost of at least $33 to $34 billion, high-speed rail reduces carbon monoxide pollution by a mere 0.9 percent. As a pollution-control device, high-speed rail is spectacularly cost ineffective.

Similarly, the EIS projects that high-speed rail will reduce greenhouse gas emissions by 1.4 percent.[62] But electric cars or plug-in hybrids could achieve the same result at a far lower cost. Since more than a third of California greenhouse gas emissions are from automobiles, substituting electric or plug-in hybrids for just 4.2 percent of driving would reduce emissions by 1.4 percent.[63] This is likely to cost far less than spending $33 billion or more on high-speed rail. In short, claims of environmental benefits are either examples of optimism bias (in the cases of energy and greenhouse gas emissions) or strategic misrepresentation (in the cases of congestion and other pollution relief).

Florida High-Speed Rail

Florida briefly considered, then discarded, a rail plan intermediate between Obama's moderate-speed rail and California's ambitious plan. The Florida legislature created a state High-Speed Rail Authority in 2002. In 2005, the authority published a detailed proposal for building a 92-mile rail line running 125-mile-per-hour trains between Tampa and Orlando. The authority estimated this line would cost between $2.0 and $2.5 billion and carry about 4 million passengers a year. Rather than pay the added cost of overhead wires and other electrical facilities, the authority proposed to power the trains with gas-turbine locomotives.

Planners estimated that the rail line would divert 11 percent of people who would otherwise drive between Orlando and Tampa.[64] Since most of the traffic on Interstate 4 between the two cities has other origins or destinations, the train would remove only about 2 percent of cars from the least-busy segment of I-4 and smaller shares from busier segments.[65] Traffic on I-4 is growing by more than 2 percent per year, so the rail line would provide, at most, about one year's worth of traffic relief. As the EIS itself noted, the traffic "reduction would not be sufficient to significantly improve the LOS [levels of service] on I-4, as many segments of the roadway would still be over capacity."[66]

The EIS also estimated that the trains would produce more nitrogen oxide pollution and volatile organic compounds than would be saved by the autos they would take off the road.[67] Further, planners calculated that operating and maintaining the gas-turbine locomotives would consume 3.5 to 6.0 times as much energy as would be saved by the cars taken off the road.[68] The EIS did not estimate the effects of the trains on greenhouse gas production, but given that greenhouse gas emissions from fossil fuels are roughly proportional to energy consumption, the trains would produce far more greenhouse gases than would the cars taken off the road.

The EIS concluded that "the environmentally preferred alternative is the no-build alternative" because it "would result in less direct and indirect impact to the environment."[69] The state high-speed rail authority has disbanded, and the project is now mainly promoted by a consortium of consultants, contractors, and manufacturers who would profit from rail construction.[70] If construction ever begins on the California project, these groups are ready to revive the idea of high-speed rail in Florida.

The Midwest Rail Initiative

The most detailed plan for Obama-style moderate-speed rail was developed by the Midwest Regional Rail Initiative, a consortium of state departments of transportation in nine Midwestern states. In 2004, these states published a report proposing a network of trains operating in eight major corridors with several branches.

Although the cover of the Midwest rail report features a photo of an electrically powered high-speed train in Europe, the report itself proposes conventional diesel-powered trains operating at speeds comparable to the Milwaukee *Hiawatha* of the 1930s. Specifically, the report proposes 110-mile-per-hour lines from Chicago to Minneapolis, Green Bay, Detroit, Cleveland, Cincinnati, and St. Louis, with 90-mile-per-hour lines to Carbondale and Quincy and from St. Louis to Kansas City and 79-mile-per-hour branches to Port Huron, Grand Rapids/Holland, and Omaha. These routes are about 800 miles longer than the FRA plan for the Midwest.[71]

The report estimates that it will cost about $6.6 billion, or $2.1 million per mile, to upgrade about 3,150 miles of track to the speed standards cited above. About $1.1 billion more will purchase 63 train sets, which will cost between $450 and $500 million per year to operate.[72] Increases in construction and materials costs since 2004 could well increase this total to nearly $13 billion, or an average of about $4.1 million per mile.[73]

On routes with top speeds of 110 miles per hour, average speeds are projected to be about 74 miles per hour, or about 40 to 45 percent faster than current Amtrak speeds.[74] The plan also calls for at least tripling the number of trains per day on all routes.[75]

In return for this $7.7 billion investment, the report projects that the Midwest rail system will carry about 13.6 million passengers per year, or about four times what the existing passenger rail system carries. Of course, Amtrak carries only a tiny share of travel in these

99

corridors, so a quadrupling of Amtrak's numbers will do little to reduce driving or congestion.

For example, in 2007 Amtrak carried fewer than 450,000 passengers on its trains in the Chicago-Detroit-Port Huron corridor (not all of whom went the entire distance).[76] By comparison, the Michigan Department of Transportation recorded 9.0 million vehicles on the least-used segment of I-94 parallel to the Amtrak route and four to six times that many vehicles on more heavily-used segments.[77] In the unlikely event that every rail rider would otherwise have gone by auto over the least-used segment of the route, a quadrupling of rail ridership will take only 9 percent of cars off of this segment and much smaller percentages off other portions of the road.

Although the proposal calls for charging fares about 50 percent higher than Amtrak's fares, it projects that many of the routes will not be able to cover their operational expenses until 2025.[78] The initial capital costs will have to be covered by federal and state funds, with no expectation that they will ever be repaid out of passenger fares.[79]

One major difference between the Midwest approach and the California plan is that the former is incremental. While California will have to spend tens of billions of dollars before a single train carries revenue passengers, the Midwest plan can be implemented one grade crossing and/or one train at a time.

The incremental approach means that, if the returns from the first projects do not produce worthwhile benefits, later projects can be stopped and avoided before too much money is wasted. However, this will happen only if someone is objectively monitoring the projects to make sure they are worthwhile. Too often, the agencies that implement these projects are run by rail advocates who are quick to claim success no matter how large the costs and how small the benefits. Meanwhile, incremental projects that are hidden in state budgets may be so small that they escape the attention of more objective budgetary watchdogs.

High-Speed Risks

Japanese and European cities are much denser than American cities, and most are served by much denser transit systems that rail passengers can rely on when they get to their destinations. If high-speed rail cannot capture or even maintain rail's share of passenger travel from the automobile in Europe and Japan, how can it work in the United States? High-speed rail must be considered highly risky.

An oversight report on the California high-speed rail project from that state's Senate Transportation Committee pointed to many specific risks of high-speed rail, including forecasting, rights-of-way, and safety risks.[80] Unlike running a bus system or even an airline, building a rail line requires accurate long-range forecasting. Planning and construction can take many years, and the service life of the rail line is measured in decades. A seemingly minor forecasting error can turn what appears to be a productive asset into an expensive white elephant.

Some of the questionable assumptions made in the Florida and California estimates of future ridership and other benefits include the following:

1. Cars and planes will not become more fuel-efficient in the future.
2. Airports will not become more efficient at moving people through security.
3. Cars that use alternative fuels will not become feasible or popular.
4. Downtowns will remain or be restored as preeminent job centers.
5. No new technologies will help reduce highway congestion.
6. People will want to go where the trains go.

Several of these assumptions are clearly wrong; as previously noted, cars are likely to be at least 38 percent more fuel-efficient by 2030, and downtowns have been losing their importance as job centers since at least 1950. Many of the other assumptions are also likely to be wrong. Any forecasts of high-speed rail ridership, energy savings, and other benefits based on these assumptions are likely to be greatly overestimated.

The last assumption—that people will want to go where the trains go—may be the riskiest of all. While many people travel between, say, San Francisco and Los Angeles, that does not mean that they travel between downtowns, which will be the primary areas served by rail. Jobs and people are spread throughout modern cities in a fine-grained pattern. As economist William Bogart observes, only about 10 to 15 percent of metropolitan jobs are located in central city downtowns—in Los Angeles it is less than 5 percent. Even when suburban downtowns are counted—only a small fraction of which would be served by high-speed rail—the total is still only 30 to 40 percent.[81] That means most people will rarely if ever find high-speed rail convenient.

This is particularly apparent in China's Shanghai magnetic levitation (maglev) train, which travels 19 miles between Pudong Airport and downtown Shanghai. Reaching speeds of nearly 270 miles per hour, it is the fastest regularly scheduled train in the world. Yet ridership is well below expectations; rarely are more than one out of four seats filled. When the *New York Times* asked air travelers why they don't use the train, they say it doesn't go where they want to go. "It may take longer, but the taxi is more convenient," says one. "Once you get to the train station, I'd just have to get a taxi there," says another, "and I don't want to change cars again."[82]

The January 2008 oversight report from the California senate committee pointed to a risky assumption that the California High-Speed Rail Authority would be able to build high-speed lines in the rights-of-way owned by private railroads such as BNSF and Union Pacific.[83] The risk was confirmed by a May 2008 letter from the Union Pacific Railroad to the High-Speed Rail Authority explicitly denying the authority the right to use any of its right-of-way.

"Union Pacific has carefully evaluated CHSAs project," says the letter, and "does not feel it is in Union Pacific's best interest to have any proposed alignment located on Union Pacific rights-of-way. Therefore, as your project moves forward with its final design, it is our request that you do so in such a way as to not require the use of Union Pacific operating rights-of-way or interfere with Union Pacific operations."[84]

One reason why the freight railroads may not want high-speed rail in their rights-of-way is safety. The California High-Speed Rail Authority presumed that it would use European-style rail equipment, which is very lightweight, in order to save energy. European and Japanese rail safety is based on *accident avoidance*, that is, everything is highly engineered to prevent accidents. This standard has worked well: There has been only one fatal high-speed rail accident, which turned out to result from poorly engineered wheels. However, partly because of the lightweight equipment, that accident caused more than 100 deaths.[85]

In contrast, American safety standards are based on *accident surviv-ability*. This means American rail equipment is much heavier than foreign high-speed trains. The California senate oversight report worried that this would create a regulatory problem: the Federal Railroad Administration would refuse to allow the use of the light-weight trains that the California High-Speed Rail Authority had in mind.[86] In addition, mixing American and European trains in the same rights-of-way, even if not on the same tracks, would create a special liability problem for the railroads: a derailment of a heavy American train could easily kill many people on an adjacent light-weight high-speed train. Indeed, many of the graphics on Califor-nia's official high-speed rail website show high-speed trains passing just a few feet away from standard freight and passenger trains.[87]

99 Percent Pay, 1 Percent Ride

The experiences of Japan and Europe and plans for California, Florida, and the Midwest teach valuable lessons about Obama's proposed plan. First, Obama's high-speed rail plan will cost far more than the $13 billion he has proposed to spend. Building truly high-speed rail in California and moderate-speed rail elsewhere would likely cost around $100 billion.

Second, Japan's experience and the Midwest rail plan show that, once a nation starts building high-speed rail, it is hard to stop. Despite the need for huge subsidies that the nation can't really afford, Japan's taxpayers are forced to pay for high-speed lines into the prefectures of every powerful politician in the country. The Midwest initiative proposes to build hundreds of miles of lines not included in the FRA plan. Texas will want a line connecting Dallas and Houston, which isn't on the FRA map either. Nevada Sen. Harry Reid will want a line to Las Vegas, and politicians from Denver, Phoenix, Salt Lake City, and many other places will press hard for lines to their cities and states.

Third, the environmental benefits of high-speed rail are negligible at best. Obama's moderate-speed trains will be powered by diesel locomotives that will burn petroleum and spew pollutants and greenhouse gases into the air. Florida found that its proposed high-speed train would do more harm than good to the environment. Even electrically powered, true high-speed rail is unlikely to be clean. California rated its proposal as sound only by projecting impossibly high ridership numbers and unrealistically assuming that future autos and airplanes would be no more energy-efficient than those today.

Fourth, the mobility benefits of high-speed rail are similarly negligible. Despite huge taxpayer subsidies of high-speed rail, the average residents of France and Japan ride their TGVs and bullet trains just 400 miles a year. With slower trains connecting lower-density cities and regions, Obama's high-speed rail system will be lucky to reach even 100 miles per capita. Even a much more comprehensive, truly high-speed network is unlikely to approach 400 miles per capita because, unlike Europe and Japan, the United States has few major city-pairs located close enough for high-speed trains to compete with airlines.

Fifth, any mobility gained by construction of high-speed rail will accrue mainly to a relatively wealthy elite. The Japanese ride trains more than anyone else in the world, but 80 percent of their rail travel is by conventional trains. The reason is pricing. Consider the fares for travel between New York and Washington. At the time of this writing, Amtrak charges a minimum of $99 to ride the high-speed Acela train but as little as $49 to ride conventional trains. Meanwhile, relatively unsubsidized bus companies asked as little as $20 for the same trip—and offer leather seats and free WiFi en route. The airlines, meanwhile, have met Amtrak's high-speed price of $99. With fares like these, the only people on the high-speed train are the wealthy and those white-collar workers whose employers pay the fare.

In short, even if the United States spends twice as much money on high-speed rail as it spent on interstate highways, high-speed trains will carry less than 10 percent as many passenger miles—and 0 percent as much freight—as the interstates. High-speed rail will not likely capture more than about 1 percent of the nation's market for passenger travel, yet the other 99 percent will have to pay for that service. Moreover, the average traveler riding subsidized high-speed trains will likely have a much higher income than the average taxpayer paying for those trains.

High-speed rail's inability to draw more riders should be no surprise considering rail's inherent disadvantages compared with driving and air travel. Driving offers point-to-point convenience, while rail deposits most travelers miles from their final destinations. Air

104

service is at least twice as fast as the fastest trains and—since most Americans no longer live or work downtown—leaves average travelers no farther from their destinations than downtown train stations. Though high-speed rail may compete a little on trips of 200 miles or so, it is not optimal at any distance.

During the 1990s and early 2000s, American cities built more than 2,600 miles of new rail transit routes. Observers could only marvel that this nation was wealthy enough to spend hundreds of billions of dollars on transportation systems used by such a tiny number of people who paid only a fraction of their costs. But, like families going deeply into debt to pay more for homes than those houses were actually worth, cities could not really afford these systems— they just charged them to the future. The recent economic crisis has shown that we were all living beyond our means. Spending $100 billion dollars or more on high-speed rail will only compound these errors.

President Obama says that he wants to rebuild America. User-fee-funded highways are used by most Americans almost every day. High-speed rail would be regularly used by only a small fraction of Americans, but the cost would be borne by everyone else. Which is the America Obama wants to build?

6. The Road to Green

Growing up in the 1960s, I was acutely aware of America's severe air pollution problems. On otherwise sunny days, brown clouds replaced the traditional grey rain clouds in the skies of my hometown of Portland, Oregon. Though Mt. Hood, Oregon's highest peak, was just 50 miles away, it was nearly invisible on most "clear" days. When Ray Atkeson, Oregon's best-known photographer, wanted an up-to-date photo of the city of Portland with the mountain in the background, he was forced to combine two pictures: one of the mountain when the city was obscured by smog and one of the city when the mountain was lost in haze.

When I went to college at Oregon State University, Ralph Nader came to Oregon and inspired students to form the Oregon Student Public Interest Research Group to do research on social and environmental issues. In the summer of 1972, I was one of the group's first student interns, and I worked on air pollution issues.

Under the Clean Air Act of 1970, every city whose air quality fell below standards set by the Environmental Protection Agency was required to develop a strategy for reducing transportation-related air pollution. I bicycled everywhere I went in Portland and had no love for the automobile—I didn't even get a driver's license for several more years. So I was easily persuaded that the solution to air pollution was to encourage people to drive less.

Because of traffic congestion, Portland's worst pollution was downtown. So I proposed that Portland's three-year-old transit agency, TriMet, contract with churches on the city's periphery to use their parking lots as weekday park-and-ride stations. This would allow commuters to leave their cars well outside of downtown.

Once downtown, people still might need to get around, so I proposed that TriMet create a demand-responsive jitney bus system. Signal boxes on every street corner would allow people to call a bus. The nearest bus would pick them up and, after picking up or dropping off other people, drop them off at their downtown destination. The hardware and software for such a system was commercially available but had never been used in the United States.[1]

Portland's traffic engineer had a very different solution to the city's air pollution problems. Cars pollute the most at low speeds, he pointed out. So his idea was to install a traffic signal coordination system on downtown's one-way streets that would allow cars to drive through downtown at faster speeds. According to his department's calculations, this program, combined with the EPA's stricter air pollution controls on new cars, would bring the city in compliance of EPA's pollution standards by 1980.

I worried that speeding up downtown traffic would simply bring in more traffic, which would offset the clean-air benefits of higher speeds. But the city adopted the traffic engineer's plan.

All across the country, cities required to comply with the Clean Air Act faced the same question. While most chose traffic engineering or other technical solutions, some attempted to promote alternatives to driving and other behavioral solutions.

More than 30 years of experience have proven I was wrong in 1972. Various technical solutions to air pollution have had a tremendous effect in cleaning the air. They also greatly contributed to improved auto and highway safety. Behavioral solutions, however, have had either no effect or such a tiny effect at such a high cost that they were not worth the effort.

Between 1970 and 2006, American driving grew by 166 percent.[2] Yet according to the EPA, total emissions of carbon monoxide from automobiles and trucks decreased by 67 percent; nitrogen oxides decreased by 48 percent; volatile organic compounds decreased by 77 percent; particulates decreased by 63 percent; and lead fell by more than 98 percent.[3]

These improvements are entirely due to technical solutions. The most important of these is tailpipe controls such as catalytic converters. New cars today emit less than 10 percent of the pollution per mile of cars built in 1970; some, less than 1 percent. New cars are cleaner every year, so as they replace older cars on the road, automotive air pollution problems are steadily disappearing.

Local programs such as traffic signal coordination have contributed to these reductions as well. Signal coordination saves people time and also saves fuel. When drivers burn less fuel, their cars emit less pollution. The city of Portland estimates that coordinating signals at 135 intersections saves motorists 1.75 million gallons of gasoline per year, which means a lot less pollution.[4]

Behavioral tools, however, have had virtually no effect on air pollution. Per capita driving has grown in cities that emphasize behavioral tools just about as much as in cities that focus on technical tools. Differences in the growth of per capita driving among cities relate more to differences in the economic health of those cities than to their transportation programs. To the extent that people can detect an effect from behavioral tools, the costs of those tools greatly outweigh the benefits.

I still think low-cost bus park-and-ride stations and demand-responsive jitneys are good transit solutions in some situations. As remedies for air pollution, though, they would have been next to useless. The pollution from the downtown jitneys quite possibly would have exceeded the pollution saved by the cars they took off the road.

The same comparison of behavioral and technical solutions holds true when addressing other social costs of driving, such as traffic accidents, energy consumption, or greenhouse gas emissions. While some might argue that these are, in fact, not social costs, the fact remains that if a city, state, or nation wants to reduce them, then technical solutions work better than behavioral ones.

When America's urban skies were darkened with pollution in the late 1960s, up to 55,000 people died on America's highways each year. This represented more than 50 deaths for every billion miles of driving. By 2007, when driving had increased by more than 175 percent, highway fatalities had fallen to 41,000, for a rate of less than 14 deaths per billion miles of driving. Driving today is more than 70 percent safer than it was before 1970, and the safest roads of all are urban interstates, where only about 5 people die per billion miles driven. Reduced fatalities resulted from improvements in both highway and auto safety, not from people driving less.

Despite the fact that behavioral tools have completely failed to reduce driving in the past, many proposals to save energy and reduce greenhouse gas emissions rely on such tools. In 2008, the California legislature passed a law requiring all urban areas in the state to increase their population densities, which is supposed to reduce greenhouse gas emissions by reducing driving.[5] Numerous transit agencies have justified rail transit proposals based on rail's

109

supposed ability to save energy and reduce toxic and greenhouse emissions. Similar justifications have been made for high-speed rail.

Ironically, my hometown of Portland has become the nation's leader in imposing behavioral tools on its residents. These include land-use plans that emphasize denser development inside the region's urban-growth boundary and transportation plans that emphasize light-rail and other rail transit over highways. The reams of publicity Portland has received for these plans emphasize intentions rather than results. Despite claims that Portlanders love transit, the sad truth is that the share of the region's residents who take transit to work declined from 9.8 percent in 1980, when the region began implementing these plans, to just 6.5 percent in 2007.[6] This is hardly an endorsement for the region's costly programs.

I believe technical tools will prove to be the best solutions to problems with energy, greenhouse gases, and any other undesirable side-effects from driving. When taking all things into consideration, alternative modes of travel, such as rail transit, consume just about as much energy and emit as much greenhouse gases (and in some cases more) as automobiles. Any savings at all from attempting to change people's driving habits would be extremely costly.

Your Mileage May Vary

The energy required to operate various forms of transportation can be calculated from data published by the Federal Transit Administration, Department of Energy, and Environmental Protection Agency. Each year, the Federal Transit Administration publishes the total amount of fuel consumed by individual transit agencies for each kind of transit: light rail, heavy rail, buses, and so forth.[7] The data do not include energy consumed by companies that contract to operate transit services for some agencies, but such contractors carry only 11 percent of transit passenger miles.

The Department of Energy publishes an annual report showing how much energy is used by passenger cars, light trucks, airlines, Amtrak, and other forms of travel.[8] The EPA's fuel economy ratings can be used to estimate the energy requirements for specific automobiles such as the Toyota Prius.[9] The Energy Information Administration publishes coefficients for converting various sources of energy into British Thermal Units and for estimating the pounds of carbon

Table 6.1
ENERGY CONSUMPTION AND CO_2 EMISSIONS PER PASSENGER MILE

Mode	BTUs	Pounds of CO_2
Ferry Boats	10,744	1.73
Automated Guideways	10,661	1.36
Motor Buses	4,365	0.71
Light Trucks	3,990	0.63
Trolley Buses	3,923	0.28
All Automobiles	3,700	0.58
Passenger Cars	3,512	0.55
Light Rail	3,465	0.36
All Transit	3,444	0.47
Airlines	3,228	0.50
Amtrak	2,650	0.43
Heavy Rail	2,600	0.25
Commuter Rail	2,558	0.29
Toyota Prius	1,659	0.26

SOURCES: Calculations based on data in Federal Transit Administration, "Energy Consumption," *2007 National Transit Database* (Washington: Department of Transportation, 2008); Stacy C. Davis and Susan W. Diegel, *Transportation Energy Data Book: Edition 27* (Oak Ridge, TN: Department of Energy, 2008), Table 2.13; Energy Information Administration, *Fuel and Energy Emission Coefficients*, (Washington: Department of Energy), tinyurl.com/smdrm; Energy Information Administration, *State Electricity Profiles 2006* (Washington: Department of Energy, 2007), Table 5; Environmental Protection Agency, *Model Year 2008 Fuel Economy Guide* (Washington: EPA, 2007), tinyurl.com/25y3ce.

dioxide (CO_2) emitted by various fuels.[10] The same agency also publishes the sources of power used to generate electricity in each state, which is necessary to estimate the CO_2 emissions from electrically powered transit.[11]

Using these data, Table 6.1 shows the average number of BTUs consumed and pounds of CO_2 emitted per passenger mile for various modes of transit and types of automobiles in 2006. Ferries and automated guideways (people movers) are far worse, on both counts, than any other form of passenger travel. Motor buses and light trucks (pick ups, full-sized vans, and SUVs) are comparable to one another, while light rail uses about as much energy as passenger cars but emits less CO_2.

The Toyota Prius, the most fuel-efficient auto sold in the United States, is also shown as an example of the potential for energy-efficient autos. The Prius uses less energy than other forms of travel but generates about the same CO_2 as heavy rail and commuter rail.

These are nationwide averages, but—as the saying goes—your mileage may vary. The number of BTUs per passenger mile crucially depends on the number of passengers on board any vehicle. Based on Department of Transportation surveys, the numbers in table 6.1 presume 1.57 occupants per passenger car and 1.73 occupants per light truck.[12] This means a typical SUV with three people in it will consume fewer BTUs per passenger mile than almost any form of transit with average loads.

Occupancies, and therefore energy consumption per passenger mile, vary greatly among transit providers as well. Transit buses in the United States carry, on average, fewer than 11 passengers. However, some commuter bus lines in the New York City, Baltimore, and Seattle areas carry an average of 20 to 30 passengers, while transit buses in many small towns carry an average of less than 4 people. Similarly, average light-rail-car occupancies range from less than 14 in Denver to more than 38 in Boston.[13]

Emissions from electrically powered transit depend on local sources of electricity. Massachusetts and Ohio, for example, rely heavily on fossil fuels for electrical power, so trolley buses in those states emit more greenhouse gases than diesel buses. Washington and California rely more heavily on hydroelectric power, so trolley buses in those states emit less greenhouse gases than diesels. Although light rail on average emits less CO_2 than automobiles, light-rail lines in states that primarily burn fossil fuels can emit more than an average SUV.

One obvious way to reduce energy consumption and emissions is to increase vehicle occupancies. Increasing auto occupancies is easier said than done, however. Historically, average auto occupancies have roughly equaled average household size minus one.[14] Most carpools are really "fampools," that is, family members traveling together to work or other destinations. Not surprisingly, efforts to increase occupancies with carpool lanes and 1-800-CAR-POOL numbers have mostly failed.

Transit loads are easier to manipulate by directing transit service to areas where demand is high and avoiding or providing smaller

112

vehicles in areas where demand is low. Most transit agencies fail to do this for political reasons. Since transit agencies rely heavily on tax dollars, they try to provide at least some service to all taxpayers in a region. Because a large share of their capital costs are funded by federal grants, they also tend to buy buses that are larger than they really need. The result is that buses often run nearly empty; in 2007, the average transit bus was about one-sixth full.[15]

While Table 6.1 suggests that rail transit is more energy efficient than the average automobile, several factors mitigate this conclusion. First, the commuter- and heavy-rail numbers are distorted by the fact that most of the nation's rail transit riders are in the New York urban area, whose population and job densities are not representative of the rest of the nation. Second, automobiles are continually becoming more fuel-efficient; since 1985, the energy cars consume per passenger mile has declined by nearly 1 percent per year, and the decline for light trucks has been even greater.[16] Meanwhile, rail transit's fuel economy has actually declined since 1985.[17] Third, rail transit must be supplemented with feeder buses, and because the fuel economy of these buses is low, the fuel efficiency of rail-plus-bus transit systems is often much lower than automobiles. Fourth, building rail transit consumes huge amounts of energy, which can partly or completely offset the operational savings.

Most New Rail Lines Are Brown

Table 6.2 lists the energy efficiency and CO_2 emissions for most of the nation's light-rail, heavy-rail, and commuter-rail lines in 2006. Streetcars, ferryboats, and trolleybuses are also listed because some cities are considering either constructing or expanding each of those modes. For good measure, the table also includes automated guideways and cable cars, even though these are not being seriously considered by any major cities.

The table shows that about half the nation's heavy-rail lines and a clear majority of light-rail lines use more energy than today's average automobile. Commuter rail fares a little better, but most of the newer commuter-rail lines—such as those in Dallas, Los Angeles, and Seattle—are contracted out and so data are not available.

National Transit Database numbers for Salt Lake City indicate that the city has extraordinarily efficient light rail, equal in energy performance to the San Diego line. However, the Utah Transit

Table 6.2
TRANSIT LINE ENERGY CONSUMPTION AND CO_2 EMISSIONS PER PASSENGER MILE

Urban Area	BTUs	Pounds of CO_2
Commuter Rail		
Chicago (NW IN)	1,587	0.33
Newark (NJT)	1,599	0.19
Boston	2,209	0.36
New York (LIRR)	2,681	0.24
Chicago (RTA)	2,693	0.40
New York (Metro-North)	3,155	0.28
Philadelphia	4,168	0.53
Heavy Rail		
Atlanta	1,983	0.29
New York (MTA)	2,149	0.16
San Francisco (BART)	2,299	0.14
New York (PATH)	2,953	0.20
Washington, D.C.	3,084	0.62
Chicago	3,597	0.37
Boston	3,631	0.44
Baltimore	3,736	0.50
Philadelphia (SEPTA)	3,745	0.48
Los Angeles	4,233	0.26
Philadelphia (PATH)	5,077	0.35
Cleveland	5,494	1.02
Miami	6,756	0.89
Staten Island	8,039	0.60
Light Rail		
San Diego	2,102	0.13
Boston	2,473	0.30
Portland	2,482	0.08
Minneapolis	2,498	0.35
St. Louis	2,613	0.48
Salt Lake City	2,830	0.56
Houston	2,849	0.39
Los Angeles	2,884	0.18
Denver	4,400	0.78
Dallas	4,466	0.60
San Francisco	4,509	0.27
Newark	4,564	0.31

Urban Area	BTUs	Pounds of CO_2
Sacramento	4,821	0.29
Philadelphia	5,459	0.69
Cleveland	5,585	1.03
Buffalo	5,774	0.43
San Jose	6,174	0.38
Baltimore	8,128	1.09
Pittsburgh	9,265	1.18
Streetcars/Vintage Trolleys		
New Orleans	3,540	0.40
Tacoma	4,396	0.09
Charlotte	5,438	0.71
Tampa	7,941	1.04
Little Rock	12,948	1.54
Memphis	17,521	2.42
Kenosha	32,910	4.94
Galveston	34,325	5.58
Trolley Bus		
San Francisco	3,341	0.21
Seattle	3,912	0.08
Dayton	6,377	1.12
Boston	7,589	0.88
Ferry Boat		
New York	4,457	0.72
San Francisco	10,173	1.65
Portland	11,464	1.86
Seattle	13,118	2.13
Savannah	38,864	6.31
San Juan	60,582	9.84
New Orleans	71,784	11.66
Automated Guideway		
Miami	7,649	1.00
Detroit	15,058	2.11
Jacksonville	54,054	7.09
Cable Car		
San Francisco	4,629	0.28

SOURCE: *2006 National Transit Database*, (Washington: Federal Transit Administration, 2007).

NOTE: Salt Lake City data adjusted for ridership overcounts revealed by transit agency.

Authority recently revealed that it has systematically overestimated light-rail ridership by 20 percent or more for several years. More reliable counting methods reveal light rail carries about 22 percent fewer riders than UTA had previously reported.[18] The numbers in table 6.2 have been adjusted to correct this overcount.

Only a handful of rail systems are more environmentally friendly than a Toyota Prius, and most use more energy per passenger mile than the average automobile. Steel wheels on steel rails require far less friction to turn than rubber tires on pavement. So why do rail systems have such mediocre performances?

One reason is that, for the safety and comfort of passengers, rail cars tend to be heavier per passenger than buses. Light-rail cars weigh about four times as much as a typical bus, yet light-rail loads are only about two-and-one-half times buses. Light-rail cars thus weigh around 60 percent more per passenger.[19]

A second problem is that electrically powered systems suffer significant losses in generation and transmission. A kilowatt-hour provides users with about 3,400 BTUs of energy. But the electricity producer must consume three BTUs of coal or other fuel to deliver one BTU to the user.[20] For this reason, trolley buses in Boston, Dayton, and Seattle consume more energy per passenger mile than diesel buses in those same cities—even though the trolley buses carry the same or greater loads.[21]

A third problem is that rail lines cost a lot to build, so they are largely limited to major corridor routes. To justify the large investment, transit agencies operate light- and heavy-rail lines at greater frequencies than buses. Where buses do run frequent service in busy corridors and then diverge into various neighborhoods at the ends of the corridors, train cars are substantially empty at those corridor ends and during much of the day.

All of these factors counteract rail's inherent efficiency advantage. As a result, rails are energy efficient only in extremely high-use corridors. And electrically powered rail lines are greenhouse friendly only in regions that use alternatives to fossil fuels to generate most of their electricity.

Getting Better All the Time

Since 1970, the fuel economy of the average passenger car has improved by more than 40 percent. Average occupancies are estimated to have declined since then, so the improvement in BTUs per

Table 6.3
IMPROVEMENTS IN ENERGY EFFICIENCY THROUGH 2006 (PERCENT)

Mode	Since 1970	Since 1984
Passenger Cars	27.9	13.6
Light Trucks	44.7	22.7
Airlines	68.6	39.1
Amtrak	25.3*	9.3
Buses	− 71.3	− 28.1
Commuter Rail	n.a.	2.2
Light and Heavy Rail	− 29.1	8.3

*Data for 1971.

SOURCE: Stacy C. Davis and Susan W. Diegel, *Transportation Energy Data Book: Edition 27* (Oak Ridge, TN: Department of Energy, 2008), Tables 2.13 and 2.14.

passenger mile is only about 28 percent. But that is still better than transit, most forms of which have actually lost energy efficiency since 1970.

The improvement in energy efficiency for light trucks is probably better than shown in Table 6.3, which presumes occupancies remained constant. In reality, most light trucks in 1970 were pick-ups and probably had much lower average occupancies than the SUVs and full-sized vans that make up the majority of light trucks today.

Most of the increase in auto and light-truck efficiencies came before 1995. Between 1995 and 2005, low fuel prices encouraged Americans to buy larger cars and trucks, so miles-per-gallon remained fairly flat. But efficiencies continued to improve in a differ-ent form: transportation researchers at the University of California (Davis) point out that the number of ton miles moved per gallon of fuel continued to increase, partly offsetting the increased weight of vehicles.[22] If gas prices rise and remain high again, Americans will buy smaller cars that will be even more efficient than those that were available a decade ago.

Buses performed the worst. Increased use of air conditioning and a tendency for transit agencies to buy larger buses than they need reduced bus fuel economy, in miles per gallon, by 17 percent. Mean-while, the extension of bus routes to suburban areas where people rarely ride buses reduced bus occupancies by 32 percent. The net effect was a 71 percent increase in energy consumption per passenger mile. Similarly, the construction of new light- and heavy-rail lines in cities that don't need such forms of transit contributed to the 29 percent decline in rail energy efficiency since 1970.

Bus energy efficiencies leveled off in the mid-1990s, but most of the other trends are likely to continue. On one hand, transit agencies continue to build rail lines in low-density urban areas where they make little sense from an economic or energy-efficiency view. On the other hand, both cars and airplanes are expected to greatly increase their fuel efficiencies.

In May 2009, a dozen major auto companies committed themselves to meeting President Obama's fuel-economy targets by increasing their "corporate average fuel economies" (CAFE) from 27.5 miles per gallon today to 35.5 miles per gallon by 2016.[23] Congress has also required that production of biofuels (which produce only one-third the net greenhouse gas emissions of fossil fuels) increase from 4 billion gallons today to 36 billion gallons by 2022.[24]

The nation's automobile fleet almost completely turns over about every 18 years, so the net effect of Obama's targets will be to increase fuel economies by more than 2 percent per year.[25] By 2020, the average automobile on the road will consume slightly less than 3,000 BTUs per passenger mile. By 2030, even if new-car efficiencies do not improve after 2020, the replacement of older cars will drop average energy consumption to less than 2,500 BTUs per passenger mile.[26]

CAFE standards are inefficient in many ways, but even without such standards, the energy efficiency of autos is likely to significantly improve in the future.[27] The same cannot be said for rail transit. Anyone claiming that a new rail transit line will be more energy efficient than autos must take into account the growing energy efficiency of automobiles. To truly save energy, a proposed rail line not only needs to be more efficient than today's autos, it must be more efficient than future autos. Since rail lines typically take 10 years to plan and construct and have an operational life (before needing energy-intensive reconstruction and rehabilitation) of 30 years, they would have to be more efficient than the average auto 20 years from now to achieve any savings at all.

Suppose a light-rail line is projected to open in 2015 and operate until 2045, when it will need to be replaced or rehabilitated. The midpoint of its life will be 2030, when autos (including SUVs) are projected to use about 2,500 BTUs per passenger mile. Since most light-rail lines consume far more than that today, new lines are not likely to save much energy.

Production of CO_2 by petroleum-fueled motor vehicles is almost exactly proportional to their energy efficiency. However, CO_2 emissions from motor vehicles can be reduced using biofuels, which offset the CO_2 emissions by obtaining energy from plants absorbing CO_2 from the atmosphere. If properly implemented, the biofuel requirement in the 2007 Energy Act means that greenhouse gas emissions per passenger mile will decline even faster than fuel consumption.

Cannibalizing Buses

Table 6.4 shows the average energy consumption of transit systems in most of the nation's top 50 urbanized areas. Only a few transit systems consume significantly less energy per passenger mile than the 3,700 BTUs consumed by the average automobile, and only two consume less than the 2,660 BTUs per passenger mile that autos are expected to use in 2030. The rail transit in many regions, including Baltimore, Dallas, Miami, San Jose, and Sacramento, is less environmentally friendly than light trucks.

Curiously, the nation's most energy-efficient transit system is not New York's but Honolulu's, which operates only buses. That system is efficient because its bus loads average nearly 18 people, compared with less than 11 for most other bus systems. New York's buses carry almost as many people, on average, which contributes as much to the energy efficiency of that region's transit as the rail lines.

One reason why many rail regions do so poorly is that new rail lines cannibalize bus systems by taking their most popular—and therefore most energy-efficient—routes. Moreover, after opening a new rail line, transit agencies typically offer their customers more bus service, not less, as corridor bus routes are turned into feeder buses for the rail corridor. Many people who have access to autos drive to the rail stations, so the feeder buses tend to operate with much smaller average loads than the corridor buses they replaced.

The result is many regions that build new rail transit lines end up using more fuel on buses carrying smaller average loads than before they built the rail lines. For example, in 1991, before St. Louis

119

Table 6.4
URBAN AREA TRANSIT ENERGY CONSUMPTION AND CO_2 EMISSIONS PER PASSENGER MILE

Urban Area	BTUs	Pounds of CO_2
Honolulu	1,577	0.25
New York	2,639	0.29
Atlanta	2,865	0.45
San Francisco	3,003	0.30
Portland	3,008	0.36
Boston	3,201	0.45
Salt Lake City	3,241	0.54
Chicago	3,357	0.46
Houston	3,528	0.57
Denver	3,596	0.59
Washington, D.C.	3,646	0.63
Orlando	3,670	0.59
Hartford	3,670	0.59
Los Angeles	3,674	0.56
Minneapolis-St. Paul	3,722	0.56
San Diego	3,893	0.54
Cincinnati	3,938	0.48
Detroit	3,998	0.64
Providence	4,076	0.66
Norfolk	4,133	0.66
Philadelphia	4,305	0.57
St. Louis	4,345	0.74
Charlotte	4,488	0.72
Baltimore	4,497	0.67
Milwaukee	4,572	0.74
Nashville	4,596	0.74
Columbus	4,643	0.50
Cleveland	4,703	0.79
Austin	4,985	0.80
Miami	5,037	0.76
Indianapolis	5,059	0.82
Tampa-St. Petersburg	5,218	0.84
San Antonio	5,351	0.84
Pittsburgh	5,357	0.82
Dallas	5,414	0.85
Memphis	5,502	0.87

Urban Area	BTUs	Pounds of CO_2
Louisville	5,521	0.89
San Jose	5,549	0.74
Buffalo	5,602	0.81
Sacramento	5,613	0.69
Seattle	5,805	0.91
Kansas City	6,106	0.97
Riverside	6,121	1.11
Richmond	6,193	1.00
Tucson	6,275	1.00
Jacksonville	6,278	1.00
Oklahoma City	6,626	1.07
Norwalk	7,243	1.17
New Orleans	8,674	1.40

SOURCE: *2006 National Transit Database*, (Washington: Federal Transit Administration, 2007).

NOTE: Las Vegas is not on the list because 100 percent of its transit is contracted out. Phoenix is excluded because 88 percent of its transit is contracted out, and the remaining 12 percent is not a representative sample. Honolulu—the nation's 51st largest urban area—is included because of its high energy efficiency.

built its first light-rail line, St. Louis buses averaged more than 10 riders and consumed 4,600 BTUs per passenger mile. In 1995, after opening the light-rail line, average bus loads declined to less than 7 and energy consumption by bus and light rail together increased to 5,300 BTUs per passenger mile. CO_2 emissions also climbed, from 0.75 pounds to 0.88 pounds per passenger mile.[28]

Other cities experienced similar declines in energy efficiencies after opening light-rail lines. Sacramento's bus loads, for example, declined from around 14 before the region's first light-rail line opened in 1987 to less than 10 afterwards. Overall energy consumption thus increased from around 3,000 to 4,300 BTUs per passenger mile, while CO_2 emissions increased from 0.48 pounds to 0.58 pounds per passenger mile.[29] In 2004, Sacramento opened a new light-rail line, but bus loads fell again to below 8, while overall energy consumption and CO_2 emissions grew to nearly 4,600 BTUs and 0.64 pounds per passenger mile.[30]

Similarly, Houston's light-rail line boosted energy consumption and CO_2 emissions per passenger mile by 8 to 10 percent.[31] Portland's

121

eastside light-rail line, which opened in 1986, increased energy use and CO_2 production by 5 to 13 percent per passenger mile.[32] Its westside line, which opened in 1998, increased energy use and CO_2 production by 7 to 11 percent per passenger mile.[33]

Not every transit system suffers a decline in energy efficiency after opening a rail line. Before opening the Hiawatha light-rail line in 2004, the Twin Cities' transit system used about 4,000 BTUs and emitted about 0.65 pounds of CO_2 per passenger mile. The light rail improved the 2006 system-wide average to 3,722 BTUs and 0.56 pounds of CO_2 per passenger mile.[34] But as the next section suggests, this small savings probably does not make up for the huge energy and CO_2 cost of building the line.

Don't Forget the Construction Cost

Even if a new rail line could save energy or reduce greenhouse gases compared with buses or autos, the energy costs and CO_2 emissions during construction are huge and may never be recovered through operational savings. Rail transit requires significant amounts of steel and concrete, for example, both of which are energy intensive and emit large volumes of CO_2.

The environmental impact statement for Portland's North Interstate light rail estimated that the line would save about 23 billion BTUs per year but that construction would cost 3.9 trillion BTUs.[35] This means it would take 172 years for the savings to repay the construction cost. In fact, long before 172 years, automobiles are likely to be so energy efficient that light rail will offer no savings at all.

Similarly, the North Link light-rail line in Seattle is estimated to save about 346 billion BTUs of energy in 2015, declining to 200 billion in 2030.[36] Construction is estimated to require 17.4 trillion BTUs.[37] If the savings remains constant at 200 billion BTUs after 2030, the savings will not repay the cost until 2095. The Federal Transit Administration says that it is satisfied with this savings, because "the light rail project is expected to have about a 100 year life."[38]

In reality, rail projects have an expected lifespan of only about 30 to 40 years, after which most of the rail line must be substantially rebuilt or replaced. Such reconstruction will require lots of energy and emit lots of CO_2, all of which must be counted against any operational savings that the systems claim to provide.

These examples show that any claims that rail transit will reduce energy consumption must be met with skepticism unless they are accompanied by evidence that the operational savings will quickly repay the construction cost. Transit agencies are often reluctant to provide that evidence even when they are required to do so by law. The environmental consequences chapter of the environmental impact statement for Dallas's Southeast Corridor light-rail line, for example, never once mentions the terms "energy," "greenhouse," or "carbon dioxide," much less estimates the energy or CO_2 costs of constructing the line.[39]

Highway construction also uses energy and emits CO_2, but each mile of urban highway carries far more passenger miles and freight ton-miles of travel than a mile of rail transit line. In 2007, for example, the average mile of American light-rail line moved only 13 percent as many passenger miles as the average lane mile of urban freeway in rail regions.[40] Highways also move millions of tons of freight that can share the cost of construction. This means the energy and CO_2 costs of highway construction, per passenger mile or ton-mile, are far lower than those of rail transit construction.

Alternatives to Rail Transit

According to analysts at McKinsey & Company, the United States can significantly reduce its greenhouse gas emissions by investing in technologies that will cut emissions at a cost of no more than $50 per ton of carbon dioxide–equivalent gases. McKinsey notes that some technologies, such as lighter, more fuel-efficient cars, can reduce emissions and actually save money in the long run. Other investments, such as retrofitting homes to be more energy-efficient, may cost some homeowners slightly more than they save but still net out at less than $10 per ton of greenhouse gases saved.[41]

Given limited resources, why choose a project that costs $10,000 per ton of reduced gases when, for every ton saved, we could have saved 1,000 tons if we had invested in projects that cost only $10 per ton? In the rare instances where rail transit or other behavioral solutions can actually save energy and reduce greenhouse gas emissions, they will do so at a cost that is closer to $10,000 a ton than $10 a ton.

Transit officials and other urban leaders who have a genuine desire to reduce energy usage and greenhouse gas emissions from their regions should consider alternatives that are far more cost effective at achieving these goals than building rail transit. Here are four potential alternatives:

- Choosing alternative transit fuels and technologies;
- Increasing average bus loads;
- Reducing fuels wasted on highways and streets; and
- Improving automotive efficiencies.

Alternative Transit Fuels and Technologies

Transit agencies wishing to reduce greenhouse gas emissions have two options, neither of which involves building rail transit. First, they can use alternative fuel sources and technologies. Second, they can improve their loadings by increasing the average number of people using each transit vehicle or reducing vehicle sizes.

Minneapolis-St. Paul is one of the few regions where a new light-rail line has saved energy. In addition, the region has reduced greenhouse gas emissions by purchasing hybrid-electric buses and converting to biodiesel fuel for its buses. Hybrid-electric buses are 22 percent more fuel-efficient than regular buses. Biodiesel's net CO_2 emissions are only a third of petroleum-based diesel fuel. In 2006, Metro Transit in Minneapolis-St. Paul began using a fuel mixture of 10 percent biodiesel, and it and other transit agencies are now experimenting with a 20 percent blend.[42]

Hybrid buses cost more than regular buses, and biodiesel costs more than regular diesel. Nonetheless, these choices are far more cost-effective at reducing greenhouse gas emissions than building light rail. Minneapolis-St. Paul spent $715 million building its light-rail line.[43] Amortized at 7 percent over 40 years, this equals a $53 million annual cost. The transit agency estimates that the light rail saves it $18 million per year in operating costs, so the net cost is $35 million per year.[44] Operating the light rail instead of carrying the same passengers on buses saves about 7,300 metric tons of CO_2, for a cost of nearly $5,000 per metric ton. This doesn't include the CO_2 emissions from construction, which reduce the net savings and thus increase the cost of any savings.

In contrast, Minneapolis-St. Paul is purchasing 172 hybrid-electric buses at a cost of $200,000 more each than a regular bus. Amortizing

124

this cost over 10 years results in an annual cost of about $28,000. The transit agency estimates that each bus will save nearly 2,000 gallons of fuel each year, which would otherwise have generated nearly 44,000 pounds of CO_2.[45] This represents a cost of about $1,300 per metric ton.

Biodiesel is even more cost effective. Converting from petroleum diesel to a 20-percent biodiesel mixture saves Minneapolis-St. Paul about 10,000 metric tons of CO_2 per year.[46] The 20-percent biodiesel mixture costs about 20 cents more per gallon and yields about 2 percent less BTUs per gallon than pure petroleum diesel, for a total net cost of less than $2 million per year.[47] Biodiesel thus costs less than $200 per metric ton of CO_2 saved, making it more than 25 times as cost-effective at reducing greenhouse gases as light rail.

Regions that rely heavily on non-fossil-fuel sources of electricity have a third option for reducing CO_2: electric trolley buses. While trolley buses are not as energy-efficient as diesel buses, they can be greenhouse friendly. Seattle's trolley buses, for example, produce just one-seventh as much CO_2 per passenger mile as Seattle's diesel buses.[48] Installing and maintaining trolley wires is costly, though nowhere near as costly as building rail transit lines. In the 1990s, for example, the Los Angeles Metropolitan Transit Authority estimated that installing and buying buses for 200 route miles of trolley wires would cost about 10 percent as much as a similar length of light rail.[49]

Increasing Transit Loads

Transit agencies can also save energy by increasing load factors, that is, the percentage of seats and standing room on transit vehicles used in the course of a day. The average transit bus has 39 seats and room for 20 more people standing, yet it carries, on average, fewer than 11 people. Some transit agencies average more than 20 passengers per bus and thus consume far less energy per passenger mile.

One way to increase passenger loads is to focus bus service in areas where ridership is highest. Such a market orientation is foreign to transit agencies that feel politically obligated to provide service to all taxpaying neighborhoods, even if those neighborhoods offer few riders.

Still, some bus operations are remarkably energy efficient. Several commuter bus lines in the New York metropolitan area consume less than 2,000 BTUs per passenger mile by focusing their services on routes and times that serve large numbers of passengers. Golden Gate Transit in San Francisco–Marin County along with transit systems in such varied cities as Cumberland, Maryland; Rome, Georgia; Brownsville, Texas; and Santa Barbara, California, all consume less than 3,000 BTUs per passenger mile.

Transit agencies that focus on corridor or commuter routes can save energy while serving suburban neighborhoods or off-peak times by using smaller buses. Transit agencies typically buy buses large enough to meet peak-hour demand and then operate those buses throughout the day. Moreover, federal funding for transit capital purchases gives agencies incentives to buy buses that are larger than they really need, even during peak hours. In any case, buying two separate fleets of buses—one for corridors and peak periods and one for suburban routes and off-peak periods—would do more to reduce energy use and CO_2 emissions than building rail transit.

Portland's TriMet transit agency, for example, has a fleet of 545 buses in fixed-route service, 90 percent of which have 39 seats or more. TriMet could supplement these buses with 500 15- to 25-passenger buses costing $50,000 to $75,000 each.[50] That would total $25 to $37 million—about the cost of one mile of light-rail line. Amortized over 10 years, this is about $5 million per year.

These smaller buses consume only about 40 percent as much fuel and emit 40 percent as much CO_2 as full-sized buses. TriMet buses produced 58,600 metric tons of CO_2 in 2006, so operating smaller buses for even one-third of vehicle-hours of service would save 11,400 tons of CO_2. Savings on fuel would offset at least $1 million of the $5 million amortized cost of buying the vehicles. Thus, the reductions in CO_2 levels would cost only about $350 per ton. While none of the transit alternatives considered here meet McKinsey's $50-per-ton threshold, they are all far more cost-effective at reducing greenhouse gases than building rail lines.

Saving Energy on Highways and Streets

The Texas Transportation Institute estimates that more than 2.9 billion gallons of fuel are wasted in congested traffic each year.[51] Relieving this congestion by fixing bottlenecks, using congestion tolls, and adding new capacity will do far more to reduce energy than rail transit. Moreover, new highways largely pay for themselves, especially if tolls are used, while rail transit requires huge subsidies.

Some people fear that relieving congestion will simply induce more driving, and the energy costs of that driving will cancel out the savings from congestion relief. The induced-demand story is as much a myth as the claim that General Motors shut down streetcar systems in order to force people to buy cars. It presumes that people have a nearly infinite demand to drive and that the only way to curb that demand is to limit the roads they can drive upon.

Not building roads out of fear of induced demand is "wrong-headed," says University of California planning professor Robert Cervero. The problems people associate with roads—for example, congestion and air pollution—are not the fault of the road invest-ments," he adds. They result "from the *use* and *mispricing* of roads."[52]

Suppressed demand is a more accurate term than induced demand. If building new roads leads to more driving, that driving represents demand that was suppressed by congestion. So long as people are willing to pay the full cost of the roads they use, it is inappropriate and counterproductive for government to try to suppress travel demand. Of course, travel demand is far from infinite and will be tempered by insuring that people do pay the full cost.

Historically, gasoline taxes and other highway user fees have paid nearly 90 percent of all the costs of building, maintaining, and policing American roads and streets.[53] (In contrast, transit fares cover only about 40 percent of transit operating costs and none of transit capital costs.) The problem with the gas tax as a user fee, however, is that it does not provide users with signals about the costs of the services they are consuming. It costs more to build a system that can meet peak-period demand, yet peak-period users pay about the same user fee as off-peak users.

The solution is to charge tolls for new highway capacity and vary the tolls by the amount of traffic, so that new highway lanes never become congested. Existing high-occupancy vehicle lanes, which often have a surplus of capacity, can also be converted to high-occupancy toll (HOT) lanes, as has been done successfully in Den-ver.[54] Toll revenues will cover the costs of new roads, but higher tolls during peak periods will reduce the need for more roads.

Tolls are one good solution but, so far, have been applied only to limited-access highways. On unlimited-access roads, traffic engi-neers can do much to reduce CO_2 emissions by improving traffic signal coordination. San Jose coordinated 223 traffic signals on the city's most-congested streets at a cost of about $500,000. Amortized over 10 years, that equals an annual cost of about $70,000 per year. Engineers estimate that this saves 471,000 gallons of gasoline each year, which translates to a 4,200-ton reduction in CO_2 emissions.[55] That works out to a cost of $17 per ton. But after deducting the fuel savings to motorists—$942,000 per year at $2 per gallon—the project actually saved money *and* reduced greenhouse gases. The project also saved people's time, improved safety, and reduced toxic air pollution.

According to the Federal Highway Administration, three out of four traffic signals in the nation are obsolete and poorly coordinated with other signals.[56] The National Transportation Operations Coalition says that deficiencies in signal coordination "are remarkably similar across the country and across jurisdictions."[57] Signal coordination easily meets McKinsey's $50-per-ton test, so cities that have not budgeted the funds to improve traffic signal coordination have no business spending hundreds of millions of dollars building light-rail lines in the forlorn hope that rail transit will reduce CO_2 emissions.

Improving Automobile Efficiencies

President Obama's fuel-economy standard requires that the average car made in 2016 get 35.5 miles per gallon. Even if this target is achieved, however, the average car on the road in 2016 will get only about 24 miles per gallon. Cities that want to accelerate the move to higher fuel efficiency will find that giving people incentives to buy fuel-efficient cars is a more cost-effective way of reducing energy consumption and greenhouse gas emissions than building rail transit.

Since 1992, American cities have invested some $100 billion in urban rail transit.[58] Yet no rail system in the country has managed to increase transit's share of urban travel by even 1 percent.[59] Between 1990 and 2005, the only rail region that managed to increase transit's share of commuting by more than 1 percent was New York, and it did so mainly by lowering transit fares. Meanwhile, transit actually lost shares of passenger travel and commuters in most other rail regions.[60] Thus, rail transit promises, at best, tiny gains for huge investments.

Considering rail transit's poor track record, persuading 1 percent of auto owners to purchase a car that gets 30 to 40 miles per gallon or better the next time they buy a car will do more to reduce energy consumption and CO_2 emissions than building rail transit. Only minimal incentives should be needed to achieve this goal, making such incentives far more cost effective than building rail transit.

7. Paying for Mobility

"All transportation is subsidized" is the frequent refrain of those who advocate even greater subsidies for their favored modes of transport.[1] Although that statement is questionable, most passenger transportation is indeed subsidized. But this begs the question of why we subsidize it when nearly all of the benefits go to the people who actually use it. Perhaps, instead of throwing more subsidies at certain forms of transportation to "balance" past subsidies to other forms of transportation, we should eliminate the subsidies entirely.

Certain things produce benefits in ways that make it difficult to pay for those things out of user fees. National defense is the classic example. Economists call such things *public goods*. This does not imply that everything owned or operated by the public is a public good, only those things that people can consume without reducing their availability to others.

Transportation is not a public good. A discerning economist might be able to find public-good aspects of transportation, food, shelter, and just about anything else. But for the most part, the benefits of transportation are captured by the people who use it. It is unfair to ask all people to pay for the transportation that only some people use.

Despite this, American history is filled with examples of government involvement in transportation. Sometimes the government proposes to provide just the initial funds to get a transportation project started. But when government begins to fund something, it often has trouble stopping. The people who benefit from that funding lobby to make sure those benefits continue. Subsidies then go out of control as interest groups favoring one mode or geographic region compete with one another to capture the greatest subsidies.

Roads and Waterways

Before steam power became dominant, the chief methods of transportation were roads and waterways. Most early settlements were located on navigable rivers. But the rivers did not go everywhere, so people supplemented the waterways with roads.

Many early roads in the United States were toll roads. Between 1790 and 1845, more than 1,500 private companies received charters to build toll roads, and a majority of those companies succeeded in building and operating such roads. A few states, notably Ohio, Pennsylvania, and Virginia, subsidized toll road companies to gain a competitive advantage over their neighbors. But most of the toll roads were financed solely by private investors who were paid dividends out of toll revenues.[2]

One argument against private roads is that they require a central planner to ensure a complete network of roads is built. Yet toll road companies often cooperated with one another to provide such a network. For example, five different companies each operated a segment of the Pittsburgh Pike, a toll road connecting Pittsburgh with Harrisburg. Another series of cooperating toll roads connected Harrisburg with Philadelphia.[3]

Despite the success of these private roads, in 1806 the federal government decided to build a "national road" from Maryland to Missouri. No doubt the theory was that accelerated construction of this road would help tie together the western portions of the young nation and defend them against French, English, or other foreign incursions. The government eventually spent about $6.8 million (roughly $135 million in today's dollars) on this road but gave up before it reached the Missouri-Illinois border. Construction of the government road cost more than twice as much per mile as private roads in similar terrain, yet the national road was poorly maintained because maintenance depended on appropriations from a fickle Congress rather than toll revenues.[4]

Meanwhile, the financial success of early canals built in Great Britain led to proposals to build canals extending the reach of navigable rivers in the United States. In 1817, New York Governor DeWitt Clinton persuaded the state legislature to provide a $7 million loan to a private company to build the 363-mile Erie Canal from Albany to Buffalo. While construction took eight years, the company building it was able to earn toll revenues on segments as they were completed.

The company eventually repaid the loan plus 6 percent interest. The completed canal proved to be a bonanza for New York City, as producers in the West found it far cheaper to ship to New York City than to competing ports such as Philadelphia and Baltimore.

Maryland and Pennsylvania each responded with a canal project. Maryland's Chesapeake and Ohio Canal extended 184 miles from Washington, D.C., to Cumberland, Maryland. Pennsylvania funded the Main Line, a combination of canals and railroads connecting Philadelphia with the Ohio River system at Pittsburgh. Unlike the Erie Canal, these canals were generally not financially successful, partly because steam railroads rendered them obsolete before they were completed.

Railroads and Land Grants

Early American railroads were built almost entirely with private funds. These railroads provided such superior transportation that by 1850 they had put most toll roads and canals out of business. Individual states still competed with one another for business—and may have offered various favors to the railroads serving those states. For example, Pennsylvania sold the state-financed Main Line to the Pennsylvania Railroad, which no doubt helped that railroad build its empire at a lower cost. For the most part, however, no federal and few state subsidies went to railroads in the eastern United States.

The Pacific Railway Act provided land grants and low-interest loans to the companies completing the railroad from Council Bluffs, Iowa, to California. Later laws provided land grants (but no low-interest loans) for railroads from St. Paul to the Puget Sound, Los Angeles to New Orleans, Los Angeles to St. Louis, and Portland to San Francisco. In total, about 170 million acres were granted to the railroads, but Congress eventually took back about 45 million acres for nonperformance, leaving the railroads a maximum of about 125 million acres.

Congress expected that the railroads would sell the land to help pay for construction. In many instances, there was no immediate market for the land. Much of it was not farmable, and the United States had a surplus of wood so there was little market for timberland. In the latter half of the 20th century, the energy and timber resources on lands granted to the Northern Pacific, Southern Pacific, Santa Fe, and Union Pacific railroads proved very profitable. But this did not help them build the railroads in the first place.

In January 1893, the Great Northern Railway completed its route from St. Paul to Seattle without any land grants (except a small grant to a predecessor railroad) or other federal or state subsidies. The railway competed directly with the Northern Pacific, and to some extent with the Union Pacific, which served some of the same territory. The Great Northern's builder, James J. Hill, knew that the other railroads had been built primarily for the subsidies, and as a result, they were poorly engineered and often followed circuitous routes. Hill built the Great Northern along the most direct route his engineers could find, so his operating costs were far lower than his competitors'.

When the economic crash of 1893 took place a few months later, the Northern Pacific, Union Pacific, and almost all other western railroads went into receivership. A company in receivership continues to operate but does not have to immediately pay its creditors—and often repudiates its bonds. Many people predicted that the Great Northern would not be able to compete and would follow the others into bankruptcy. But Hill managed to stay out of receivership, and the Great Northern remained the only transcontinental built in North America without government subsidies that never went bankrupt.

By 1930, American railroad mileage peaked at about 260,000 miles.[5] As noted in chapter 5, only 18,700 of these miles were built with land grants or other federal subsidies. Some local subsidies, such as funds or land donations from cities or towns, might have been provided, but these mostly determined where a railroad would locate, not whether it would be built. Railroads today argue that congressionally mandated rate reductions for government shipping and travel have effectively repaid the full value of all land grants and subsidies.[6]

Railroads fiercely competed for business between major cities such as New York and Chicago or St. Paul and Seattle. But many midpoints were monopolized by one railroad. Farmers were upset to find that the railroads often charged more to ship from, say, Missoula to Chicago than from Seattle to Chicago. Railroad explanations that the greater volumes shipped from Seattle allowed quantity discounts fell on deaf ears. Concerns about rail monopolies fed the growing Progressive movement and had a profound influence on 20th-century transportation policy.

Urban Transit

Early urban transit ventures were privately financed. Because many of them used public rights-of-way, they often had to obtain franchises from city councils. Other than rights-of-way, transit companies received no subsidies or other public support through the end of the 19th century.

The first urban transit in the United States was probably a ferry in Boston that began as early as 1630. Ox carts reputedly carried passengers in New York City as early as 1740. But the first popular public transit was the *omnibus* (a Latin word meaning "for everyone"), a large, horse-drawn wagon with seats and shelter for passengers. New York City saw its first omnibus in 1827, and within a few years, other major American cities had them as well.[7]

The omnibus advanced to the horse-drawn railcar in 1832. These so-called "horsecars" proved to be very popular; at some point, more than 500 American cities had at least one horsecar line, and horsecars could be found in such remote locations as Deadwood, South Dakota; Lewiston, Maine; and Selma, Alabama. Mules pulled cars in more than 30 Texas cities, including Corpus Christi and Dallas.

In 1838, the first steam-powered commuter trains started carrying suburban workers to Boston. This type of train was developed only in the largest metropolitan areas, such as Chicago, New York, Philadelphia, and San Francisco. Most of the patrons of all these early forms of mechanized transit were upper class or middle-class, white-collar workers.

The first elevated transit line was built in New York in 1871. It was powered by steam, but many cities discouraged the use of steam locomotives because of the noise and pollution. In 1873, San Francisco saw the first cable cars, a system in which steam power in a central location towed rail cars. By 1890, close to 30 other American cities had installed cable cars.

The biggest transit revolution was provided by electric streetcars, which were perfected and installed in Montgomery, Alabama, and Richmond, Virginia, in the late 1880s. Electric streetcars were so much more efficient than previous forms of travel that "trolley fever" quickly spread across the nation. Transit companies quickly converted almost every cable car and horsecar line to an electric system powered by trolley wires, and built many new lines as well. Eventually, electric streetcars could be found in more than 850 American cities and towns.

The next step, in 1893, was construction of the first electrically powered interurban rail line connecting the 15-mile distance from

Portland to Oregon City, effectively turning the latter into a suburb of the former. Within a few years, more than 300 railways and power companies were operating interurbans in 40 states.[8]

Chicago built the first electric-powered elevated rail line in 1895. But elevated lines were unpopular because of their unsightly nature. Electric power allowed companies to build underground railways that could avoid traffic without asphyxiating passengers or darkening streets. Boston submerged one of its streetcar lines in 1897. Parsons Brinckerhoff built the first true heavy-rail subway in New York City in 1904. New York also saw the first motorized bus (shortened from omnibus) in 1905 and the first trolley bus in 1921.

Up to 1904, urban transit was privately financed and unsubsidized. In that year, the North Dakota legislature, influenced by public fears of railroad monopolies, built the first state-owned streetcar line in Bismarck. In 1905, New York City took over the previously private Staten Island Ferry. In 1906, Monroe, Louisiana, became the first city to build a streetcar line.

Private transit companies faced several financial difficulties. Many streetcar lines were built by real-estate developers to attract people to their housing projects. A developer would subdivide land on the city fringe, build a streetcar line from the development to downtown, and sell lots and homes. The profits on the real-estate development paid for the capital cost of the streetcar line. Transit fares covered only the operating cost. That worked fine for a few decades, but when the time came to replace the streetcars, rails, and other equipment, the companies often lacked the capital.

One way to raise funds was to increase fares. But city or state governments regulated the fares, and proposals to raise fares were regularly rejected by public utility commissions. This left many transit companies with aging streetcar fleets in precarious financial positions.

Progressive politicians saw public takeover of transit companies as a potential solution. Since public agencies would not have to pay dividends to stockholders, the Progressives believed, they could operate transit at a lower cost and would not have to raise fares. San Francisco was the first major city to operate its own streetcars, the San Francisco Municipal Railway (Muni), in 1912. New York City started operating and acquiring subway lines in 1932. In 1938, Chicago obtained the first federal grants to support construction of a publicly owned rail line.

In cities where transit remained private, the local electric power companies often consolidated the streetcar lines under a single owner. This gave rise to concerns about monopoly power. In 1935, Congress ordered power companies to divest their transit operations. Since transit was already struggling due to the rise of the automobile and the Depression, this act put many companies on the brink of bankruptcy.

One solution was to convert streetcars to buses, which did not require as much infrastructure support. Of the more than 700 American cities served by streetcars in 1910, at least 230 either went out of business or converted to buses by the end of 1929. Another 300 converted during the 1930s and 100 more in the 1940s.[9]

The rapid conversion of streetcars to buses gave rise to the irrepressible myth that automobile and oil companies bought transit systems in order to demolish them and force people to drive gasoline-powered cars.[10] The truth is that General Motors, Firestone Tire, Chevron, and Phillips Petroleum purchased National City Lines, which owned bus companies in as many as 60 cities, in order to sell those companies their products—buses, tires, and fuel. In 1949, the Justice Department successfully sued General Motors for violating antitrust law, and it and the other companies sold their shares of National City Lines.

During the years General Motors and the other companies owned National City Lines, more than 300 streetcar lines converted to buses, but less than 30 of them were under National City ownership.[11] In many cases, the conversion was made the very year National City acquired the company, suggesting that the decision to convert had been made before National City got involved. Nor did National City Lines convert all the streetcar lines it owned to buses. When National City bought the St. Louis transit system in 1939, for example, it purchased more modern streetcars for the system and continued to operate streetcars until 1963, when it sold the system to a public agency—which quickly converted all streetcars to buses.[12]

Fifty American cities still had streetcars in 1949, the year General Motors and the other companies sold their interest in National City. Over the next 18 years, all but six of those cities converted streetcars to buses. By 1967, only Boston, Cleveland, New Orleans, Philadelphia, Pittsburgh, and San Francisco still had streetcars; New York and Chicago were the only other cities that still had other forms of

137

rail transit. The fact that more than 95 percent of the streetcar-to-bus conversions were made by private companies or public agencies that had no affiliation with General Motors shows that the conversions were made for efficiency reasons, not monopolistic ones. All General Motors wanted to do was sell its buses to companies that were buying buses.

In 1964, some of the nation's largest transit systems, including all of the rail systems except the one in New Orleans, had been taken over by public agencies. Yet the vast majority of bus systems were still private. That changed quickly when Congress promised to make capital grants available to public agencies—but not private companies—that operated or acquired transit systems. Within a decade, all but a handful of transit systems were taken over by tax-subsidized public agencies.

Contrary to popular belief, Congress did not pass the Urban Mass Transit Act of 1964 to provide mobility for low-income and other people who could not drive. Instead, Congress was reacting to proposals by various railroads to discontinue interstate commuter trains serving Boston, Chicago, New York, and Philadelphia.[13] At the time, these four urban areas plus San Francisco had the only commuter trains in America. Urban leaders argued that the commuter trains were essential to maintain jobs in Manhattan and other downtown areas.

The Urban Mass Transit Act was designed to provide federal support for interstate commuter trains. Of course, politics quickly demanded that federal support go to mass transit services in every state and metropolitan area. The various fixed-guideway funds and formulas were aimed at ensuring a minimum of support to existing train services. By 1991, the rail construction lobby had grown powerful enough to get its own fund, the New Starts fund. The $160 billion spent on rail construction since then is a monument to the slippery slope of federal involvement in what should be state, local, or private activities.

Far from operating more efficiently because they did not have to pay dividends, public transit agencies soon began hemorrhaging money. When Portland's private bus company sought permission to raise fares from 35 to 40 cents in 1969, it was instead taken over by a public agency. The fares remained 35 cents, at least for a short time, but the agency spent more than a dollar per ride. A regionwide payroll tax, which employers paid whether their employees used transit or not, made up the difference.

By this time, Americans were convinced the automobile was the most convenient form of travel ever invented. Heavily subsidized transit systems in San Francisco, New York, and other cities failed to persuade them otherwise. Relatively unregulated systems in some sunbelt cities fared no better.

Yet private, unregulated transit would probably look very different today from the socialized transit that has come to dominate American cities since 1964. Instead of running nearly empty buses or trains to distant suburbs, modern transit would probably look more like the jitneys of Atlantic City or the *públicos* of Puerto Rico: low-capacity vehicles providing more personalized service between more origins and destinations and possibly during more hours of the day.

The Highway Era

American highway users owe their first debt of gratitude not to early automobile drivers but to early bicyclists. Cycling became popular after the 1885 invention of the *safety bicycle*, which—unlike the high wheelers that preceded it—was easy for anyone to ride. In 1892, the League of American Wheelmen began publishing *Good Roads* magazine to promote the idea of paved rural roads for its members to ride on. Auto drivers joined the movement when the automobile became popular after the turn of the century.

The first question was: who should build the roads? One possible answer was to have privately financed and built toll roads. In fact, the first highway built exclusively for automobiles was William K. Vanderbilt II's 48-mile Long Island Motor Parkway, which opened as a toll road in 1908. Originally conceived as a racetrack, Vanderbilt realized he could cover some of the costs by charging a $2 toll on the 364 non-race days each year. Considered the world's first limited-access highway, with concrete pavement and banked corners, Vanderbilt advertised "40 miles per hour, no police traps, no dust." (Racers could average more than 60 and reach top speeds of more than 100 miles per hour.) Having paid off much of its cost out of tolls, the two-lane road was turned into a bike path in 1938 when it could no longer compete with a parallel toll-free state parkway.[14]

139

Despite the success of the Long Island Parkway, memories of controversies about railroad monopolies were fresh in peoples' minds. Even the railroads supported public ownership of highways, anticipating that such roads would make it easier for farmers to bring their products to the railheads.

Having settled the ownership issue, the next question became: how to pay for the roads? That was answered in 1919, when Oregon dedicated the nation's first tax on motor fuels to roads. By 1931, every state had followed suit. In 1932, the federal government imposed its own gas tax, but unlike the states did not initially dedicate it to highways. Gas taxes, tolls, and other user fees quickly grew to cover most of the costs of building, maintaining, and operating highways.[15]

User fees provide an important link between users and producers. Fees tell users how much it costs to provide a good or service and discourage them from using too much. Fees tell producers what a good or service is worth to users and encourage them to provide more if willingness to pay exceeds the costs. Gas taxes provide such a link: highway officials know, for example, that if they build a road to nowhere, no one will use it, which means it won't generate the gas tax revenues needed to pay for it.

Still, the link provided by gas taxes is not as direct as tolls, which are location- and—if allowed to vary over the course of a day—time-specific. Moreover, legislators circumvent the gas–tax link when they divert funds away from the things users are paying for or otherwise dictate how those funds should be spent. Between 1942 and 1956, federal, state, and local governments collected more highway fees than they spent on roads, so it is hard to argue that roads were subsidized.[16] At the same time, this was hardly a model of free markets at work.

In the 1920s and 1930s, New York and nearby states began building limited-access highways, some of which were supported with tolls. However, the federal government's Bureau of Public Roads, led by Thomas MacDonald, strongly opposed toll roads. As chief of the bureau from 1919 to 1953, MacDonald was "Mr. Highway" for much of the 20th century. MacDonald's friends considered him the epitome of a civil servant, bringing scientific precision to a contentious political process. His critics considered him a megalomaniac trying to consolidate power in his bureau. Nowhere was this dichotomy more apparent than on the issue of tolls.

In the 1920s, to discourage pork barrel spending, he persuaded Congress to spend federal highway funds only on roads his bureau had decided were worthy of being called "federal-aid highways." But in 1938—out of a fear, some said, that collecting tolls would allow states to by-pass his agency—he persuaded Congress to reject a proposal to build a national network of tolled superhighways.[17]

MacDonald justified his opposition to tolls by arguing that the extra cost of collecting tolls would double the amount drivers would eventually have to pay for new roads. This was probably an exaggeration, but no one disputed that collecting tolls cost more than collecting gas taxes, whose collection costs have historically averaged about 2.5 to 3.0 percent of revenues.[18] In a letter written in 1947, when combined federal and state gas taxes averaged 4.6 cents per gallon, MacDonald estimated that raising taxes to 7 cents a gallon would fund all the roads the nation needed. By comparison, toll roads typically charged about 1 cent per mile, the equivalent (considering the fuel economies of that time) of 12 to 16 cents per gallon.[19]

MacDonald also believed that would-be toll-road builders faced a dilemma. Because most highways did not charge tolls, toll roads built to conventional standards could not compete with parallel nontoll roads. But roads built to considerably higher standards might never be able to recover the higher costs from tolls.[20]

By 1947, however, that theory had already been tested by the Pennsylvania Turnpike, the nation's first truly long-distance limited-access highway. MacDonald's Bureau of Public Roads "tried to sabotage the construction" of the turnpike, says one toll-road advocate, because the state of Pennsylvania planned to make it a toll road. MacDonald predicted that the new road would attract only about 700 vehicles a day. In the first 10 days after it opened in 1940, it carried 14 times that number each day. Even the state had underestimated demand for the road, though only by 50 percent, not McDonald's 93 percent.[21]

The success of the Pennsylvania Turnpike led other states to build their own cross-state toll roads, including Maine (1947), New Hampshire (1950), New Jersey (1952), Ohio (1955), New York (1956), Indiana (1956), Massachusetts (1957), Florida (1957), and Connecticut (1958).[22] MacDonald would have his revenge, however: By forbidding the use of federal funds for any new toll roads, the Federal Aid Highway Act of 1956 shut down the toll road boom in all but a handful of states.

During this same period, the first steps toward today's interstate highway system were taken. In 1939, MacDonald's bureau published a report titled *Toll Roads and Free Roads*. The first half of the report argued that tolls might work in a few heavily used routes but could not support a national highway system. The second half proposed a 27,000-mile "Interregional Highway System." This became the nucleus of the interstate highway system.[23] A 1943 update, *Interregional Highways*, expanded the proposal to 39,000 miles.[24] In 1944, Congress authorized MacDonald's agency to designate a 40,000-mile "National System of Interstate Highways." However, it did not provide any funds to construct such a system.

As World War II neared an end, the need for such a system was widely recognized. Germany's autobahns greatly impressed American soldiers from General Dwight Eisenhower on down.[25] Big-city mayors thought that highways would revitalize downtowns. Urban planners saw the highways as an opportunity to replace "blighted" slums and particularly hoped to use road money to condemn not just rights of way but entire neighborhoods for urban renewal.[26] Some governors believed Congress should repeal the federal gas tax and let the states handle highway finance, but they were considered a minority.

Two main obstacles faced the interstate highway system: everyone wanted a piece of the action, and most wanted someone else to pay for it. Elected officials from some states worried that they would get less federal money than their residents paid in federal gas taxes. Cities worried that a truly interstate system would largely pass them by, forcing them to find their own funds for local radial and ring roads. Some states resented the Bureau of Public Roads' proposals that left off routes that local groups considered important, such as what is now Interstate 70 west of Denver.[27] It took more than a decade to iron out these issues.

Tolling might have prevented some of the sectional disputes, as money would have been spent wherever roads could be supported by toll revenues, not where the politically powerful wanted to spend it. Eisenhower supported tolls, but truckers objected to delays from stopping at tollbooths, which could often become congested.

Another question was whether the states should be allowed to finance construction by selling bonds that would be repaid out of their share of federal gas taxes. President Eisenhower favored this approach, but Tennessee Sen. Albert Gore—father of the future vice-president and then chair of the Senate Subcommittee on Roads—objected, arguing that the interest costs would be excessive and the system should be funded on a pay-as-you-go basis.[28]

To sweeten the pot, the Bureau of Public Roads added several thousand miles of mostly urban roads to the proposed system. This included urban interstates to please members of Congress who represented big cities and several new roads such as the extension of Interstate 70 west of Denver, which the Bureau of Public Roads had previously opposed because of the high cost of construction in the Colorado Rockies. In late 1955, the bureau presented members of Congress with a book, known as the Yellow Book for the color of its cover, containing maps of tentative road locations in more than 100 urban areas.[29]

After more than a decade of debate and legislative gridlock, Congress passed a bill in 1956 dedicating, for the first time, all federal gas, tire, and vehicle taxes to highway construction. According to historian Mark Rose, "the key to success was providing something for everyone, without imposing high taxes on truckers."[30] In June 1956, the bill was delivered to President Eisenhower, who signed it without examining the Yellow Book that formed the basis for the final plan.[31]

The new law enshrined MacDonald's position on tolls as national policy for more than a generation. Congress decreed that no federal funds could be spent on any new toll roads. Existing toll roads were grandfathered in, but with prejudice: MacDonald believed tolls should be lifted when construction costs were repaid, leaving the highways at the mercy of the gas tax for maintenance. Congress agreed, decreeing that toll roads not accepted as interstates could only be linked to the system if states promised to end tolls when bonds were retired.

This led to a curious situation in Pennsylvania. The Pennsylvania Turnpike was designated I-70 west of Breezewood, but east of Breezewood, I-70 and the turnpike diverged. The Pennsylvania Turnpike Commission was unwilling to stop collecting tolls when the bonds were paid off, so vehicles driving through Breezewood on I-70 are forced to exit to city streets to change between the freeway and the tollway.[32]

The anti-toll provisions of the interstate highway law greatly slowed expansion of the nation's toll network. Only Florida, Kentucky, Oklahoma, and Texas built significant mileage of toll routes between 1956 and 1991, when Congress somewhat relaxed the toll strictures.

Gas taxes might have been a suitable way of paying for the interstates but for two things. First, the initial tax was set too low because estimates of the costs and time required to build the interstate highway system failed to include the increased cost of the urban and other segments added to make the system more politically attractive. Urban roads are more expensive because of higher right-of-way costs and the need for more over- and underpasses, and the Rocky Mountain extension of I-70 proved to be the most expensive rural interstate built. Costs increased further when another 1,500 miles were added in 1968, and more miles were added in later years.[33] Inevitably, construction took far longer than the original projection of 12 years.

Second, before the system was half complete, the United States entered a period of severe inflation. A cents-per-gallon gas tax is not indexed to inflation, and Congress increased the federal tax only once—by a single penny—between 1956 and 1983. Thus, construction costs grew far faster than highway revenues.[34] This further delayed completion of the system. In retrospect, if Eisenhower's plan to finance the system through bond sales had been adopted, the system would have been completed much sooner and interest on the bonds might have been less expensive than paying inflation charges due to these delays.

Virtually complete by 1992, the system ended up costing about $132 billion.[35] Adjusting for inflation to today's dollars brings the total cost to about $425 billion.[36] That's nearly three times the original $25 billion projection (about $155 billion in today's dollars), which of course did not include the urban and other additions to the system.

Despite inflation, gas taxes worked better than funding the highways out of general funds. User fees covered virtually all of the costs, so the interstates added nothing to the national debt or local tax burdens. After passage of the 1956 law, congressional interference in the job of constructing the roads was minimal. For all its flaws, the gas tax system seemed to work: The states built highways that people wanted to use, and people paid gas taxes to drive on them.

Nevertheless, the 1960s and 1970s saw a growing anti-auto, anti-highway movement. At issue were the urban interstates, most of which had not been in the Bureau of Public Roads' initial proposals. Urban mayors insisted on adding these to the bill, arguing that urban residents were paying most of the gas taxes, so they should get their share of the highways. Urban planners gleefully encouraged highway engineers to route these roads through blighted areas so they could contribute to slum clearance and urban renewal. Tens of thousands of people lost their homes, and most ended up paying more for housing elsewhere.

The first sign that something was wrong might have been in 1959, when President Eisenhower's peace was disrupted by construction of I-395 in Washington, D.C. He had endorsed the Bureau of Public Roads' plan to build interstate highways between cities but said he knew nothing about the Yellow Book's addition of thousands of miles of urban roads to the plan. He believed that highways used mainly by commuters should be paid for by local governments, and he went so far as to launch a presidential inquiry to see if he could revoke that part of the plan. Of course, he was unable to do so.[37]

In 1961, an architecture critic named Jane Jacobs scathingly attacked urban renewal policies in her book, *The Death and Life of Great American Cities*. While not specifically questioning the need for highways, she persuasively argued that urban planners had no idea how cities really worked or how to distinguish a true slum from a vibrant urban neighborhood. "The destructive effects of automobiles are much less a cause than a symptom of our incompetence at city building," Jacobs wrote. Planners "do not know what to do with automobiles in cities because they do not know how to plan for workable and vital cities anyhow—with or without automobiles."[38]

Eisenhower's protest and *The Death and Life* were harbingers of the highway revolts of the 1960s and 1970s. Fueled by the growing civil rights movement and the fact that urban planners had targeted many black and other minority neighborhoods for clearance, the anti-highway slogan became, "No white men's roads through black men's homes."[39]

Considering that it was the big-city mayors and urban planners of the 1950s who insisted on routing interstate freeways through the cities and minority neighborhoods, it is ironic that later generations of big-city mayors and urban planners would blame the highway engineers for destroying cities and neighborhoods. "Since 1956, the federal government has spent hundreds of billions of dollars to gouge our urban centers with six- and eight-lane freeways, which separated people and markets," complains Milwaukee's Mayor Norquist. "The freeways dispersed the economy, destroyed thousands of homes and businesses, and sucked millions of middle-class residents and businesses out to the suburbs."[40]

Although the freeways did devastate some neighborhoods, it isn't clear that they really harmed the cities. In 1950, long before a single urban interstate had been built, the suburbs were already growing 10 times faster than the central cities, and downtowns were rapidly declining.[41] In fact, as Harvard transportation professor Alan Altshuler notes, by relieving inner-city congestion, interstates might actually have slowed the decline of downtown areas.[42]

Canadian urban areas lack the extensive freeway networks found in their American counterparts. Yet most, like Calgary and Ottawa, are nearly as sprawling as those in the United States. The ones that are not, like Toronto and Vancouver, have imposed draconian land-use rules to stop sprawl that have made their housing markets some of the least affordable in the world.

On the other hand, the automobile of the 1960s was far from perfect. Ralph Nader's book, *Unsafe at Any Speed*, showed that auto manufacturers were indifferent to auto safety.[43] (What Nader didn't say was that companies that had tried to sell their cars on the basis of safety, such as Kaiser in 1953 and Ford in 1956, had not succeeded.) Automobiles were also clearly responsible for much of the growing air pollution problem that darkened urban skies in the 1960s.

Many people looked at the costs of the automobile without considering the benefits, and their solution was to get rid of cars and highways. Books with titles such as *Road to Ruin, The Death of the Automobile, Autokind vs. Mankind*, and *Highways to Nowhere* appeared in the late 1960s and early 1970s.[44] "The politics of stasis," says historian Mark Rose, "replaced the politics of growth."[45]

Although the highway revolt led to the cancellation of many urban interstates, these were mostly later additions to the system; the vast majority of the road miles in the 1955 Yellow Book were eventually built. A few routes remain under construction today, but these too are mostly later additions to the system. For highway historians, the 1992 opening of I-70 through the Colorado Rockies "symbolized the completion of the original U.S. interstate highway system."[46]

Highway Trust Funds

The *fiduciary trust* is an ancient concept in British and American common law. This law goes into effect whenever someone, known as a *trustor*, gives money or resources to a second party, known as the *trustee*, to manage on behalf of a third party or parties, the *beneficiary* or beneficiaries. Within the terms specified by the trustor in the *trust instrument*, the trustee is obligated to act with undivided loyalty to the beneficiaries.

Ever since Oregon dedicated the first state gas tax to highways in 1919, most states have treated their gas tax revenues as trusts, with the legislatures as trustors, the state highway or transportation departments as trustees, and highway users as the beneficiaries. In 1956, Congress specifically adopted this model when it dedicated all federal taxes on gas, tires, and motor vehicles to a *Highway Trust Fund*.

But can the auto drivers who pay taxes into the Highway Trust Fund really trust Congress? In a perpetual trust, once the trustor signs the instrument, the trustor has no further dealings with the trust: He or she cannot change the instrument and has no standing to challenge how the trustee uses the trust (only a beneficiary can do that). Congress, however, decided to let the gas tax expire every six years. This gave it the right to change the terms of the Highway Trust Fund, sometimes drastically, whenever it reauthorizes the tax.

The first major change came in 1973, when Massachusetts Governor Francis Sargent wanted to cancel a controversial interstate freeway in Boston without losing the federal money that would have gone to the project. He proposed that Congress allow states to cancel freeways and spend the money on mass transit instead. To him, this seemed perfectly logical: the money "belonged" to Massachusetts, and so Massachusetts should be allowed to spend it however it wanted. Congress agreed to this, and soon Portland, Sacramento, and other urban areas joined Boston in spending gas taxes collected for interstate highways on mass transit instead.[47]

This law provided the foundation for the rail transit boom that began in the 1980s. Congress specified that the money could be spent only on transit capital improvements, not operating costs. If invested in buses, the federal share of the cost of an interstate freeway might be enough to more than double the bus fleets of the local transit agency. But the agencies did not have enough money to operate that many new buses. Rail transit was the answer because it could absorb a huge amount of capital funds without imposing significantly higher operating costs on the agencies. In other words, cities that traded interstates for transit ended up choosing rail *because it was expensive*. Since one rail line would serve only part of an urban area, political "equity" effectively committed them to build additional expensive rail lines to other parts of the region.

The second breach of the Highway Trust Fund came when Congress included 10 earmarks in the Federal Aid Highway Act of 1982. Between 1916 and 1981, Congress had passed at least two dozen federal aid highway acts apportioning money to the states and giving the Bureau of Public Roads general direction about how to spend it. But Congress had never before earmarked money to specific projects. While 10 was a small number, it set a precedent for 152 earmarks in 1987, 538 in 1991, 1,850 in 1998, and about 7,000, costing more than $24 billion, in 2005.[48] In May 2009, members of the House of Representatives proposed about the same number of earmarks as in 2005, but their total cost of $136 billion was nearly six times greater.[49]

Another even more serious breach also came in 1982, when Congress belatedly increased gas taxes in response to inflation. Since 1956, Congress had increased the tax only once, from 3 to 4 cents per gallon in 1959. In 1982, Congress proposed to double the tax to 8 cents. However, members of Congress from urban areas demanded that transit receive a share of the increase.

Highway advocates who had fought for decades against diversion of state gas taxes to nonhighway purposes resisted this proposal. However, in order to get the tax increase, highway supporters in Congress reluctantly agreed to add a penny tax that would be dedicated to transit. Transit would receive 20 percent of all future gas tax increases as well. Perhaps in compensation, the 1982 bill repealed the 1973 provision allowing states to spend the money from canceled interstates on mass transit.

These breaches to the Highway Trust Fund resulted from the weakening reputation of the engineers who staffed the Federal Highway Administration (the name of the Bureau of Public Roads since 1966). Thanks to years of bashing by urban planners who blamed the highways for destroying cities and environmentalists who blamed autos for polluting the air, highway engineers were no longer considered scientific managers. Instead, many viewed them as single-minded developers who didn't care about the social and environmental impacts of what they built.

Urban planners in particular argued that they could do a better job of planning transportation than engineers. While the engineers narrowly focused on things like safety, traffic flows, and pavement quality, the planners promised to look more broadly at things like air pollution, land use, and livability.

As chapter 8 will describe in detail, in passing the Intermodal Surface Transportation Efficiency Act in 1991, Congress imposed a never-ending comprehensive transportation planning process on states and metropolitan areas. This process gave urban planners every opportunity to inject their nonquantifiable values, such as "sense of community," while providing no assurances that the quantifiable things engineers worried about, such as safety and congestion relief, would receive any consideration.

ISTEA's financial effects were even greater. The name said it all: Congress was no longer passing highway bills; it was passing *intermodal surface transportation* bills. Auto and truck drivers still paid all of the costs, but increasing shares of what they paid were diverted into transit and other nonhighway projects.

Among other things, ISTEA created a "flexible" surface transportation fund: it could be spent on either highways or transit. This fund, of course, was carved out of the portion of the Highway Trust Fund that was dedicated to highways, not transit. Ultimately, about 15.6 percent of gas tax collections were dedicated to transit. The flexible fund meant that states and metropolitan areas could spend more than that amount on transit if they wanted, but not less.

ISTEA also created a "new starts" fund dedicated to "fixed-guideway" transit, which usually meant rail. Any metropolitan areas foolish enough not to begin planning for rail transit would lose their share of this fund.

Congress also gave up any pretense that the increasing number of earmarks in ISTEA and subsequent surface transportation laws (passed in 1997 and 2005) had anything to do with highways or even transportation. Some earmarks went for roads, bike paths, and transit projects. Others went for nontransportation projects such as national park visitor centers. Others went for projects that were only remotely related to transportation, such as the conversion of old train depots into museums.

After deducting the earmarks, Congress divided the remaining gas taxes into numerous funds, each of which was apportioned to states and/or metropolitan areas using complicated formulas. The following funds now come out of the highway share of gas taxes, known as the *highway account*: [50]

- Interstate Maintenance Fund (18.1 percent in 2007)
- National Highway System Fund (22.0 percent, which can be used for building new roads)
- Surface Transportation Fund (23.3 percent, for either highways or transit)
- Bridge Fund (14.8 percent)
- Congestion Mitigation/Air Quality Fund (6.1 percent, much of which goes for transit)
- Appalachian Highway System Fund (1.3 percent)
- Recreation Trails Fund (0.2 percent for off-road vehicle trails)
- Metropolitan Planning Fund (0.8 percent)
- Coordinated Border Infrastructure Fund (0.5 percent)
- Safe Routes to School Fund (0.4 percent)
- Highway Safety Improvement Program (3.9 percent)
- Rail Highway Crossings Program (0.6 percent)
- Equity Bonus Fund (7.8 percent, to guarantee each state at least 91.5 percent of the amount the state's residents paid into the Highway Trust Fund—increased to 92 percent in 2008)

Despite the name "highway account," only the Interstate Maintenance, National Highway System, Bridge, Appalachian Highway, and Highway Safety Improvement funds, which total 60.3 percent of the highway account, are spent exclusively on highways. Meanwhile, the *transit account* includes the following funds:

- Urbanized Area Fund (46.3 percent)
- New Starts (18.5 percent)
- Fixed Guideway Modernization Fund (18.5 percent)
- Growing and High Density States Fund (5.2 percent)
- Nonurbanized Area Fund (4.9 percent)
- Job Access and Reverse Commute Fund (1.9 percent, to help inner-city welfare recipients reach suburban jobs)
- Special Needs Fund (1.5 percent, for seniors and people with disabilities)
- Metropolitan Transportation Planning Fund (1.0 percent)

- New Freedom Program (1.0 percent, for people with disabilities)
- National Research Program (0.8 percent)
- Administrative Oversight (0.8 percent)
- Statewide Transportation Planning Fund (0.2 percent)
- Rural Transportation Program (0.1 percent)

Except for New Starts, research, and oversight, most of these are *formula programs*, which means they are distributed to states and/ or metropolitan areas based on formulas. These formulas use such factors as the amount of diesel consumed in each state (National Highway System Fund), population density (Urbanized Area Transit Fund), and the age of the rail system (Fixed Guideway Modernization Fund). The formulas for the highway funds, which are mostly divided among the states, tend to be fairly straightforward. For example, one-third of the Interstate Maintenance Fund is distributed to states based on the interstate system lane miles in each state, one-third on the vehicle miles traveled on the interstate system, and one-third on the state's contributions to the Highway Trust Fund from commercial vehicles.[51]

Formulas for transit funds, which are divided among hundreds of urbanized areas, tend to be more convoluted. For example, 9.32 percent of the Urbanized Area Fund is divided among areas that have 50,000 to 199,999 residents based on their populations and population densities. Of the other 90.68 percent, 33.29 percent goes to urban areas of 200,000 people or more with fixed guideway transit based on the route miles and vehicle revenue miles of fixed guideway transit. The remaining 68.71 percent goes to urban areas of 200,000 people or more with bus transit based on their bus vehicle revenue miles, population, and population density. Regions of 750,000 people or more with commuter rail are guaranteed certain minimums, with an "incentive" payment for low operating costs per passenger mile.[52]

Most of these factors are beyond the control of state and metropolitan planners. Planners cannot significantly alter a state's or metropolitan area's population, vehicle miles traveled, or the annual contributions to the Highway Trust Fund. Through urban-growth boundaries and similar tools, regions can increase population densities, but only after many years.

The one thing metropolitan areas can do to immediately increase the flow of federal funds is to build rail transit. Areas with rail transit

Table 7.1
USER FEES AND SUBSIDIES, 2006 (BILLIONS, EXCEPT SUBSIDIES PER
PASSENGER MILE IN CENTS)

Mode	User Fees	Government Subsidies	Government Expense	Passenger Miles	Subsidy Per Passenger Mile
Highway	$116.4	$25.1	$146.3	4,933.7	0.6¢
Transit	11.9	30.1	42.0	49.5	60.9
Amtrak	1.8	1.5	3.3	5.4	28.6
Airlines	27.1	7.9	35.0	590.6	1.3

SOURCES: *Highway Statistics 2006* (Washington: Federal Highway Administration, 2007), Table HF-10; *2006 National Transit Database* (Washington: Federal Transit Administration, 2007), spreadsheets "operating expenses," "capital use," and "fare revenues"; *2006 Annual Report* (Washington: Amtrak, 2007), pp. 27, 33, 35; *National Transportation Statistics* (Washington: Bureau of Transportation Statistics, 2008), Tables 3-27a and 3-29a.

NOTE: Highway user fees and subsidies do not add up to total highway expenses; the difference is interest and bond revenues.

are eligible for New Starts money, Fixed Guideway Modernization Funds, and nearly one-third of the Urbanized Area Fund. In fact, just over half of the transit account is dedicated to regions with rail transit. This gives metro areas that do not have rail transit a huge incentive to plan a rail line.

In 1980, only eight major metropolitan areas had some form of fixed-guideway transit. By 2009, counting automated guideways (people movers) and vintage trolleys, this number had increased to 39, with at least one more scheduled to open in 2010. Since 1980, after adjusting for inflation, cities have spent close to $200 billion building rail transit lines that mostly provide no better service than could have been provided by buses. The incentives provided by federal transit funding are in large part responsible for this huge waste of resources.

Taxes and Fees Today

Chapter 1 noted that subsidies to passenger travel in 2000 averaged 0.1 cents per passenger mile for air, 0.8 cents for highways, 14 cents for Amtrak, and 50 cents for transit. Table 7.1 shows that, by 2006, most of these subsidies had risen, with the biggest relative increase going to air travel (mainly because airport subsidies in 2000 were anomalously low). Still, user fees are the main source of funds for highways and air service, while taxes provide most of the funds for transit and nearly half the funds for Amtrak. Moreover, because highways and airlines carry hundreds of times as many passenger miles as transit and Amtrak, the net subsidies per passenger mile to the former are quite small.

Highway users both subsidize other transportation users and are subsidized by general taxpayers. Most of the subsidies to highways come at the local level, while the net subsidies at the federal and state levels are from highway users to transit and other programs.

At the federal level, close to $5.4 billion of gas taxes are siphoned off to mass transit, while $1.8 billion of general funds support roads—mostly for the Federal Emergency Management Agency and land-management agencies such as the Forest Service and Department of the Interior. Thus, highway users lose a net $3.6 billion. States divert $12.7 billion of highway user fees into mass transit and other nonhighway programs. At the same time, they spend $9.9 billion of general funds on roads, for another $2.9 billion loss to highway users.

The main subsidies to highways come from local governments, few of which collect gas taxes or other user fees. Collectively, they bring in $4.6 billion in user fees, $1.1 billion of which is diverted to transit or other uses. But local governments also spend $32.8 billion of general funds on roads, for a net local subsidy to roads of $31.7 billion.

All levels of government together spend $44.5 billion of nonuser fees on roads. But they also divert $18.6 billion from user fees to transit and other programs for a net subsidy of about $25.1 billion. If none of the subsidy is attributed to the 1.3 trillion ton-miles of freight carried on the highways, this subsidy averages less than 0.6 cents per passenger mile. Some road costs are paid for out of interest and bond sales, so the exact subsidy depends on what combination of user fees and taxes go to repay those bonds.

While highway user fees covered at least 85 percent of highway costs, transit fares covered just 28 percent of 2006 capital and operating costs.[53] Total transit subsidies of $30.1 billion included $5.4 billion of federal gas taxes and $4.1 billion of state gas taxes.[54] The rest of the transit subsidies came from a variety of state and local taxes, mostly sales taxes. Total subsidies averaged more than 60 cents per passenger mile.[55] Note that transit subsidies are greater than highway subsidies even though highways carry nearly 100 times as many passenger miles of travel.

Amtrak's annual report stresses that just 4 percent of the federal transportation budget is used to support the company's passenger trains.[56] That does not seem excessive until you realize that Amtrak carries less than 0.1 percent of the nation's passenger miles of travel. State and local governments provided nearly $300 million in support to Amtrak, while the federal government gave Amtrak $1.26 billion.[57] The net subsidy averages close to 29 cents per passenger mile.

Airline subsidies are the most difficult to estimate because the Bureau of Transportation Statistics stopped keeping track of state and local expenditures on airports and airlines in 2003. According to available data, 2006 subsidies totaled somewhere around $8 billion, or about 1.3 cents per passenger mile. Most of these subsidies come from cities convinced that they have to have a big airport to maintain the prestige needed to attract new businesses. Data before 2003 suggest that the increase from 0.2 cents per passenger mile in 2000 to 1.3 cents in 2006 is not a general upward trend; instead, subsidies just happened to be unusually low in 2000.

One mode isn't listed in Table 7.1 because it receives virtually no subsidies: intercity bus service. In 2006, intercity buses carried nearly three times as many passenger miles as transit, and 27 times as many as Amtrak. While Trailways and Greyhound have declined, they have been replaced in many markets by cut-rate buses such as Megabus, Coach, and Bolt. The growth of these systems refutes the notion that transportation has to be subsidized.

The Future: User Fees or Taxes?

The current system of funding transportation is obviously dysfunctional. Gasoline taxes made sense when there was no congestion and no inflation, motor vehicles averaged about 10 miles per gallon, and tolls were expensive to collect. None of these are true today.

Gasoline taxes fail to signal users that some roads are more congested than others or at certain times of day. When the demand for a highway exceeds supply, some form of rationing is required. The free-market method of rationing is to charge a toll that is high enough to keep the road from becoming congested. The political method of rationing is queuing—forcing people to waste time standing in lines. The advantage of the market method is that the collected tolls can be put to good use, perhaps building new facilities to relieve congestion. The time people waste in queues is a deadweight loss to society.

Gas taxes not only fail to keep up with inflation, they fail to keep up with more fuel-efficient cars. The average motor vehicle on the American highway today uses 30 percent less energy per mile than the average vehicle in 1960. After adjusting for both inflation and fuel economy, federal and state gas taxes per mile driven peaked in 1960 at 3.9 cents per mile (in 2007 dollars). Today, the average American motorist pays less than half of this amount for every mile driven.[58]

One reason why gas taxes have failed to keep up is that voters have not been enthused about raising them, or about supporting legislators who raise them. Opponents of new roads vote against such taxes. But many supporters of new roads also oppose tax increases because they suspect that their gas taxes are diverted to other purposes or are inefficiently used by state transportation departments. Even though the goals of these two groups are completely opposite, their members have prevented both states and Congress from letting taxes keep pace with inflation and fuel economy.

Meanwhile, the cost of collecting tolls has declined dramatically with the introduction of electronic tolling. Based on data from 11 toll systems, toll roads expert Peter Samuel estimates that collection costs range between 12 and 23 percent of toll revenues. While this is still higher than the cost of collecting gas taxes, Samuel argues that the extra cost is worthwhile because the tolls provide highway managers with better incentives to meet user needs.[59]

The electronic toll revolution has led many people to suggest that tolls should pay for new highways while gas taxes pay to maintain existing roads. Several states have studied the idea of building new toll roads. However, the most successful new toll projects have been built by county or regional toll road authorities, such as the ones in and around Dallas and Houston, Texas. These authorities seem to suffer less from bureaucracy and opposition from anti-road forces.

Another approach being considered by a few states is to tax vehicles by the mile instead of by the gallon. This would prepare transportation departments for vehicles powered by electricity or other nonpetroleum fuels. One proposal is to add a geographic positioning system (GPS) transmitter to each vehicle so that charges could vary depending when people drive and what roads they use.

Oregon, the first state to dedicate a gasoline tax to highways, has pioneered work on a vehicle-mile fee. Under a system successfully tested by several hundred Oregon motorists, a GPS device installed in each vehicle tracked how many miles were driven in various zones. The device includes a display screen informing the driver how much they are paying to drive in a particular zone or road. In lieu of the gas tax, drivers were charged the appropriate per-mile rates whenever they bought gasoline.[60]

This system avoids any intrusions on people's privacy. When drivers buy gasoline, the on-board vehicle device transmits only the total charges the vehicle has incurred, not where and when the car actually went.[61] However, there is a trade-off: "When a system completely protects privacy," notes the state, "the ability of an agency to audit payments, and the ability of a customer to challenge a bill, becomes difficult."[62]

The state also concluded that full-scale adoption of this system would not significantly increase the costs of collecting the vehicle-mile fee above the costs of gas tax collections.[63] The system would impose modest one-time-only costs on both drivers and fuel dealers, namely the costs of installing the GPS devices in the vehicles and billing equipment in the fuel stations.

Although not specifically tested in Oregon, the same system is easily adaptable to a congestion-pricing system in which the charges vary to keep roads from becoming congested.[64] For a truly dynamic pricing system, in which tolls vary depending on the amount of traffic rather than by time of day, the GPS devices would need to communicate with highway tolling systems. This could still be done without threatening privacy if, for example, the toll system simply transmitted the charge to the GPS.

Given the success of Oregon's experiment, the state's governor has proposed that the state "transition away from the gas tax as the central source of funding for transportation."[65] At least six other states are looking at similar plans.[66]

While transportation departments experiment with better ways of collecting user fees from auto drivers, transit agencies are focused more on capturing more tax dollars from nontransit users. Indeed, tolls provide highway users with no immunity from diversions of the fees they pay into the pockets of the transit-industrial complex.

Since 1968, more than $12 billion in tolls from seven New York City bridges have subsidized the city's transit system.[67] Virginia transferred control of the once-private Dulles Toll Road to the Metropolitan Washington Airports Authority so the profits from tolls could subsidize a rail line to Dulles Airport.[68] San Antonio recently proposed to merge its toll-road authority and transit agency so tolls could subsidize construction of a new light-rail line.[69] Similarly, Portland, Minneapolis, and other cities have dedicated some of the airport landing fees they collect from passengers to subsidize their light-rail lines.

User fees create the best incentives for both users and providers. But Amtrak and the transit industry have become addicted to taxes and to spending those taxes on high-cost modes when much less expensive alternatives are available. Until broken of this addiction, highway and airline users must be wary that the fees they pay are not diverted to subsidize other forms of transportation.

8. Faith-Based Transportation Planning

In 2006, planners in Sacramento, California, admitted that transportation plans written for their region "during the past 25 years have not worked out."

- Despite building light rail and making other efforts aimed at "luring drivers out of their autos," the share of transit riders who "have access to an automobile [and] can otherwise choose to drive" was decreasing.
- Despite efforts to promote alternatives to driving by discouraging sprawl and promoting high-density infill, sprawl "continues to out-pace infill. . ., and businesses increasingly prefer suburban locations."
- "Even though gasoline prices are at an all-time high, the total amount of driving has more than doubled since 1980."
- Revealingly, the report added, "lack of road building and the resulting congestion have not encouraged many people to take transit instead of driving."[1]

Planners did have one piece of good news: "total smog emissions from motor vehicles are now half what they were in 1980." However, this was not because of anything the planners had done but because "technology has reduced auto emissions by 98 percent from 1980 models."[2]

Sacramento planners remained undaunted by these results. Their new long-range transportation plan "continues the direction of" previous plans. The new plan proposes to use "transportation funds for community design, to encourage people to walk, bicycle, or ride transit" and to give "first priority to expanding the transit system."[3] In particular, planners want to spend nearly $3.0 billion on transit capital improvements but only $2.0 billion on improvements to state highways.[4] The Sacramento Area Council of Governments, which wrote the plan, also agreed to use "'smart growth' strategies" such as "mixed use and compact development, infill," and similar land-use policies—some of which will be subsidized with transportation funds—designed to "reduce the number and length of auto trips."[5]

Yet the planners' own analyses project that the new plan will work no better than the previous ones. The huge investments in transit are expected to expand transit's share of total travel from 0.9 percent in 2005 to just 1.1 percent in 2027. Transit's share of rush hour commuting will likely increase from 2.6 percent to merely 3.0 percent.[6] Despite spending nearly $300 million on bicycle and pedestrian improvements, cycling and walking's share of travel and commuting are projected to decline. Even though "congestion will continue to worsen inside the urban area," planners predict that per capita driving will continue to grow.[7]

Novelist Rita Mae Brown was the first to define insanity as "doing the same thing over and over again and expecting a different result."[8] By this definition, not only are Sacramento planners insane, but so are planners in other cities who deliberately imitate plans written in Sacramento, Portland, and other cities that have unsuccessfully tried to change residents' transportation choices.

Since 1962, Congress has required all metropolitan areas—regions of more than 50,000 people—to write long-range metropolitan transportation plans and to update those plans at least every four to five years.[9] Sacramento is one of a growing number of regions whose transportation plans focus on using behavioral tools—density, rail transit, transit-oriented development, pedestrian-friendly design—to address congestion, toxic pollution, greenhouse gases, and other problems created by the automobile.

Buried deep within many of these plans are candid admissions that the authors agree with Dom Nozzi's claim that "congestion is our friend."[10] "Congestion signals positive urban development," say Portland planners, who have decided to allow rush-hour congestion on most major highways in the region to deteriorate to stop-and-go conditions.[11] In fact, they add, "transportation solutions aimed solely at relieving congestion are inappropriate" in most of the region.[12]

Minneapolis-St. Paul's transportation planners decided that "expansion of roadways will be very limited in the next 25 years." "As traffic congestion builds," the plan states hopefully, "alternative travel modes will become more attractive."[13] Planners may say they need to plan regionally to reduce congestion. What they often mean is that they want to plan regionally to *increase* congestion in the unlikely hope that (as the Sacramento plan put it) the "lack of road building and the resulting congestion [will encourage] people to take transit instead of driving."[14]

In addition to their other costs, behavioral tools are highly intrusive. Instead of providing a level playing field, smart-growth government favors certain property owners, housing types, and modes of transportation over others. No individuals can say that government planners are forcing them to live or travel a certain way. But when planners divert highway user fees into transit with the expectation that highway congestion will increase, they are imposing huge costs on auto drivers and giving huge subsidies to transit riders. Similarly, when planners restrict low-density development and subsidize high-density housing, they are consciously denying many families access to the form of housing that most Americans say they prefer—a single-family home with a yard.

As expensive and intrusive as the behavioral tools are, the biggest indictment against them is that they simply do not work. As Sacramento planners found, transportation plans can emphasize alternatives to the automobile, but most people still drive. Cities can subsidize the construction of mixed-use developments, but most people living in those developments still travel mostly by car. Regions can impose compact, high-density development, but the percentage of travel by car will not significantly decline.

Behavioral tools may even make matters worse. Higher-density development combined with minimal new road construction necessarily means more traffic congestion. Cars in stop-and-go traffic use more energy and emit more toxic fumes and greenhouse gases (which many metropolitan transportation plans fail to account for).[15] Even if residents of compact cities do drive slightly less than residents of so-called sprawl, the energy and pollution costs of congestion may more than use up any savings.

Despite the problems, the number of regions adopting these tools seems to grow each year. Part of the blame can be placed on the urban planning profession, which promotes these ideas incessantly and which is slow to learn from its mistakes.[16] But much of the blame should be placed on Congress, which effectively gave authority over the nation's urban transport systems to urban planners in the Intermodal Surface Transportation Efficiency Act of 1991.

161

A review of transportation plans for the nation's largest urban areas reveals that too many focus on behavioral tools when technical tools could solve congestion, pollution, and other problems at a much lower cost. But even if planners followed a rational process, long-range metropolitan transportation planning as mandated by Congress would fail. Long-range regional problems are simply too complex for anyone to predict or fix. Congress should repeal long-range planning requirements in federal law and replace them with a short-range planning process built around incentives and user fees.

History of Urban Transportation Planning

In 1962, Congress required that urban areas use "a continuing, comprehensive transportation planning process carried out cooperatively by states and local communities." This became known as the "3Cs" process for "continuing, comprehensive, and cooperative." The law even required that between 1.5 and 2.0 percent of federal highway funds be spent on this planning process.[17]

Congress did not provide detailed guidance about what the plans should consider. But in 1963, the Bureau of Public Roads defined a planning process that included identifying local goals and objectives, forecasting future travel needs, developing and evaluating alternative transportation networks, and recommending a plan that could be funded with available financial resources. The plans, the bureau added, should cover 10 basic elements: economic factors affecting development, population, land use, transport facilities including mass transit, travel patterns, freight facilities, traffic control, zoning and land-use codes, financial resources, and social and community values such as parks and historical sites.[18]

Up to this point, nearly all federal funding for urban areas was limited to interstate freeways and other major roads, so plans did not need to be very complicated. In 1964, Congress passed the Urban Mass Transportation Act, providing federal funding, out of general funds, for mass transit. But initially, Congress allocated very little money to transit.[19]

In 1975, the Department of Transportation issued rules requiring joint highway and transit planning. The rules required every state to create or designate a *metropolitan planning organization* (MPO) for each urban area. The MPOs were expected to write long-range transportation plans; however, the emphasis in the new rules was on short-term plans known as the *transportation improvement program*, or TIP, which identified the actual projects to be built in the immediate future. While long-range plans typically looked ahead 20 years or more, the TIPs covered only the next 5 years. The TIPs, says one historian, "changed the emphasis from long-range planning to shorter range transportation system management, and provided a stronger linkage between planning and programming."[20]

San Francisco began operating the Bay Area Rapid Transit (BART) system in 1972. BART's planners expected the system would lead to higher-density development in rail corridors, thus giving more people easy access to rail service.[21] But subsequent evaluations revealed that BART had little impact on local land uses. If anything, one analysis found, population densities increased more in areas distant from BART lines than near BART stations.[22] This occurred partly because existing residents opposed any changes in zoning and land uses near BART stations.

In response, in about 1980, the Urban Mass Transit Administration (forerunner of today's Federal Transit Administration) required communities proposing to spend federal money on rail transit to commit themselves to "local supportive actions," such as rezoning areas around transit stations for higher densities, to increase rail transit ridership.[23] This was the first time that any federal transportation rule required cities to regulate land uses in order to be eligible for federal funding.

The 1991 reauthorization of federal transportation funding, known as the Intermodal Surface Transportation Efficiency Act, made long-range transportation planning far more important, and the requirements for it more elaborate, than ever before. Metropolitan planners were required to consider air pollution, the connections between land use and transportation, and various other quality of life issues. Historically, transportation engineers had handled the highly quantitative issues involved in planning: safety, efficiency of movement, and so forth. But the broader issues raised by ISTEA were beyond the engineers' training or abilities. In fact, they were beyond anyone's training or abilities, but members of the urban planning profession believed they could handle such questions.

Planning under ISTEA was complicated even further by the Clean Air Act Amendments that Congress passed in 1990, the year before ISTEA. This law constrained what urban areas could do if the Environmental Protection Agency rated them out of compliance with air

163

pollution rules. Even though congestion was a major cause of air pollution, the law discouraged regions with severe pollution problems from building more roads to relieve congestion and instead encouraged them to use behavioral tools to discourage driving.

When combined with the Clean Air Act Amendments, ISTEA contrasted strongly with the planning process developed by the Bureau of Public Roads in the 1960s. The earlier process considered land uses, regional growth, and personal travel preferences to be outside the realm of transportation planning. ISTEA regards all of those things as variables that the planners can manipulate: planners restrict development over here, force increased growth over there, and redesign cities to shape people's future travel decisions. While the Bureau of Public Roads goal was to provide a safe and efficient transportation system, ISTEA's goal is to promote the general welfare by reducing pollution, saving energy, improving the efficiency of land use, and taking other steps to make cities more "sustainable."

In a 1950 conference organized by the Bureau of Public Roads, economist Shorey Peterson noted, "It is in the character for the engineer to be mainly concerned, not with broad matters of public interest, but with specific relations between road types and traffic conditions." Peterson specifically warned against trying to account for the "public interest" when planning roads. "Control of road improvements through judging its relation to the general welfare is as debatable, as devoid of dependable benchmarks, as deciding the proper peacetime expenditure for national defense or the right quantity and quality of public education," said Peterson. "Controlled in this way, highway projects are peculiarly subject to 'pork barrel' political grabbing."[24]

Federal transportation funding since passage of ISTEA has proven Peterson correct. Federal transportation earmarks, unheard of before 1980, exploded from 10 in 1982 to nearly 7,000 in 2005.[25] Cities are competing to outdo one another in building the most expensive rail projects. And in a growing number of urban areas, transportation planning seems to be about almost anything but transportation.

A Rational Planning Process

Before reviewing long-range transportation plans, it is important to know how the planning profession itself believes such plans should be written. The so-called *rational planning model* is supposed to find the best way to achieve society's goals. "In this model," summarizes one planner, "goals are first identified and priorities set among desired consequences of policy. Alternative strategies (means to the goals) are then examined and a choice made of the 'best' alternative."[26]

The process developed by the Bureau of Public Roads in 1963 is based on this model. Planners first define their goals and criteria. At least some of the criteria should be measured in terms of quantifiable outputs so that the plan and its alternatives can be fairly evaluated. For example, tons of toxic air pollution are quantifiable, "sustainability" is not. Planners should also ensure that their criteria are *outputs*, not inputs. The amount of walking people do is an output; the "walkability" of a neighborhood is an input. When planners rely on vague terms like sustainability and walkability, they run the risk of writing plans that can only be judged by their intentions, not their results. An appropriate set of criteria might include the number of transportation-related fatalities, hours wasted in congestion, tons of air pollution, and BTUs of energy consumption.

Next, planners need to forecast future travel needs and expectations. The best travel models today are based on detailed observations of how people actually live. These observations, usually collected from thousands of people in the form of travel diaries, are used to predict how people will respond to changes in their incomes, educations, family sizes, travel costs, congestion, transportation alternatives, and urban design features such as density and mixed-use developments.

Even if the travel diaries are an accurate reflection of how people live today, many things about the future remain unknowable, including local population growth, energy prices, other transportation costs, and how people will respond to those costs. This means many of the inputs needed for travel forecasts will necessarily be based on best guesses.

One way planners can handle this uncertainty is through a *sensitivity analysis*, which asks how transportation outputs vary in response to fixed changes—say, plus or minus 20 percent—in assumed inputs. If changing a particular input does not greatly change the outputs, then accuracy is not important. If a particular input does have a large effect on outputs, then planners should put more effort into making certain that information about the input is as accurate as possible and in reporting to the public the effects on the plan if the assumption proves inaccurate. They could even build *feedback* mechanisms into the plan so it can automatically change if some of the assumptions prove wrong.

The next step is to devise alternative transportation plans. To do this, planners must list all possible transportation projects: new roads, new transit lines, new bicycle and pedestrian facilities, other improvements such as traffic signal coordination, and new ways of managing facilities such as high-occupancy vehicle lanes or toll lanes. To this list some planners might add different forms of land-use regulation such as urban-growth boundaries, incentives for infill development, form-based zoning codes, and other rules designed to change people's travel preferences.

For each project, planners should estimate the cost to taxpayers, the cost to everyone else, and the benefits in terms of the criteria developed in the first step: for example, the effects of the project on fatality rates, congestion, pollution, and energy consumption. Capital costs should be annualized by amortizing them over the life of each particular project so that both benefits and costs can be compared on an annual basis. Each of the benefits can then be divided into each project's annual dollar cost to get cost per life saved, cost per hour of congestion relief, cost per ton of air pollution relief, and cost per BTU of energy saved. The projects can then be ranked using these criteria.

For the actual alternatives, planners might develop a transit-emphasis alternative, a highway-emphasis alternative, and so forth. But that would be unnecessarily polarizing. A better way is to build alternatives around each of the major criteria: a maximum-safety alternative, a minimum-congestion alternative, and so forth. The maximum-safety alternative would include all of the projects with the highest safety rankings that the region can afford with available funds. Thus, the region might have four alternatives—safety, congestion, pollution, and energy—each of which costs the same but produces different levels of outputs and meets the criteria in different ways.

At this point, planners could compare the projects and criteria to see which are complementary and which conflict. For example, traffic signal coordination can improve safety and reduce congestion, pollution, and energy use. But building a new highway might reduce congestion at a cost of consuming energy during construction. Planners could first ask: Is it possible to redesign the project so that it produces a net energy savings? If not, then planners have to consider trade-offs: How much energy are we willing to spend to save an hour of congestion? Some trade-offs, such as people's time and energy, are easy because both can be valued, but others, such as fatalities, require more subjective judgment.

Given these trade-offs, planners should design a preferred alternative that attempts to provide the best possible balance of outputs for the fixed amount of funds available. The alternative should also specify where it makes sense to spend more money if more becomes available through, say, a local tax increase or increased federal grants.

After the plan is adopted, planners should monitor the results to ensure that the plan's goals are being achieved. If possible, monitoring should include feedback mechanisms so that the plan can self-correct if any of its assumptions prove wrong. For example, if a particular project turns out to cost much more than planners originally projected, the plan could provide for substituting alternative, more cost-effective projects.

Each of these steps should include consultation with the public to ensure first, that planners do not neglect any important criteria, potential transportation projects, or alternatives; and second, that any balancing planners make in developing the preferred alternative meets public approval. Moreover, the plan should be transparent; that is, it should be clear to any reader how planners made each step along the way toward development of their preferred alternative.

In sum, a rational transportation plan should include the following:

- Quantitative output criteria by which the plan can be judged;
- State-of-the-art forecasts of travel needs and travel behavior;
- Sensitivity analyses for questionable assumptions;
- A list of all possible transportation projects with projections of costs and benefits, with the benefits firmly associated with each major criterion;
- Project rankings in terms of cost per each criteria-related benefit;
- Several alternatives, consisting of various collections of potential projects, possibly one for each major criterion;
- Estimates of the financial costs and the transportation, environmental, and other benefits of each alternative;

- A preferred alternative that proposes a list of projects in an attempt to balance the various criteria;
- Consultation with the public at key stages along the way, with assurances that the planning process is transparent so reviewers can understand why planners made their recommendations;
- Monitoring to ensure that the plan is working as intended with feedback mechanisms that would add or subtract projects if more money becomes available or if certain assumptions prove wrong.

Metropolitan Transportation Plans

To compare metropolitan transportation planning with the standard rational planning model, I read the most recent plans for more than 70 regions, including plans covering the 67 largest urban areas (New York, NY, through Albany, NY) and several smaller ones (Bakersfield, Colorado Springs, Des Moines, Durham, Ft. Collins, Fresno, Little Rock, Madison, Raleigh, and Savannah). None of these plans come close to the rational process described above or even the more basic process defined by the Bureau of Public Roads in 1963.

None of the plans included sensitivity analyses of critical assumptions, and none bothered to project potential benefits or cost-effectiveness of projects considered for the plans. Most plans failed to include any realistic alternatives, and many failed to project the effects of the proposed plan on transportation. As a result, plans lacked transparency: taxpayers and other readers of most plans would have no idea how projects were selected or whether those projects or the plans themselves were cost effective at meeting plan goals, or even, in many cases, whether the plans met any goals.

Criteria. Most metropolitan transportation plans include goals and objectives that serve as evaluation criteria. However, most of the criteria in most of the plans are qualitative. Even when the criteria are potentially quantifiable, planners rarely list the quantitative measures they use to evaluate alternatives.

As previously noted, such things as hours of congestion delay, tons of air pollution, or transport-related fatalities are easily quantifiable. But many plans include such unquantifiable goals as these:

- Promote livable communities[27]
- Foster vibrant communities[28]
- Build community structure[29]

- Promote environmental justice[30]
- Provide a multimodal transportation system[31]
- Increase accessibility[32]
- Create walkable districts[33]
- Protect wetlands[34]
- Preserve open space and agricultural land[35]
- Discourage urban sprawl[36]
- Plan for workforce housing[37]
- Safeguard historical, cultural, and archeological resources[38]
- Support economic development[39]

Many of these goals, such as livable communities or community structure, are not quantifiable at all. Other goals are quantifiable, but not in terms that are comparable to other goals. How many units of environmental justice are people willing to trade off to protect more open space? How many units of workforce housing are people willing to trade off to safeguard historical resources? How many units of economic development are people willing to trade off to add another mode to their multimodal system? Most plans contain numerous such goals, leaving no way to identify an optimum plan.

Some goals, such as accessibility and walkability, are actually inputs, not outputs. Just because planners judge a neighborhood to be walkable doesn't mean that anyone is actually walking. One plan defines *accessibility* as "the number of opportunities (such as jobs, shopping, etc.) that can be reached from a given location within a given amount of travel time by auto, transit, or non-motorized modes."[40] This is an input, not an output.

Other terms, such as sustainable, livable, and multimodal, are code words, and in most cases they are codes for the same thing: alternatives to the automobile. "Sustainable" often means non-petroleum-based transportation. "Livable" means cities designed for pedestrians and cyclists, not autos. "Multimodal" means money spent on any transportation mode except autos—even if most people continue to use autos.

Part of the problem is that Congress has required planners to include or consider a number of vague goals, such as supporting economic vitality, enabling global competitiveness, promoting energy conservation, and improving accessibility.[41] Having set the precedent by requiring unquantifiable, vague, and/or conflicting goals, Congress has effectively encouraged planners to add more such goals of their own.

Most plans offer little hint into how planners account for the trade-offs among these goals. But the plan for Nashville does include a system of scoring projects that provides a revealing glimpse into planners' priorities. Here are the most important scores:

- Public transit capital improvements—21 points
- Positive impact on transit—9 points
- HOV use—4 points
- Travel demand management (carpooling, vanpooling, etc.)— 9 points
- Bike/pedestrian facilities—8 points
- New highway lanes—8 points
- Congestion pricing—2 points
- Eligibility for federal and state funding—50 points[42]

The Census Bureau says that nearly 97 percent of all Nashville-area commuters get to work by car, less than 2 percent walk or bicycle, and less than 1.5 percent take transit.[43] Yet bike-pedestrian facilities score the same as new highway lanes, and transit scores nearly four times as many points as new highway lanes. Far and away, projects "eligible for federal and state funding" score the most points.[44] In other words, if someone else will pay for it, no matter what the project is, Nashville will build it.

Nashville's scoring system makes the biases of regional planners readily apparent. Most transportation plans do not include such a scoring system, which helps hide whatever biases planners may have. As will be shown below, many plans spend far too much on forms of transport that move very few people, indicating that the biases of Nashville's planners are shared by many metropolitan transportation planners.

Forecasts and Sensitivity Analyses

Nearly all plans contain at least some forecasts of population growth and future travel demands. Few describe how reliable the travel forecasts might be. No plan reports that planners did any sensitivity analyses to deal with questionable assumptions and forecasts.

170

Project Listings with Benefits and Costs

Most plans list projects that will take place under the proposed plan. Some plans include additional projects that planners consider desirable but for which no funding was available.

Typically, the metropolitan planning organizations (MPOs) compile these lists by asking state, regional, and local transportation agencies to list the projects they would like to complete in the next 20 years or so. The Jacksonville plan calls this the "wish list."[45] MPOs rarely, if ever, add alternative projects to the list. In most cases, these wish lists end up far exceeding the total financial resources available to the region. Thus the MPOs have to determine which projects will get funded and which will not. This is the essence of the long-range plan.

This process is open to abuse. If we assume that government agencies regard tax dollars as a common-pool resource, then they will have an incentive to submit lengthy wish lists. Indeed, they may be induced to propose expensive solutions (such as rail transit) when low-cost solutions (such improvements to bus transit) would work just as well.

For example, the Ft. Collins plan used an elaborate scoring system to rank projects within several categories—highway, transit, bike/ pedestrian, and so forth. When it came time to select from the high-ranking projects among those categories, the MPO essentially punted, saying it would "spend the resources that have been allocated to each project category at an equal rate."[46] In other words, if funding was available for only half of all projects, it would fund half (by dollar value) of each category's projects. This, of course, would motivate the various agencies to make their project lists as long as possible.

Transportation planning models allow planners to estimate the effects of individual projects on congestion and other outputs. Yet none of the plans list any effects, other than financial costs, for their projects. In one case, an MPO assessed the effects of individual projects on congestion but did not include this assessment in the plan itself. For its 2025 long-range plan, the San Francisco Metropolitan Transportation Commission published a separate "evaluation report" that listed dozens of highway and transit projects.[47] This MTC report included one set of tables listing the cost of each project and a separate set of tables estimating the number of hours of congestion relief each project would provide.

Unlike the plan itself, this report was not available for download on the Internet. But anyone who obtained a copy could calculate the cost per hour of delay and rank projects by this measure. The report shows no evidence that the MTC ever made this calculation itself. Its plan proposes to fund several projects that have the highest costs per hour of delay saved, while it does not fund many projects with much lower costs. Clearly, the MTC does not consider this to be an important criterion.

This evaluation report has been used by low-income advocates in a discrimination lawsuit against the MTC, charging that the agency is building expensive transportation facilities for high-income neighborhoods while neglecting low-cost transportation improvements that would serve low-income neighborhoods.[48] Not surprisingly, the MTC published no comparable report for its more recent 2030 plan.

Alternatives

The biggest gap in metropolitan transportation planning is the lack of alternatives. Of the more than 70 plans reviewed, only two—those for Jacksonville and Salt Lake City—include real alternatives and evaluate the effects of those alternatives.

Some plans consider no alternatives at all. The proposed plans appear completely arbitrary or perhaps based on some hidden (or not-so-hidden) agenda. Perhaps planners do not want to reveal to the public how badly the plans perform when compared with alternatives. Other plans list alternatives that are alternatives in name only. Take the following examples.

Many plans include a "no-build" alternative, meaning no new capital improvements after the ones already in progress are finished. Planners usually project a huge increase in congestion under this alternative, which allows them to say that the preferred alternative "reduces" congestion—when in fact it merely increases it by a smaller amount than the no-build plan. In Austin, Texas, where more than 90 percent of commuters drive to work, planners predict that a no-build option will increase the amount of time people waste in traffic by more than 100 times, but under the proposed plan, it will increase by "only" 4 times.[49] Since no other alternatives were evaluated, people have no way to know whether some other plan could have prevented such an increase.

Some plans, including Portland's, add a "priority" or "needs" alternative, which could also be called the "wish-list" alternative, as it includes all of the projects submitted to the MPO by the various transportation agencies in the region. Since the total cost of all projects can be many times the total funds available, the needs alternative, like no-build, is not a realistic option.

The 2030 plan for Sacramento includes the 2025 plan as an "alternative" to the proposed plan. Given that part of the 2025 plan has already been accomplished and the 2030 plan extends five more years into the future, the 2025 plan is not a real alternative.

A few plans, such as Pittsburgh's, consider different "vision scenarios." Pittsburgh includes four: current trends, dispersed development, compact development, and corridor/cluster development. These are all land-use alternatives, of course, not transportation alternatives. But whatever they are, Pittsburgh planners made no effort to evaluate the transportation or other effects of each scenario. Instead, they settled on a preferred scenario and based their transportation plan exclusively on that.

Buffalo's 2025 transportation plan considers three alternatives. Alternative A emphasizes highway capacity improvements, B emphasizes transit improvements, and C emphasizes investments to promote economic development. The proposed plan ultimately calls for equal investments in all three.[50]

The exceptions are Jacksonville and Salt Lake City. In addition to a no-build alternative, Jacksonville also considered highway-emphasis and transit-emphasis alternatives.[51] Salt Lake City offered three alternatives: continuation of the previous plan, freeway emphasis, and arterial emphasis. Despite the names, the differences among the alternatives are actually minor. All three include five light-rail and commuter-rail lines, as if those lines are not in question. They also include several streetcar lines, though not necessarily on the same streets.[52]

Projections of Costs and Benefits

An important step in the federally mandated planning process is ensuring that the proposed plan is feasible considering available financial resources. Most plans, therefore, estimate the monetary costs of the proposed plan. But many do not bother to estimate the benefits or other effects of the plan. Will the plan lead to more or less traffic congestion? Will heavy investments in transit shift travel from automobiles? Will such shifts reduce congestion and air pollution? Planners for Boston, Ft. Lauderdale, Miami, Minneapolis-St.

173

Paul, San Diego, the San Francisco Bay area, and many other major urban areas could not be bothered with answering these and other questions relating to plan performance.

For example, Albuquerque's plan notes that, in 2005, 77.4 percent of commuters drove alone to work and only 1.4 percent rode transit. Their plan provides "extensive opportunity for commuters to move away from the 'Drive Alone' category to other non-'SOV' [single-occupant vehicle] modes," including commuter rail, bus rapid transit, and bikeways. However, planners did not estimate how many people would actually take advantage of such opportunity. Opportunities, of course, are inputs; actual use would be an output.

Buffalo planners went to the trouble of identifying alternatives to their 2025 plan but failed to estimate the effects of those alternatives.[53] Moreover, Buffalo does not include any alternatives in its more-recent 2030 plan.[54]

The Jacksonville plan includes estimates of such things as number of hours of congestion delay, average rush-hour travel speeds, and numbers of transit riders for each alternative as well as the selected plan.[55] Jacksonville's plan is unusual in that it was written by outside consultants rather than in-house planning staff; perhaps other MPOs should go this route.

For each of their alternatives, Salt Lake City planners estimate the impacts of the number of hours of congestion delay, average commuting speeds, tons of air pollution, and many other effects.[56] Curiously, they do not report a comparable evaluation of the preferred alternative. The plan devotes 65 pages to the impacts of the selected plan (compared with 17 pages for the three alternatives, 16 of which describe methods and 1 of which presents results), but readers will search in vain to find total hours of congestion delay, average commuting speeds, tons of air pollution, or many of the other impacts estimated for the alternatives.[57] This greatly reduces the usefulness of the alternatives.

Preferred Alternative

Every plan includes a preferred alternative, though of course, since many present no other alternatives, they simply call the preferred alternative "the plan" or the "fiscally constrained plan." Most plans include projections of the effects of the plan on future transportation: congestion, pollution, the share of travel using transit, and so forth.

But without alternatives for comparison, members of the public have no way of knowing whether the selected plan is the best way to deal with metropolitan transportation issues.

For example, as evidence that the draft Los Angeles metropolitan transportation plan is cost-effective, planners say that the projected benefits are slightly more than twice the expected costs.[58] But this does not prove that a plan is cost effective. Suppose a plan consists of three projects, each of which costs a dollar. One project produces $5 worth of benefits, one $0.75, and one $0.25. All three projects together earn twice the benefits of their costs, but the second and third projects are neither efficient nor cost-effective. Further, merely knowing the benefit-cost ratio of selected projects says nothing about whether potential projects that were rejected or not considered at all might have produced even greater benefit-cost ratios.

Transparency

Few of the plans are transparent to members of the public. How did planners select the projects being considered in the plans? How did they select the projects to be funded under the proposed plan? How did they weigh the relative importance of congestion relief, safety, pollution abatement, land-use manipulation, or providing alternatives to the automobile? The plans provide few answers to these questions.

Monitoring and Feedback

Most of the plans claim that the agencies will monitor implementation. However, few include many details about how the monitoring process will work, and none include any feedback mechanisms or triggers that might require plan amendments or revisions. For the most part, planners seem to include language about monitoring more to fulfill federal planning guidelines than because they believe monitoring is important or can improve on-the-ground decision-making.

Substantive Problems with Transportation Plans

Although fewer than 7 percent of Portland-area commuters take transit to work, Portland, Oregon, has become famous for its plans that emphasize compact urban development and public transit over new highways. But in January 2007, the Federal Highway Administration sent Metro, Portland's MPO, some unusually critical comments about its draft metropolitan transportation plan. Those comments include the following:

- "It is difficult to find the transportation focus" in the plan. "The current focus is about land use and attaining land use goals through other means, specifically by controlling transportation."
- "The plan should allow for highway expansion as a viable alternative. The transportation solution for a large and vibrant metropolitan region like Metro should include additional highway capacity options."
- "The plan should acknowledge that automobiles are the preferred mode of transport by the citizens of Portland—they vote with their cars everyday."[59]

The letter also criticized Portland's zoning codes that allow unusually narrow streets, the region's failure to do anything about high crime rates on its light-rail lines, and street designs that require buses to block traffic instead of pulling into loading bays when stopping for passengers. If nothing else, this letter revealed that many transportation professionals are not persuaded that behavioral solutions are the answer to Portland's transportation needs.

The lack of alternatives, sensitivity analyses, and transparency in the planning process allow regional planning agencies to gloss over the fact that many plans are not really about solving transportation problems. Instead, like Portland's, too many are about social engineering, that is, changing people's behavior by artificially increasing the costs of some modes of transport while artificially reducing the costs of others. Even if members of the public supported such behavioral modification, the plans provide no way of knowing whether it works, that is, whether the plans produce any meaningful changes in behavior and whether those changes are worth the cost.

Polls frequently show that urban residents consider traffic congestion to be one of the most serious problems with living in American cities.[60] As previously noted, the Texas Transportation Institute estimates that congestion costs American commuters $78 billion per year.[61] Most metropolitan transportation plans pay lip service, at least, to relieving congestion. But few end up doing anything more than slowing the rate of increase in congestion, and a few don't even promise to do that.

Two symptoms reveal whether regional transportation planners are placing undue emphasis on behavioral tools rather than technical tools to accomplish their goals. First is the share of the region's capital funds that planners propose to devote to transit. Second is the emphasis planners place on regulating land use to achieve transportation objectives.

Overemphasis on Transit

New York is the only American metropolitan planning area where transit carries more than 15 percent of commuters to work. In only four other areas—Boston, Chicago, northern New Jersey, and Washington—does transit carry more than 10 percent of commuters. Yet more than 30 metropolitan transportation plans—well over half of those for which data are available—propose to spend more than 20 percent of their region's capital funds on transit.

New York's plan to spend 56 percent of the region's capital funds on transit is not significantly out of line with the 40 percent of the region's commuters who use transit (Table 8.1). But the Twin Cities' plan to spend 70 percent of the region's capital funds on transit is far out of line with the 4.8 percent of commuters who take transit to work.

The transportation plan for St. Louis rejects the regional transit agency's proposal to spend $4.9 billion on light-rail lines and other capital improvements. The plan notes that the transit agency's projected revenues could not even cover its operating costs, much less the cost of light-rail expansion. The plan adds that county voters rejected a tax increase needed to support transit operations and that, even with that tax, the agency's revenues would be insufficient to support the proposed expansions.[62]

With the exception of St. Louis, all regions propose to spend a greater share of capital funds on transit than transit's share of commuters. Transit also costs more, per passenger mile, to operate and maintain than highways. Moreover, tax subsidies are needed to cover more than 70 percent of transit capital and operating costs, while subsidies to highways total only about 12 percent of highway costs.[63] So, in one sense, all of the urban areas in table 8.1 except St. Louis are spending too much on transit. But, assuming that some

Table 8.1
SPENDING ON TRANSIT (PERCENT)

Metro Area	Transit's Share of Funds	Commuters
Minneapolis-St. Paul	70	4.8
San Francisco	68	9.6
Miami	68	5.5
Hartford	67	3.0
Honolulu	57	8.7
New York	56	39.9
Boston	55	11.6
Philadelphia	55	9.7
Ft. Lauderdale	53	2.6
Springfield	49	1.5
Denver	47	4.3
Portland, OR	43	7.6
Atlanta	38	4.0
Houston	37	3.2
Seattle	36	7.0
Phoenix	34	2.5
Albany	33	2.9
Durham	33	4.9
Ft. Collins	32	1.0
San Diego	31	3.1
Washington, D.C.	31	14.7
Albuquerque	28	1.5
Memphis	28	1.6
Buffalo	28	3.6
Los Angeles	27	4.5
Salt Lake City	27	3.9
Tucson	25	2.5
Savannah	25	2.5
Dallas	24	1.9
Sacramento	23	2.4
Baltimore	23	7.6
Cleveland	21	4.9
Little Rock	21	0.9
Madison	19	4.9
Portland, ME	19	2.1

Metro Area	Transit's Share of Funds	Commuters
El Paso	18	2.4
Tampa	18	1.4
Bridgeport	17	9.3
Jacksonville	16	1.4
Richmond	13	2.1
Bakersfield	13	1.6
Austin	12	3.8
Akron	11	0.9
Detroit	11	1.7
Oklahoma City	11	0.7
Charlotte	10	2.6
Cincinnati	10	2.8
Las Vegas	10	3.5
Milwaukee	10	3.5
Birmingham	9	3.2
Anchorage	5	1.5
St. Louis	0	2.8

SOURCES: Transit's share of funds from the most recent draft or final metropolitan transportation plan for each region. Transit's share of each region's commuters from *2005 American Community Survey* (Washington: Census Bureau, 2006), Table GCT0804, "Percent of Workers 16 Years and Over Who Traveled to Work by Public Transportation" for urbanized areas or for counties in cases (such as New York) where metropolitan regions do not coincide with urbanized areas.

NOTE: Regions not shown on this list, such as Chicago and Pittsburgh, did not include enough data in their plans to calculate these numbers.

basic level of support is needed for people who have no access to autos, the really serious problems are in regions that are spending more than about 20 percent of their funds on transit *and* are spending several times more on transit than transit's share of commuters.

In deciding to spend a large share of its funds on transit, Salt Lake used a scoring system to rank projects on the basis of congestion relief, cost effectiveness, safety, environment, and community factors. Several rail transit projects scored very high with this ranking. However, a state auditor found major math errors.[64] Correcting the errors reduced the ranking of one rail project from 2 to 19 and a second project from 7 to 18, and it pushed several projects ahead of those rail projects. Together, these two downgraded projects combined absorbed 80 percent of state funds.[65] "Instead of providing funding for both road and transit projects which are essential to congestion relief," noted the auditor, planners "used almost all of the funds for transit projects."[66]

On reviewing the auditor's report, the council of governments decided to ignore the new ranking and continue funding the transit projects. "The reason for selecting the same projects is that transit provides a balanced transportation system," said the council.[67]

The council was also unfazed by a report issued at about the same time finding that Salt Lake City's transit agency has systematically overestimated light-rail ridership by about 20 percent.[68] If existing light-rail lines carry fewer people than the agency has claimed, then new light-rail lines will probably do less to relieve congestion than planners predict.

The president of the council of governments responded by saying, "I'm satisfied that regardless of what the numbers are, UTA makes an impact." Despite the new numbers, "I only see us going forward" with transit.[69] In other words, the actual amount of congestion relief or the cost-effectiveness of that relief is irrelevant despite the scoring system in the planning process. Clearly, in this case, the planning process is less important than the preconceived notions of the members of the council of governments who make the final decisions.

Those preconceived notions are often wrong. In 1979, University of California economist Charles Lave observed that many people assume "that public transportation is vastly more energy-efficient than automobiles" and "that investing money to improve transit facilities will attract many more passengers."[70] Both of these assumptions, Lave said, were wrong when he was writing. They remain wrong today: transit is not particularly environmentally friendly, and even if it were, no American metropolitan area has been able to attract more than about 1 percent of commuters out of their cars by making huge investments in transit.[71] Those metropolitan transportation plans that estimate future transit usage confirm this: none project that transit will significantly gain market share over the automobile.

Transit planners prefer to compare mode shares in terms of trips, as in "transit carries 5 percent of trips and autos 90 percent." But this is misleading when dealing with congestion and mobility because transit trips tend to be slower and shorter than auto trips, and a shorter trip offers less mobility than a longer one. A 10-mile trip potentially accesses four times as much land area, and four times as many potential destinations, as a 5-mile trip. So passenger miles are a better indicator of mobility.

Portland, Oregon, planners, for example, optimistically project that their plan will increase the share of trips on transit from 3.55 to 5.11 percent.[72] This is equivalent to increasing transit's share of passenger miles from 2.0 to 2.9 percent.[73] Similarly, the plan for Denver projects transit's share of trips will increase from 2.3 to 3.1 percent, which is the same as increasing transit's share of passenger miles from 1.4 to 1.9 percent.[74] Such gains are a trivial return from spending 40 to 50 percent of each region's transportation capital dollars on transit. This is especially true considering that growth will put a lot more cars on the road and that diverting funds to transit will prevent the region from building more roads to those cars to drive upon.

Overemphasis on Land-Use Regulation

The second symptom of the excessive use of behavioral tools is an undue reliance on land-use programs to alter transportation choices. At least 27 plans place a strong emphasis on manipulating land uses to promote alternatives to auto driving, and another 13 place at least some emphasis on this goal. In contrast, the rest of the plans mostly regard land use as something transportation planners must respond to, not something they can or should try to control.

"Traditionally, development patterns have been allowed to determine the distribution of travel demand, which government has then accommodated by expanding infrastructure," says Cincinnati's 2030 plan. "In contrast, growth management involves governments in influencing the timing, location, pattern, intensity, and budgeting of development so as to reduce the need for transportation facilities as well as address environmental, social, and fiscal issues."[75]

Reflecting changes in planning jargon, Cincinnati's 2004 update of its plan uses identical language but substitutes the words "smart growth" for "growth management."[76] Both versions "recommended that local governments adopt and implement comprehensive land use and transportation policies which support SOV [single-occupant vehicle] alternatives."[77] Because this is only a recommendation, not

181

Table 8.2
PLANNING EMPHASIS ON LAND-USE REGULATION

Strong	Moderate	None or Minor
Albuquerque	Albany	Akron
Atlanta	Buffalo	Anchorage
Austin	Chicago	Bakersfield
Baltimore	Cincinnati	Birmingham
Boston	Cleveland	Charlotte
Bridgeport	Ft. Lauderdale	Columbus
Denver	Little Rock	Dallas
Ft. Collins	Miami	Des Moines
Hartford	Raleigh	Detroit
Honolulu	Sarasota-Manatee	Durham
Houston	Springfield	El Paso
Los Angeles	St. Louis	Fresno
Madison	Washington, D.C.	Hampton Roads
Minneapolis-St. Paul		Indianapolis
Nashville		Jacksonville
Northern New Jersey		Kansas City
Orlando		Las Vegas
Philadelphia		Louisville
Pittsburgh		Memphis
Portland, OR		Milwaukee
Sacramento		Montgomery
Salt Lake City		New York
San Diego		Oklahoma City
San Francisco		Omaha
Seattle		Phoenix
		Portland, ME
		Providence
		Richmond
		Rochester
		San Antonio
		Savannah
		Tampa
		Tucson

SOURCE: Reviews of most recent draft or final long-range metropolitan transportation plans for each region.

a mandate, Cincinnati's plan falls in the "moderate emphasis" category.

Plans like Cincinnati's that moderately emphasize land use may promote transit-oriented developments through subsidies, or sometimes merely by exhorting local governments to zone for such developments. They do not rely on coercive land-use measures such as growth boundaries.

The plan for St. Louis, for example, says that transportation facilities "should be supported by land use policies that harmoniously mix residential, retail, and office development near transit stations." While a 2020 plan considered spending up to $1.5 billion on "sustainable development," neither that plan nor any subsequent plan has rated this project a high enough priority to reach the final list.[78]

Like the moderate plans, plans with a strong land-use emphasis promote transit-oriented developments, often with tax-increment financing and other subsidies. But unlike the moderate plans, strong plans also employ coercive measures such as growth boundaries. Outside the growth boundaries or some other boundary, they use large-lot zoning or other restrictions to prevent development. Inside the boundary, they promote more compact development, perhaps through minimum-density zoning or perhaps merely with subsidies to high-density infill.

Goal 7 of Sacramento's 2006 plan says, "Influence land use policies to improve access to jobs, services and housing to everyone in the region by using market forces and the regulatory process."[79] The plan proposes to "rein in sprawl" and promote "compact development" by dedicating $500 million of transportation funds to subsidies to developers of high-density, mixed-use projects.[80]

The 2030 plan for the San Francisco Bay area proposes to use land-use regulation to limit greenfield development to 15,600 acres instead of the 128,000 acres that planners project would be developed without such regulation.[81] The plan also dedicates $27 million per year to subsidize transit-oriented developments.[82]

The regulation and enforcement of land-use policies in transportation plans are simplified when the same agencies plan handle both issues and when those agencies are granted strong powers by either the states or the communities within the metropolitan area. Oregon state land-use rules require every city or metropolitan planning organization in the state to draw urban-growth boundaries, so naturally these boundaries were incorporated into the transportation plans for Portland and other Oregon urban areas. Cities and counties in the Denver area have agreed to let Denver's metropolitan planning organization draw an urban-growth boundary, something that a majority of municipalities can impose on any dissenters by virtue of the MPO's ability to withhold federal grants from recalcitrant cities.

In addition to the urban-growth boundary, Denver's transportation plan includes restrictions on large-lot subdivisions and financial and other incentives for transit-oriented and other high-density developments.[83] Portland's transportation plan links to the region's 2040 land-use plan.[84] The latter emphasizes "maintaining a compact urban form" through an urban-growth boundary and increasing the density of neighborhoods within the boundary so that the region can grow with minimal expansions to the boundary.[85]

Los Angeles' transportation plan ties to an aggressive land-use plan that focuses on transportation outcomes. Although the details are somewhat vague, the plan proposes to put nearly 40 percent of all new residents in high-density infill developments in transit corridors on just 2 percent of the region's land area.

Just as spending billions on transit does little to increase transit ridership, little evidence suggests that either compact urban areas or transit-oriented development will significantly reduce auto driving. Los Angeles' land-use plan, along with new rail transit lines and bike paths, is projected to reduce the length of average commutes by 2 percent, increase transit's share of trips from 2.1 to 3.0 percent, and increase walking and cycling's share of trips from 8.3 to 9.2 percent. The net result is a projected 3.3 percent reduction in per capita driving.[86]

This may sound small, but Los Angeles planners are more optimistic about the effects of land-use changes on transportation choices than planners in other regions. Plans for both Denver and Portland project an increase in per capita driving despite new rail-transit lines, increased population densities, and scores of new transit-oriented developments.[87]

Such predictions are not exactly a revelation to planners. Denver's MPO, the Denver Regional Council of Governments, began assessing the viability of behavioral strategies for reducing congestion and air pollution more than three decades ago. A 1977 report found that more compact development would have little effect on driving and no effect on air pollution.

The number of trips people make by car is primarily a function of household income, noted the report, and not very sensitive to development patterns or housing types. The report cited a study in Boston that simulated shifting 20 percent of the region's population from the suburbs to the urban core and found it would reduce driving by only 1 percent.[88]

Even if more compact development could shorten the length of trips, noted the report, the number of trips is what counts for air pollution. Catalytic converters only work after engines warm up to normal operating temperatures, so most pollution from today's cars comes from "cold starts." Thus, a 2-mile auto trip generates almost as much pollution as a 20-mile trip. "Cold start engines mean number of trips is more significant than VMT" (vehicle-miles traveled), warned the report.[89]

Nor will changes in density combined with huge investments in transit make a difference. "Likely, no more than 15 percent of total personal trips can be accommodated by transit—most see no more than 10 percent."[90] Even that number is optimistic considering that, even in the New York urban area, less than 10 percent of all travel is by transit, while the number is less than 5 percent in every other American urban area.

A 1979 report analyzed various strategies such as transit improvements, high-occupancy vehicle lanes, increased parking charges, and other "transportation system management strategies." Any one of these strategies had fairly insignificant effects on driving, and even when combined, the strategies reduced per capita driving by less than 10 percent.[91]

Despite these findings, plans issued by the Denver Regional Council of Governments since 1977 have increasingly relied on behavioral tools to reduce driving. For example, a 1981 plan focused on promoting "activity centers" of mixed-use developments throughout the Denver region in the hope that such developments would reduce driving.[92] The most recent plan calls for building nearly 80 such transit-oriented developments throughout the Denver metro area.[93]

Why Long-Range Transportation Planning Can't Work

Despite the high costs and minimal benefits of behavioral tools, more than a third of the plans reviewed for this report rely heavily on such tools, and another 20 percent use them to some degree.

Moreover, virtually none of the plans seriously evaluated alternatives or attempted to find the most cost-effective solutions to congestion, air pollution, and other regional transportation problems. Whether due to laziness or a desire to cover up the inefficiency of their plans, most plans used an abbreviated Rational Planning Model that left out alternatives and other important steps.

The failure of planners to use the Rational Planning Model illustrates the bankruptcy of the long-range transportation planning process required by Congress. But these problems cannot be remedied by simply insisting that planners strictly follow the Rational Planning Model. Even if that model were followed to the letter, the process would still fail for several reasons.

First, a long-range plan requires information about the future that is essentially unknowable. Forecasts of future populations, construction costs, energy costs, travel demands, job locations, housing preferences, tax revenues, and other information will, in many cases, be no better than guesses or, in some cases, wishful thinking. Yet, on the basis these guesses, many cities are committing billions or tens of billions of dollars to transportation projects that may prove to be useless.

Second, comprehensive plans that attempt to account for such diverse factors as vibrant communities, workforce housing, cultural resources, and economic development are simply too complicated to analyze or comprehend. As previously noted, many of these variables are not quantifiable, and many of the ones that can be quantified cannot be easily weighed against other variables.

Third, as Shorey Peterson predicted in 1950, whenever a plan must deal with long-range unknowns or nonquantifiable benefits or costs, the final decision ends up being political rather than rational. Decisions are made by politicians whose preconceived notions may be entirely at odds with reality, as in the case of the Salt Lake City commission that supported rail transit even when its corrected analysis found that it made no sense. Furthermore, decisions that are entirely up for grabs and not based on any rational process give special interest groups a powerful incentive to influence the process in their favor.

Fourth, long-range planning offers planners and decisionmakers little or no incentive to ensure the decisions they make are the right ones. They are spending other people's money, and the people whose money they are spending will have to live with the decisions long after the planners have changed jobs or retired and the politicians have left office.

Finally, if new information becomes available indicating that a long-range plan is flawed—if, for example, costs are higher or benefits lower than expected—correcting the problem can be very difficult even in a regularly scheduled update. Any long-range plan will generate special-interest groups that benefit from the plan, and they will work very hard to prevent any changes in the plan.

Government planners can't accurately predict what we will want or need in the future, so long-range transportation plans may lock agencies into plans and projects that will make no sense. Twenty years ago, no one could have predicted the Internet; or that telecommuters would outnumber transit riders in the vast majority of urban areas; or that intercity bus service (driven by on-line ticket sales) would be growing for the first time in decades; or that FedEx, UPS, and DHL would be making daily deliveries on almost every residential street in America. Just as plans written 20 years ago would be wrong about these things today, plans written today and projected out 20 years from now will also be wrong.

Yet, as Peter Drucker observed, "any government activity almost at once becomes 'moral.'"[94] Once a plan is written, no matter how flawed, those who stand to benefit view it as an entitlement. So what if costs turn out to be double the original predictions? So what if the benefits turn out to be far smaller than hoped? The plan must be carried out.

In short, any long-range plan is guaranteed to be wrong. Yet, if it is a government plan, it is very hard to change. As a result, long-range transportation plans are locking more and more urban areas into dubious programs of increased congestion (in the hope of discouraging a few vehicle miles of travel), unaffordable housing (in the hope of encouraging a few more people to crowd into transit-oriented developments), and costly rail projects whose environmental and transportation benefits are dubious at best.

Short-term planning can focus on today's problems, including congestion, safety, and deteriorating infrastructure. Transportation agencies that solve those problems will bequeath a much better urban environment to the future than ones that ignore those problems in an attempt to create some unattainable vision. Because short-term planning depends less on distant forecasts, it is less likely to make mistakes that lock regions into bad plans. Short-term planning should also focus only on quantifiable values directly related to transportation, not on broader community concerns that are difficult to measure and debatable in any case.

Safe, efficient transportation literally drives our economy and has made America one of the wealthiest nations in the history of the world. The recommendations to Congress in chapter 10—to repeal long-range transportation planning requirements, offer regions incentives to achieve transportation goals, and encourage more user-fee-based financing of new transportation facilities—will assure Americans that the fees and taxes they pay for transportation are used as effectively as possible.

9. Dude, Where's My Driverless Car?

New York's 1939–1940 World's Fair promised the public a glimpse into the "World of Tomorrow." No exhibit at the fair came closer to keeping this promise than Futurama, the pavilion sponsored by General Motors. Twenty-eight thousand people a day waited in long lines to enter this exhibit. Once inside, they were seated in chairs that floated over a huge, 35,000-square-foot diorama depicting the United States in the then-distant-future year of 1960, complete with cities, towns, farms, plains, mountains, and canyons. More than a half-million miniature buildings and 1 million tiny trees went into this model.

The star of the show was a network of thousands of scale miles of "magic motorways" along which 16,000 tiny autos and trucks zipped among cities and farms without delay or congestion. Despite a decade of depression, despite the fact that little more than half of American families owned a car, big American cities like New York, Chicago, and Los Angeles were terribly congested in 1939. The mobility promised by Futurama astonished the nearly 10 million Americans—close to 1 out of every 10 people in the country—who saw it and who proudly wore buttons after they left that said, simply, "I have seen the future."

Futurama was easily the most popular exhibit at the fair. Years later, writer E. L. Doctorow, who saw the exhibit when he was nine years old, remembered that the lesson of Futurama was, "General Motors is telling us what they expect from us: we must build them the highways so they can sell us the cars."[1]

In fact, the message was not nearly so crass, and it did not even come from General Motors. The entire exhibit had been planned and designed by an artist named Norman Bel Geddes long before General Motors even agreed to sponsor it.

Theater Designer to Highway Futurist

Though he tried to position himself as an industrial designer in a class with Raymond Loewy (who happened to design the Chrysler exhibit at the fair), Bel Geddes had spent most of his career in theater design. His goal as a set designer was to make the audience feel a part of the play. For one production, for example, he stunned the audience by transforming the entire interior of a New York theater into the nave of a gothic cathedral, complete with pews in the place of theater seats.[2]

In addition to his role designing theater sets, Bel Geddes considered himself a futurist. In 1927, he began designing cars, ships, planes, and trains of the future: vehicles that were not only beautiful but capable of much higher speeds. "Today, speed is the cry of our era, and greater speed one of the goals of tomorrow." He published many of these designs, which helped inspire the streamlined modern style in future autos, trains, planes, and buildings, in a 1932 book called *Horizons*.[3]

In response to the book, Shell Oil Company hired Bel Geddes to build a scale model of his vision of a city of the future for use in its advertising. However, when Bel Geddes approached both Shell and General Motors about expanding the model for the 1939 fair, neither was interested. GM already had plans to duplicate its entry from the 1933 Chicago fair, where the company installed an auto assembly line so people could watch cars being built and even order one for delivery later the same day.[4]

Bel Geddes did manage to obtain the tentative interest of the Goodyear Tire Company in entering an exhibit in the fair, but the company pulled out before the fair was to open. Desperate, Bel Geddes returned to GM, arguing that doing the same thing it had done in Chicago was admitting "that it hasn't had a new idea in five years." The auto company gave him the green light just 11 months before the fair was to open.[5]

He brought his expertise in theater design to Futurama, presenting fairgoers with a surprise at the end of the ride: after seeing a futuristic city street in the last scene of the diorama, awestruck members of the audience left their chairs and found themselves on a full-sized version of that very street, complete with cars (naturally made by GM) and shops (featuring general GM products).

With their gentle curves, easy grades, and interchanges capable of handling 50-mile-per-hour traffic, motorways in Futurama's diorama bore many resemblances to the interstate highway system that would indeed be under construction by 1960. Bel Geddes acknowledged the influence of the Bureau of Public Roads in his book, *Magic Motorways*.[6] He also accurately predicted some of the changes these highways would produce. "Travel radius increases," he wrote. "Decentralized communities come into existence, population trends are changed. Cities tend to become centers for working, the country districts centers for living."[7] His vision of cities included skyscrapers scattered over the landscape, more closely resembling the edge cities of today than the downtown-centric cities of 1939. These predictions came true, even if World War II delayed them a few years.

Bel Geddes' vision went well beyond these easy predictions, however. His multiple-lane motorways of the future would feature separate lanes dedicated to 100-, 75-, and 50-mile-per-hour traffic. Each of the lanes would have "an electrical conductor imbedded within the road surface, carrying an electric current producing an electromagnetic field" that would "control both the speed of the car and its path of travel." On entering the motorway, drivers would select by pushbutton which speed they wanted to go and relinquish control of their vehicles to the road.[8]

His cars of the future would not only have sensors capable of detecting the electro-magnetic fields in the road, they would be equipped with radios that would constantly transmit their positions to nearby vehicles. Cars and trucks would thereby be able to maintain safe distances from one another. Since machines could react to changes in flows quicker than people, Bel Geddes' magic motorways could move more traffic with no congestion and almost complete safety. With this system, Bel Geddes promised, "your grandchildren will snap across the entire continent in 24 hours on a new kind of highway and in a new kind of car that is controlled by the push of a button."[9]

Actually, Bel Geddes brought up electro-magnetic fields and radio communication merely as examples. Radar was still a state secret; laser beams and computer processors were not even on the horizon. Yet Bel Geddes realized that new technologies such as these could easily replace his suggestions. Whatever technologies were eventually used, his main point was that driverless highways and cars were the next step in the nation's transportation future.

The interstate highway system fulfilled Bel Geddes' vision of motorways but not his vision of magic, that is, driverless cars. As a result, many of those highways are heavily congested, top speeds remain well below 100 miles per hour, and highway technology has not significantly advanced since the 1950s. Futurama should remind us that we can do better. As Bel Geddes wrote, "Because today we move more freely than our ancestors, we have a tendency to overlook the fact that we should be able to move ten times more freely."[10]

Driverless highways and vehicles could produce tremendous benefits, at least equal to the benefits generated by the original interstate highway system. First, moving from human-controlled to electronically controlled vehicles would nearly quadruple the capacity of existing roads to move traffic. At 60 miles per hour, modern freeway lanes can move no more than 2,200 vehicles per hour. By safely reducing the distances between vehicles, driverless lanes could move at least 8,000 vehicles per hour at the same speed. In most urban areas, this would nearly eliminate the need for new highway construction for several decades.

Second, because computer reaction times are so much faster than a human's, driverless highways would eliminate the kind of congestion that results when one car in a line briefly slows down. A highway lane capable of moving 2,200 vehicles per hour at 60 miles per hour might be capable of moving only 1,600 vehicles per hour at 30 miles per hour. If that highway lane is loaded with, say, 1,800 vehicles per hour and one car slows down to 30, however briefly, traffic will remain at 30 miles per hour—or less—until flows fall below 1,600 vehicles per hour.[11] This is why people often find themselves stuck in congestion that has no visible cause.

Third, by virtually eliminating driver error, which causes a majority of fatal highway accidents, these systems would greatly increase highway safety.[12] Reducing accidents would not only save lives, it would save the time of people who would otherwise be stuck in congestion caused by accidents.

By reducing congestion, driverless cars would increase average urban speeds, giving people access to more resources. By offering more precise driving, driverless cars would make possible higher top speeds on existing roads. Though few of today's roads may be suitable for Bel Geddes' 100 miles per hour, speeds in many areas could be raised above today's typical limits of 65 to 75 miles per hour.

Driverless systems would save energy by eliminating stop-and-go congestion. In the long run, driverless cars would reach higher speeds without increasing fuel consumption. Today's automobiles are designed to allow occupants to survive in the event of a variety of accidents. But driverless cars would likely reduce most kinds of accidents, allowing manufacturers to build lighter-weight cars that would still be safer and far more fuel-efficient today's cars.

While no system is perfect, an electronic system is much less prone to error than one relying on humans. People whose desktop computers suffer frequent system crashes may find this hard to believe, but the truth is that automobiles are already loaded with scores of microprocessors controlling fuel injection, automatic transmissions, cruise control, anti-lock brakes, airbags, climate control, instrument panels, and literally thousands of other functions. These microprocessors are controlled by up to 100 million lines of software code—close to 15 times as many lines as are used to operate Boeing's latest 787 aircraft. Automobile owners will soon be able to install software upgrades simply by plugging their car into a computer communications port.[13] Making cars driverless would, in many cases, require little more than the installation of one or two sensors and another piece of software.

Driverless Vehicles Today

Bel Geddes predicted Americans would travel in driverless vehicles by 1960. Yet, 50 years later, driverless vehicles still seem like something out of science fiction. In fact, as noted in chapter 2, advances in highway and driving technologies seem to have ended some time in the 1950s.

To be fair, some advances have been made in roadway and auto technology since the 1950s, but most have been oriented to safety, fuel economy, and power rather than to speed and traffic flows. Of the latter kinds of advances, most are not yet widespread enough to significantly improve traffic flows and speeds.

One of these advances, electronic tolling, is significant enough that *USA Today* listed it as one of the 25 most important inventions of the past 25 years.[14] As previously noted, electronic tolling not only eliminates delays at the tollbooths, it eases the use of congestion pricing, in which tolls are adjusted to rise enough that roads never become congested. Although more than a dozen states use electronic tolling, congestion pricing has so far been implemented on only a dozen or so highways in nine states, plus a number of bridges and tunnels, mostly in the New York City area.[15]

Other advances have been made to automobiles and involve the use of radar or lasers to detect other vehicles around the car. Adaptive cruise control detects if a vehicle is in front of the car and automatically adjusts speed, using either the accelerator or brakes, to maintain a safe distance behind that vehicle. All the driver has to do is set a top speed and steer. Adaptive cruise control not only increases highway safety, it reduces the kind of congestion caused by slow human reflexes. Traffic engineers at the University of Minnesota estimate that congestion will significantly decline when as few as 20 percent of cars on the road are using adaptive cruise control—which is expected by 2010.[16]

Supplementing adaptive cruise control, Nissan, Honda, and Toyota are now selling cars with "lane keep assist systems" that steer themselves on highways. A camera detects lane stripes, and the car stays between the stripes. Legally, drivers must keep their hands on the wheel, but the car will resist efforts to deviate from the lanes without signaling a lane change. Such cars have been available in Japan since at least 2001, in Europe since 2004, and will begin to enter the United States in 2010.[17]

New cars are also being made with collision avoidance systems that use radar or lasers to detect vehicles behind or in drivers' blind spots.[18] Volkswagen, Raytheon, and other companies have taken these systems the next step by developing cars that can safely change lanes in traffic, for example, to overtake slow-moving vehicles.[19]

Some other intermediate technologies are on the horizon. One is the idea of intelligent intersections that wirelessly communicate with motor vehicles. Such an intersection might warn on-coming vehicles that vehicles will be crossing their path or that a light is about to turn red or green.[20] The Institute of Electrical and Electronics Engineers has drafted a communications standard for wireless communications among vehicles and between vehicles and traffic control devices.[21] The combination of all these technologies—adaptive cruise control, collision avoidance, lane keep assistance, and wireless communications between intersections and vehicles—effectively enables driverless cars on major highways.

Despite the glacial pace of implementing these improvements, the reality is that all of the driverless technologies envisioned by Bel

Geddes in 1939 are available today and have been successfully demonstrated in practice. Coincidentally, many of the successful demonstrations have been supported by General Motors, the sponsor of Bel Geddes' Futurama exhibit.

Real-life demonstrations of driverless technologies extend back more than a decade. In 1997, the California Partners for Advanced Transit and Highways—a consortium that included the California Department of Transportation, University of California, and General Motors, among many others—demonstrated a driverless system much like the one proposed by Norman Bel Geddes. CalTrans installed magnets in the high-occupancy vehicle lane on newly built Interstate 15 in San Diego. PATH then ran a platoon of eight driverless Buicks down this lane, spaced just one car length apart, at 60 miles per hour. Individual cars were able to change lanes on command.[22]

PATH has since installed the magnetic devices on Donner Pass and other mountain roads for detection by snowplows and the eventual automation of snow removal.[23] PATH also installed magnets on a street in Berkeley to demonstrate a driverless bus system.[24] AC Transit, which serves Berkeley, Oakland, and other parts of Alameda County, estimates that this technology could be used for bus-rapid transit at less than 15 percent of the cost of building light-rail lines.[25] However, except for a few other demonstration projects, this system has yet to be implemented on a day-to-day basis.

The other demonstrations came in response to an X-prize-type challenge from the Defense Advanced Research Projects Agency. In 2004, DARPA offered a $2 million prize to the research team that provided the best demonstration of a driverless car negotiating a prescribed course in a desert terrain. None were successful, but in 2005, four teams completed the challenge and the prize went to the Stanford Racing Team, which was supported by Volkswagen, Intel, and Google, among others.[26]

In 2007, DARPA offered another $2 million prize for a more difficult challenge: negotiating an urban course complete with buildings, streets, traffic signs, pedestrians, and moving vehicles. This challenge was won by the Tartan Racing Team, sponsored by Carnegie Mellon, Caterpillar, Continental Tire, and General Motors.[27] The vehicle they used was equipped with more than a dozen sensors and controlled by a microprocessor programmed with more than 500,000 lines of code.[28]

The PATH and DARPA demonstrations illustrate two different models for driverless cars. The PATH model, which might with justice be called the Bel Geddes model, involves modifying both highways and cars. As Bel Geddes wrote, the "automatic control of a car could not be put into the car alone or into the highway, alone. The major part will be in the car, but its complementary elements must be in the highway."[29]

The disadvantage of this system is that only properly modified highways can be driverless. State transportation departments may be expecting that in-vehicle technologies such as lane-keep assist systems will overcome the need to place magnets in roads. But even lane-keep assist systems require well-maintained highway paint stripes; magnets might actually be less expensive and more reliable in the long run.

The advantage of the Bel Geddes model is that it is simple enough that the cost to auto owners is relatively low. Cars being built today with automatic transmissions, electric steering, anti-lock brakes, and adaptive cruise control already have nearly all of the technology needed for Bel Geddes-type driverless highways. They would only need a sensor to detect the magnets in the roads, a microprocessor to control the system, software, and a way to sense or communicate with other vehicles. Altogether, this should cost no more than, say, an inexpensive laptop computer. Retrofitting cars without some or all of these technologies would cost more, but within a few years, these technologies could be built into nearly all automobiles.

In contrast, the DARPA model requires minimal modifications to the roadways. Instead, all of the hardware and software to make cars driverless would be built into the vehicles themselves. The advantage of this system is that it allows cars to operate in driverless mode on any highway or street. The disadvantage is that the cost of the required equipment and the complexity of the programming would be greater—as evidenced by the fact that only 6 of 11 teams that attempted the DARPA urban challenge managed to finish the course. Advocates argue, however, that the costs of sensors, computer processors, and software are declining so rapidly that the DARPA model makes more sense.

After the Tartan Team won the DARPA urban challenge, cosponsor General Motors predicted that driverless cars would be available by 2018.[30] That's under the DARPA model; using the Bel Geddes

196

model, such cars could be available much sooner. Under either model, however, 2018 is optimistic given the formidable institutional obstacles to driverless vehicles. According to GM vice president of research Larry Burns, "Government regulation, liability laws, and other issues pose a bigger impediment to driverless cars than any technical hurdles."[31]

The biggest roadblock can be described as the chicken-and-egg problem: Who is going to pay extra for a driverless car if there are no driverless roads? What highway department is going to provide driverless roads if there are no driverless cars? While this would seem to be mainly an obstacle to the Bel Geddes model, it affects even the DARPA model. The law in every state requires drivers to be in control of their vehicles at all times; driverless cars would violate this law. Laws can be changed, but again, what state would change the law if there are no driverless-car owners demanding such a change?

Four Scenarios

The American automobile fleet turns over about every 18 years.[32] This means that, once perfected, driverless vehicles could become dominant within a decade and universal soon after that. Most of the people reading this book are likely to see widespread adoption of driverless vehicles in their lifetimes. But this advance can be hastened or slowed by government action or restraint. Here are four ways in which the chicken-and-egg problem and other obstacles to driverless vehicles might be overcome.

The Do-Nothing Model

Driverless vehicles will eventually be introduced even if no government policy actively promotes them. Early models will initially operate on private roads. For example, many private forestland owners manage their own road systems and might introduce driverless vehicles on those roads to transport timber from forest to mill. Similarly, driverless passenger services might start on private systems such as golf courses and freight yards.

Shipping companies might propose that states allow convoys of trucks, with the first truck operated by a driver followed by one or more driverless trucks which are programmed to follow the first one. Driverless buses may initially work on routine journeys such as between air terminals and parking lots. Eventually, states will

197

legalize driverless cars on highways or city streets. The disadvantage of the do-nothing model is that it may take an extra decade or more before the full benefits of driverless vehicles can be realized.

The Computer Model

Whether you are the proud owner of a Mac, a Dell, or any other brand of personal computer, most of the components in the sleek outer casing of your machine are identical to or closely resemble off-the-shelf products that anyone with a little expertise could buy and assemble into a functional computer (though it would probably cost far more than to simply buy a ready-made machine). Nearly all of the parts inside a typical laptop, including the processor, graphics chip, memory chips, disk drives, screen, and keyboard, communicate with one another using hardware and software standards developed by the computer industry.

A consortium including Intel, Compaq, Microsoft, Digital, IBM, and Northern Telecom originally developed the standard USB port now available on most computers. A consortium including Apple, Texas Instruments, Sony, IBM, DEC, and Thomson originally designed the somewhat competing Firewire port. Similar standards govern communications between hard drives and other devices inside the computers. Regardless of who originally creates the standards, they are openly published with the hope and expectation that a wide variety of manufacturers will make products that use them.

The computer model of groups of manufacturers voluntarily developing, sharing, and integrating new technologies works for several reasons. First, computer technologies are rapidly advancing and users are willing to replace their machines every few years. People who do nothing but write on their computers may find this cycle of obsolescence to be absurd, but people who manipulate photos, edit videos, or do other memory- and processor-intensive work look forward to machines that can help them do their work faster.

Second, many parts of a personal computer, such as the central and graphics processors, are expensive to develop but cheap to copy. Companies that insist on using proprietary components must pay the development costs themselves, while manufacturers using off-the-shelf products can share those costs with other manufacturers. For example, Macs used Motorola-based processors for many years, while other personal computers used Intel processors. Apple switched to Intel when it became clear that the cost of designing competitive chips was too great for Apple's small market share.

Finally, computer buyers prefer models that are compatible with a wide variety of other products. Few would be willing to purchase a computer that would only work with printers, cameras, and other external devices made by the same company that manufactured the computer.

In any case, successful adoption of driverless vehicles will clearly require the development of industry standards. Several questions will have to be answered: Should driverless vehicles follow the Bel Geddes model, incorporating some sort of driverless features into highways, or the DARPA model, building all driverless capabilities into the vehicles themselves? Should driverless vehicles operate on the same roads as driver-operated vehicles, or should some roads be set aside for driverless operations and others for driver-operated vehicles? What kind of communications should take place among vehicles and between vehicles and highway features such as intersections? Who is liable if a driverless vehicle gets into an accident: the owner or the manufacturer?

The HDTV Model

The short story behind high-definition television (HDTV) is that the Federal Communications Commission encouraged television manufacturers to develop a new standard and then smoothed the way for that standard to be put in place on a rigorous timetable. This model could be adapted to highways by having the Department of Transportation play the role of the FCC in promoting driverless standards and then mandating that those standards be applied to some or all highways by a certain date.

The long story behind HDTV makes this model a lot less appealing. Unlike rapidly changing computer technology, changes in television technologies have been slow, and the political nature of the FCC is largely responsible. For example, CBS began broadcasting in color in 1950.[33] Yet it took 17 more years before all three major networks broadcast most of their programming in color. Much of that delay was caused by FCC dithering and political maneuvering by the major networks trying to get an advantage over their competitors.[34]

The same thing happened with HDTV. The FCC initiated efforts to introduce HDTV in 1987, and the basic digital HDTV standard

199

was developed by 1994.[35] But this was followed by years of political debate and lobbying over the best use of the extremely valuable portions of the radio spectrum that the FCC allocated to television broadcasters. At certain points in this debate, it appeared that HDTV would never be implemented.[36] One of the FCC's early targets was to have HDTV completely replace conventional broadcasting by May 1, 2002. They missed this target by seven years, which in the computer industry would be several generations of new products.[37]

Still, the European Commission seems to be following the HDTV model. It launched an intelligent car initiative in 2006 aimed at removing the barriers to implementing intelligent vehicles. This initiative aims to build a consensus among the key players involved, remove the legal and institutional barriers, and stimulate consumer demand for the new technologies.[38] Among other things, the program has dedicated a radio frequency for road safety and traffic management.[39]

The Cell Phone Model

The cell phone model is a hybrid. Like the computer industry, cell phone technology changes rapidly as users purchase successively powerful new phones capable of texting, photography, video, and internet communications. Competition is the driving force behind advances in cell phone technology, with at least five major networks (AT&T, Nextel, T-Mobile, US Cellular, and Verizon) supplemented by many local providers. Like television broadcasting, however, cell phones use a share of the radio spectrum, keeping the hand of government in the mix. Still, thus far, the cell phone model seems superior to the glacial pace of technological change in the television industry.

Lessons from the Four Scenarios

The government monopoly on highways may be the main obstacle to the introduction of new technologies. User fees such as gas taxes are set by the political system, not the market. This forces highway agencies to continually scramble to find funds for basic maintenance, leaving them few resources to think about future innovations. A completely private highway system would offer competition among many destinations. Just as deregulated railroads introduced innovations such as piggy-back and container services to compete for business over major routes, private highway owners would offer innovations such as driverless highways.

The need to introduce new technologies to improve our transportation system may be one of the best arguments for privatizing highways. Unfortunately, the political efforts required to privatize roads will take so long that privatization will probably not hasten introduction of driverless vehicles. For this reason, the recommendations in chapter 11 focus on a process based on the computer model in which the states (as owners of the nation's major roads) and auto manufacturers set standards and introduce cars that meet those standards as rapidly as possible.

Objections to Driverless Cars

The main opposition to driverless vehicles is likely to come from the same anti-mobility coalition that opposes today's automobiles. Even if driverless cars were powered by renewable, nonpolluting sources of energy, many would still object to them because of their contributions to sprawl.

Driverless highways can potentially carry four times as much traffic as driver-operated roads. Yet opponents will claim that this extra capacity would quickly be filled up by people who were induced to drive more. As noted in chapter 6, so-called "induced demand" is more accurately described as "suppressed demand." As long as people pay the costs, anything that increases mobility should be regarded as good, not bad.

No doubt driverless vehicles will contribute to the further decentralization of urban areas, that is, "sprawl." The question is, What's wrong with that? The opponents of decentralization claim that Americans were forced to sprawl by misguided government policies such as Federal Housing Administration "redlining" of inner-city neighborhoods, or that they were encouraged to sprawl by government subsidies to roads and other infrastructure. The solution in either case is to fix the policies, not to prohibit sprawl through heavy-handed land-use regulation and anti-mobility plans.

Driverless vehicles and driverless highways represent the next mobility revolution. Like previous revolutions, from the steamboat and canal to the automobile, the driverless revolution is likely to produce massive economic, social, and personal benefits. Moreover, as with the automobile, but unlike previous revolutions such as the railroad, those benefits are likely to be shared by nearly everyone in America. The question is not whether to promote driverless vehicles but what policies will lead to the most rapid and widespread adaptation of driverless technologies.

10. Reforming Federal Transportation Policy

Once a relatively insignificant part of the federal budget, transportation spending now totals some $70 billion a year. This makes it the largest source of discretionary spending after national defense and explains why the House Transportation Committee is the biggest committee in congressional history.[1] Transportation earmarks, nonexistent before 1980, numbered more than 7,000 and totaled more than $24 billion (to be spread over five years) in 2005, giving various interest groups 24 billion reasons to thank their senators and representatives.

In 2007, the Department of Transportation spent about $66 billion. Slightly more than half, or $38 billion, went for highways, most of which was passed through to states and metropolitan areas.[2] In addition, several other federal agencies, such as the Department of the Interior (which includes the Forest Service), have their own budgets for roads on their lands. The Federal Emergency Management Agency also spends money repairing roads following natural disasters.

The next-biggest chunk of transportation spending, slightly less than $15 billion, went to the Federal Aviation Administration. Most of this was spent on air traffic control, but about $3.5 billion in 2007 was used for airport improvement grants.[3]

The third-largest item in the Department of Transportation's budget is about $10 billion per year for transit.[4] As with highway money, most of this is passed through the Federal Transit Administration to local transit agencies in the form of grants or following Congress's apportionment formulas. Amtrak, which is not in the Department of Transportation, also typically receives about $1.5 billion in federal money each year.

The Federal Railroad Administration is the next-largest agency in the department, with a budget of about $1.5 billion per year. The FRA monitors railroad safety, administers loans and grants (mostly to short-line railroads), and oversees the federal government's high-speed rail program.

The Department of Transportation also includes agencies dealing with maritime issues, pipelines, research, the St. Lawrence Seaway, and various other programs. None of these agencies spends more than about $300 million a year, and all of them put together spend less than $1 billion per year.[5]

The 2009 stimulus bill nearly doubled transportation spending for the year. The bill allocates about $52 billion for transportation, including $27.5 billion for highways, $8.4 billion for transit, $8 billion for high-speed rail, $4.5 billion for waterways, $1.3 billion for Amtrak, $1.1 billion for airports, and $1.5 billion that states can spend on highways, transit, or ports.[6] The stimulus bill increases the proportion of transit-highway funds dedicated to transit from the historic rate of 15.5 percent to 22.5 percent. This may foreshadow a desire of many members of Congress to increase transit's share in upcoming legislation.

What makes transportation so politically attractive to members of Congress is the fact that nearly all of the highway and transit money, and a large chunk of the railroad and aviation money, consists of grants to states and metropolitan areas. As noted in chapter 7, this money is divided into earmarks, competitive grants, and formula grants. Thus, members of Congress can earmark money to particular projects, lobby the agencies to make competitive grants into their states or districts, and tinker endlessly with the formulas used to apportion the formula grants to states and metropolitan areas. All of these tasks politicize what should be a straightforward process of spending the money collected from transportation users on the things that those users need the most.

Alternatives

Why the federal government needs to be involved in transportation at all remains an open question. With the possible exceptions of air traffic control and maritime work, virtually everything that the Department of Transportation does can be handled as well or better by state or local authorities. As for air traffic control, at least 17 countries, including Australia, Canada, Germany, Ireland, and Switzerland, have improved their air traffic control through some form of privatization.[7]

204

Federal involvement in highways and transport is really just a big shell game. States collect gas tax revenues and turn them over to the federal government, which redistributes them back to the states using politically driven formulas. Some states and metropolitan areas are "recipients," meaning they receive more from the federal government than their residents pay in federal gas taxes. Others are "donors," meaning they receive less than their residents pay. For highways, the recipient states tend to have low population densities while the donors have higher densities. The transit account somewhat redresses this imbalance by dedicating most of its money to urban areas with rail transit, which often tend to be denser.

The question is why this redistribution is necessary at all. It made some sense when Congress created the interstate highway system in 1956: states like Wyoming and South Dakota might have had a hard time paying for their segments of the system out of the gas taxes they collected. But modern electronic tolling systems allow users to pay directly for the roads they use. Federal involvement only weakens the connections between users and transportation providers.

When Congress was considering reauthorization of federal surface transportation programs in 2004 and 2005, a few representatives offered proposals that would have phased out federal involvement in transportation. In 2003, Rep. Jeff Flake (R-AZ) proposed to gradually reduce federal gas taxes from 18.4 to just 2 cents per gallon and use it solely to maintain the interstate highway system.[8] In 2005, Rep. Scott Garrett (R-NJ) urged that states be allowed to opt out of the federal gas tax, allowing them to keep the user fees they otherwise send to Washington.[9]

These are commendable proposals, but they received support from only a handful of senators and representatives. Political change usually is incremental. In the spirit of that notion, I offer the following proposals as ways to improve federal transportation programs without foreclosing the options for more revolutionary changes such as those proposed by Flake or Garrett.

Proposals

1. Apportion Funds Based on User Fees, Population, and Land Area

As described in chapter 7, complex formulas apportion most federal surface transportation funds into at least three dozen different accounts. These arcane formulas result from political debates and negotiations that seek to find a "fair" allocation of revenues among modes and geographic areas. But the result may not be fair and is certainly not efficient. The current highway formulas may not be fair because they take money from densely populated states ("donor states") and give it to sparsely populated states ("recipient states"). The transit formulas are not efficient because they reward transit agencies that build or retain high-cost rail transit systems and penalize agencies that focus on low-cost bus systems.

These complex formulas should be replaced with a simple formula that does not dictate how funds can be spent. Instead, it should distribute funds to the states according to simple measures such as population, land area, and the transportation user fees collected in the state. Making user fees a prominent part of the formula would give state and metropolitan planners incentives to invest in efficient transportation projects that cover much if not all of their costs out of user fees. It would also discourage them from relying on general taxes to pay for transportation projects, because—unlike user fees—such taxes would not be matched by federal funds.

The user fees included in the formula would be gasoline taxes, motor vehicle registration fees, weight-mile taxes, tolls, transit fares, and any other fees collected by transportation agencies and dedicated to transportation. They would not include any gasoline taxes or other fees that are spent on nontransportation purposes. And, again, the formula would not include general sales, property, or income taxes that state or local governments might appropriate to transportation.

The current formulas for apportioning highway funds use such factors as lane miles, vehicle miles, and the ratio of diesel fuel used on the highways in each state (which is apparently a proxy for truck traffic). None of these are truly goals and can be seen as creating perverse incentives to, for example, build too many lane miles of roads. Population (the people to be served by transportation networks), land area (the area to be served), and user fees (representing how people value transportation) are much better factors that avoid such perverse incentives.

A formula that allocates 50 percent of the funds based on user fees, 45 percent based on population, and 5 percent based on land area produces results that are reasonably close to the current allocations. The main losers from such a formula would be states that, because of low gas taxes or other factors, do not collect many user fees. For example, the two biggest losers would be Wyoming and Georgia, which have two of the nation's lowest gas tax rates of 14 and 8 cents per gallon, respectively.[10] Wyoming contributes 0.5 percent of all federal highway taxes, but collects only 0.2 percent of state and local user fees, so its share of federal funds would decline by 55 percent. Georgia contributes 3.9 percent of all federal highway taxes but collects only 1.2 percent of state and local user fees, so its share of federal funds would decline by 41 percent.[11]

These and other states could increase their share of federal funds by increasing gas taxes or other transportation user fees. This would lead to a "race to the top" in which state and local areas increasingly relied on user fees rather than sales, property, or other general taxes to pay for transportation facilities.

Beyond the allocation formula, Congress might want to direct states to allocate a certain percentage of their funds to urban areas based on population, user fees, or other criteria. Congress could also limit federal matching funds to no more than a fixed amount—say 50 percent—for any capital project (and that fixed amount should be the same for all types of projects). Beyond these stipulations and the cost-efficiency criteria in proposal 2, below, Congress should keep to a minimum any specifications for how funds should be used.

2. Require That Short-Term Plans Be Efficient or Cost-Efficient

Like electricity or phone service, transportation is a public utility and should act like one. Electric and phone companies do not worry about the effects of their investments on urban sprawl or livable communities. Instead, they provide services to anyone who will pay the cost. While they may have long-term goals, their planning horizons tend to be short, and their plans are flexible and often able to rapidly change in response to new technologies, tastes, or demands.

Electricity shortages are rare, and telephone users hardly ever get an "all-circuits-busy" message. Yet urban roadway congestion costs tens of billions of dollars per year. While aggravating, congestion has become so commonplace that Americans don't even notice that, among public utilities, it is the exception rather than the rule. This congestion results partly from transportation planning focused more on capturing federal and other tax dollars for economic development and special interest groups than on providing effective transportation.

207

As chapter 8 describes, in addition to mandating long-range plans, Congress currently requires states and metropolitan areas to write short-term transportation plans, known as transportation improvement plans (TIPs). Such a short-term planning process can overcome many of the defects in long-range planning, with no need to forecast populations, costs, or travel needs in the distant future. Congress should specify that short-term planning must focus on a few quantifiable variables, primarily safety and congestion, and possibly air pollution and/or energy efficiency. When limited to these variables, planners can apply the Rational Planning Method, as described above, to regional transportation decisions.

However, current law contains few requirements that would ensure that TIPs are either efficient or cost-efficient (see chapter 3 for the distinction between efficiency and cost-efficiency). To correct this flaw, Congress should require that states and metropolitan areas follow a four-step process:

1. Transportation improvement plans should identify goals that are true outputs. Congress may want to specify certain goals, including safety, congestion relief, clean air (in nonattainment areas), and energy efficiency. Under no circumstances should goals include such factors as reduced miles of driving, increased population densities, or per capita transit ridership, as these are only means to output-oriented goals.
2. TIPs should identify all possible transportation projects that could achieve one or more of those goals.
3. TIPs should rank all of the projects according to their cost-efficiency in achieving each of the goals. Rankings should take into account both the amortized capital cost and the operating cost of each project, including dollar, energy, and other costs. Within the parameters of available funds, the projects that are most cost-efficient in meeting each goal should comprise one alternative in the plan.
4. Given these alternatives, TIPs should define a preferred alternative that achieves some appropriately weighted average of all of the goals.

3. Create a Citizen-Enforcement Process to Ensure Efficiency and Cost-Efficiency

Congress should place the burden of proof that transportation improvement plans are efficient or cost-efficient on the state agencies and metropolitan planning organizations writing the plans. To enforce this burden and to discourage state and metropolitan planners from allowing a bias toward politically favored projects, the secretary of transportation should create an appeals process whereby citizens could ask the secretary to review and reject plans that might not be efficient or cost-efficient.

Citizens could challenge plans based on their failure to consider a full range of projects, because they selected a project or alternative that is not cost-efficient in meeting the goals, or because they fabricated data to make it appear a project is cost-efficient when it is not. States or urban areas whose plans are not cost-efficient would be denied a share of their federal funds until they are made cost-efficient.

Similar appeals processes already exist in many other agencies. For example, the Forest Service allows citizens to appeal its plans, and the Department of the Interior has a Board of Land Appeals. These appeals processes provide a low-cost way of settling disputes and ensuring that local officials follow national laws and policies. The Department of Transportation's appeals process would be unique in that it would focus on cost-efficiency, something that has not been an enforceable standard in most other agencies.

Citizens not satisfied with the secretary's decision could take the plans to court. Since the efficiency and cost-efficiency criteria are clear and easily quantifiable, minimal litigation should be needed to set standards that state and metropolitan transportation agencies must follow. Once those standards were set, agencies would have an incentive to meet them to avoid having their plans overturned by the secretary.

4. Eliminate Long-Range Transportation Planning

Congress currently requires states and metropolitan areas to write and regularly update long-range (20 years or more) transportation plans.[12] Yet, as chapter 8 revealed, these plans actually do more harm than good. No one can predict transportation needs 5 years from now, much less 20 years. Once written, however, plans often get politically locked in no matter how actual needs or facts change.

For example, as a part of a political deal among all of Denver's local governments, Denver wrote a transportation plan that included building a commuter-rail line to the distant suburb of Longmont.

209

When the plan was written, planners estimated it would cost $16 per trip to carry riders on the line. Since then, projected costs have increased by 59 percent, and projected ridership has declined by 45 percent. The line is now projected to cost $60 per trip.[13] Yet neither Denver's transit agency nor Denver's metropolitan planning organization is seriously considering not building the line.

Since no one can accurately predict the future, Congress should not require states and metropolitan planning organizations to pretend they can. Congress should also eliminate requirements that at least 1.25 percent of federal transportation funds be spent on planning. Beyond the steps listed in proposal 2, Congress should not specify any detailed planning processes such as public involvement or clean air conformance.

5. Allow Unlimited Use of Road Tolls

As cars become more fuel-efficient and alternative fuels become available, the gas tax is increasingly ineffective as a way of raising funds for transportation. In the long run, tolls are a better way of paying for roads, especially roads that are likely to become congested.

When Congress first created the interstate highway system in 1956, it rejected tolls as a way of paying for roads because of the congestion and delays created at tollbooths. Today's electronic tolling systems, including automatic recording of license plates of vehicles without toll transponders, eliminates this objection. Tolls have an added advantage over gas taxes in that they can vary according to the actual cost of the road and by the amount of traffic to smooth out the peaks and troughs in travel demand and thereby eliminate congestion.

While Congress has removed the absolute prohibition against tolls, current law still contains several restrictions against tolls. For example, U.S. Code 23, section 129, authorizes a limited number of toll projects. Beyond this, U.S. Code 301 requires that all other federally funded roads be "toll free." These limits and restrictions should be eliminated.

6. Eliminate Clean Air Mandates

When Congress passed the Clean Air Act in 1970, air quality was a serious problem in most urban areas, and automobiles were guilty of causing much of that problem. The Clean Air Act's requirement that automakers design cleaner cars has largely eliminated that problem in most urban areas.[14] At the same time, efforts to reduce air pollution by getting people to drive less have been largely unsuccessful.[15]

Despite these results, the Clean Air Act Amendments of 1990 combined with the 1991 transportation reauthorization law "arguably made air quality the premier objective of the nation's surface transportation programs."[16] Yet, because they focus on ineffective behavioral controls aimed at reducing per capita driving, many of the clean-air requirements in the law are not cost-efficient. Some, such as restrictions on adding highway capacity in congested areas, are actually counterproductive, because new capacity can reduce the pollution generated by cars in congested conditions.

While clean air should remain an important cost-efficiency goal of the short-term transportation plans as described in proposal 2, it should not be the overriding goal. Nor should Congress prescribe solutions that may not be cost-effective or effective at all in cleaning the air.

7. Avoid Earmarks

Congress did not earmark any transportation funds until the 1982 reauthorization, which included 10 earmarks. Since then, earmarks have grown exponentially to about 7,000 in 2005.[17] Some are clearly not efficient because they are not even spent on transportation purposes. For example, about 30 earmarks in the 2005 reauthorization were for visitors' centers in various national parks and other public lands. A few of these were related to transportation, but many were not.

Beyond this, earmarks are almost by definition not efficient, because if they were, they would be funded by an efficient planning system and no earmark would be necessary. Some members of Congress may argue that the current transportation planning system is inefficient and the earmarks are aimed at overcoming this lack of efficiency. But making the process efficient would be better than hampering it with even more earmarks.

8. Remove Employee Protective Arrangements from Transit Law

Urban mass transit is the most disappointing performer and least-productive part of the nation's transportation system. Since 1964, when Congress first passed the Urban Mass Transportation Act, transit costs have risen far faster than either revenues or ridership. This signals a tremendous decline in productivity.

"It's uncommon to find such a rapid productivity decline in any industry," wrote University of California economist Charles Lave in 1994. "If transit productivity had merely remained constant since 1964," Lave wrote, "total operating costs would be more than 40 percent lower" in 1985, the last year for which he had data.[18] By 2006, operating costs per trip were 2.3 times as much as they were in 1964 (after adjusting for inflation), while average fares had fallen by 24 percent.[19] All of this additional cost came out of taxpayers' pockets.

Thanks to this decline in productivity, transit is the most expensive form of travel in the United States. In 2006, Americans spent about 13 cents per passenger mile flying, 23 cents driving, and 56 cents on Amtrak, but they spent 85 cents per passenger mile for public transit. While users pay nearly all of the costs of flying and driving, and 60 percent of the costs of Amtrak, taxpayers subsidize more than 70 percent of the costs of transit.[20]

One reason for transit's loss in productivity is the lack of any cost-efficiency requirements in federal transit funding. Instead, much of that funding, such as New Starts money, is distributed on a first-come, first-served basis, which actually encourages transit agencies to propose high-cost projects rather than cost-efficient ones. Proposals 2 and 3 regarding cost-efficiency should fix this problem.

Another reason for the decline in productivity, however, is the "employee protection" requirement in federal transit law.[21] This provision effectively gives transit labor unions the right to veto any federal grants to transit agencies, forcing the agencies to agree to union demands.

One way transit agencies can increase productivity is to contract out transit service to private operators such as First Transit and Stagecoach. For example, Denver contracts out about half of its bus routes and pays contractors only 53 percent as much per bus mile as it spends on its own directly operated routes.[22]

Given this cost advantage, transit agencies that now operate their own routes could almost double service to transit riders, at no additional cost to taxpayers, by contracting out. Despite this, 92 percent of transit riders in 2007 were carried by directly operated services.[23] The reason is that unions object to contracted services because the contracting companies are often nonunion. Most contracting is done in places where transit has not traditionally been unionized, such as Phoenix and Las Vegas. Denver contracts half its service only because the Colorado legislature requires it to do so, a law the unions would like to change.[24]

As a result, while the labor productivity of almost every other industry steadily increases, transit's labor productivity—the number of trips carried per employee—declined by more than 1 percent per year between 1990 and 2006.[25] Cost-efficiency requirements combined with the repeal of the employee protection requirement would help the transit industry reverse this decline.

9. Privatize Air Traffic Control and End Airport Subsidies

User fees should easily pay the costs of airports and air traffic control. The main reason for airport subsidies is the hope that they will stimulate economic development. From a federal viewpoint, however, this is a zero-sum game, as subsidies that attract economic development to one town effectively draw it away from another. As previously noted, air traffic control has already been privatized in some form or another by at least 17 countries, and the United States should follow suit.

11. State and Local Transportation Policy

In 2006, Massachusetts spent more than two-thirds of state gas taxes and motor vehicle registration fees on mass transit. Connecticut, Maryland, New Jersey, and New York also dedicated more than 30 percent of these fees to transit, while New Mexico and Rhode Island spent more than 20 percent on transit.[1] Texas spent most of its gas taxes and vehicle fees on nontransportation programs, while California, Georgia, New Mexico, Oklahoma, Rhode Island, South Dakota, and Vermont all allocated 20 to 35 percent of highway user fees to nontransportation programs.[2]

Highway tolls seem to be a little more secure against such diversions than gas taxes and vehicle fees. Only California, Maryland, and New York devote a significant share of toll revenues to nonhighway programs: between 30 and 35 percent in California and Maryland, 19 percent in New York, 8 percent in Pennsylvania, and 6 percent in Massachusetts.[3] This is partly because toll authorities in many states are completely self-financing and independent of state transportation departments.

Counting fuel taxes, vehicle fees, tolls, and other user fees, states diverted nearly $12.7 billion, or 17 percent, of highway user fees to mass transit or nontransportation programs in 2006. Most of this amount was diverted by California, New York, and Texas.[4] At the same time, however, states appropriated $9.8 billion of general funds to highways, meaning highway users lost a net of about $2.9 billion out of the $73.5 billion they paid in user fees.[5] Taxes spent on roads exceeded diversions in 27 states and the District of Columbia.

Why do state legislatures play this game, taking money out of highway funds with one hand, putting it back with another? The fact that highways have relatively stable and apparently abundant sources of funds leads to resentments from other programs, such as transit agencies, that demand their "fair share" of transportation dollars. Such diversions are followed by pleas from highway agencies that roads are deteriorating and require more funds. Legislators gain power both when they please special interests by diverting funds and when they replenish those funds from general tax dollars.

County and city road departments are worse off, as most do not collect gas taxes or other user fees. As table 11.1 shows, some states share a healthy portion of their highway user fees with local governments, while others keep nearly all of those user fees for themselves. A few local governments do collect gas taxes, tolls, and other user fees, but general funds spent on local roads exceed those user fees in every state. Of those that collect user fees, a few devote a large share of those fees to mass transit or other nonhighway purposes.

New York City, for example, milks more than half the tolls from the Triborough Bridges to subsidize the region's transit system.[6] Large chunks of local gas taxes in Brevard, Broward, Duval, and Miami-Dade counties are used to subsidize Florida transit systems.[7] Of course, such diversions merely require that more local taxes be spent on roads.

Table 11.2 shows that $42.5 billion in general taxes was spent on roads in 2006, most of which ($31.0 billion) was spent by local governments rather by state or federal governments. These taxes were only partially offset by the $18.6 billion in highway user fees diverted to other purposes. Total expenses exceeded total user fees by nearly $40 billion (partly made up for by $13 billion in net interest and bond proceeds not shown in the table), which represents a substantial amount of money. However, when divided by the trillions of passenger miles of highway travel, it averages only six-tenths of a penny per passenger mile.

While highway subsidies average 0.6 cents per passenger mile, transit subsidies are 100 times greater. Table 11.3 shows why: transit fares cover only 4 to 40 percent of operating costs in all major urban areas except New York, where they cover 70 percent of operating costs. Transit agencies spent an average of 42 cents on capital improvements for every $1 they spent on operations in 2006, and none of those capital costs were covered by fares.

Partly because of the heavy subsidies, transit agency finances are less stable than those of highway agencies. While highway vehicles are operated and paid for by users, transit agencies must operate the vehicles themselves. If highway revenues decline in a recession, highway agencies can defer maintenance until the next economic boom. If transit revenues decline, transit agencies must curtail actual

216

Table 11.1
DISPOSITION OF 2006 STATE HIGHWAY USER FEES (PERCENT)

State	State Roads	Local Roads	Transit	General Funds
Alabama	56	39	0	0
Alaska	89	0	0	0
Arizona	49	47	0	2
Arkansas	67	28	0	2
California	50	17	0	28
Colorado	80	16	3	0
Connecticut	60	4	30	0
Delaware	98	0	0	0
Florida	92	5	0	3
Georgia	59	11	1	22
Hawaii	55	10	1	32
Idaho	50	43	0	1
Illinois	68	26	0	0
Indiana	34	54	0	0
Iowa	26	65	2	0
Kansas	54	37	0	2
Kentucky	78	21	0	0
Louisiana	99	1	0	0
Maine	86	6	0	0
Maryland	30	22	32	9
Massachusetts	38	0	53	1
Michigan	37	51	5	1
Minnesota	54	43	0	0
Mississippi	53	41	0	6
Missouri	77	22	0	0
Montana	38	37	1	14
Nebraska	35	59	0	0
Nevada	60	24	0	2
New Hampshire	81	10	0	0
New Jersey	73	4	18	3
New Mexico	37	18	22	20
New York	63	6	26	1
North Carolina	76	6	4	12
North Dakota	43	50	3	1
Ohio	50	43	0	1

Table 11.1—(Cont'd)
DISPOSITION OF 2006 STATE HIGHWAY USER FEES (PERCENT)

State	State Roads	Local Roads	Transit	General Funds
Oklahoma	62	3	0	30
Oregon	73	11	3	2
Pennsylvania	90	6	1	1
Rhode Island	46	3	20	24
South Carolina	65	10	1	18
South Dakota	63	1	0	27
Tennessee	61	23	3	8
Texas	41	3	1	52
Utah	75	19	0	1
Vermont	40	24	0	35
Virginia	69	19	4	2
Washington	52	37	2	2
Washington, D.C.	0	78	11	0
West Virginia	95	0	0	2
Wisconsin	45	40	8	3
Wyoming	77	18	0	0
Total	60	19	6	12

SOURCE: *Highway Statistics 2006* (Washington: Federal Highway Administration, 2007), table SDF.

NOTE: Distribution of total highway revenues, including fuel taxes, vehicle fees, and tolls. Most state totals do not add up to 100percent; the difference is collection expenses.

operations, thus hurting transit users. The 2008 financial meltdown, for example, has forced scores of transit agencies to make or plan severe cuts in service.[8]

When gas prices rose in 2007 and 2008, transit watchers were treated to the spectacle of agencies having to cut service during a time of record demand because their fuel costs rose faster than transit fares. This would not have been an issue if agencies relied on user fees to cover most or all of their expenses.

Proposals for State and Local Transportation

Federal funds can heavily influence transportation decisions because state and local officials so often view federal money as "free"

Table 11.2
2006 HIGHWAY DATA BY STATE

State	User Fees	Diversions	Taxes	Expenses	Subsidy
Alabama	$1,661	$94	$1,269	$2,813	1.2¢
Alaska	258	31	331	792	6.6
Arizona	1,810	124	1,235	2,634	0.8
Arkansas	1,073	70	209	1,299	0.4
California	12,620	2,915	4,370	13,242	0.1
Colorado	2,022	120	743	2,367	0.4
Connecticut	1,316	323	221	1,094	−0.4
Delaware	545	14	123	742	1.3
Florida	7,241	527	2,746	9,582	0.7
Georgia	2,399	388	1,197	3,313	0.5
Hawaii	477	100	44	549	0.4
Idaho	573	30	96	788	0.9
Illinois	4,746	185	1,230	6,168	0.8
Indiana	2,699	125	343	2,725	0.0
Iowa	1,373	77	680	1,860	0.9
Kansas	1,086	62	725	1,813	1.5
Kentucky	1,878	84	229	1,843	0.0
Louisiana	1,502	83	856	2,450	1.3
Maine	599	25	252	875	1.1
Maryland	3,077	1,077	421	2,698	−0.4
Massachusetts	2,002	790	1,448	2,793	0.9
Michigan	3,301	274	1,589	4,691	0.8
Minnesota	1,937	93	1,281	3,721	1.9
Mississippi	1,090	98	250	1,485	0.6
Missouri	1,974	116	992	3,176	1.1
Montana	551	72	79	775	1.2
Nebraska	714	33	643	1,305	1.9
Nevada	1,137	55	257	1,564	1.2
New Hampshire	697	22	62	748	0.2
New Jersey	3,413	625	1,146	4,140	0.6
New Mexico	985	308	235	1,023	0.1
New York	6,949	2,140	3,444	9,829	1.2
North Carolina	3,318	494	1,039	3,690	0.2
North Dakota	334	22	171	600	2.1
Ohio	4,473	218	856	4,917	0.2
Oklahoma	1,859	451	176	1,553	−0.4

Table 11.2—(Cont'd)
2006 HIGHWAY DATA BY STATE

State	User Fees	Diversions	Taxes	Expenses	Subsidy
Oregon	1,392	102	357	1,928	0.9
Pennsylvania	5,413	283	1,026	6,281	0.5
Rhode Island	361	145	83	500	1.0
South Carolina	1,464	234	273	1,737	0.3
South Dakota	347	71	313	761	2.8
Tennessee	2,290	267	193	1,865	−0.4
Texas	11,437	4,332	2,520	12,960	0.4
Utah	808	42	410	1,190	0.9
Vermont	296	85	141	430	1.0
Virginia	3,188	287	1,295	3,606	0.3
Washington	2,394	155	804	3,609	1.3
Washington, D.C.	149	18	96	281	2.2
West Virginia	901	43	261	1,342	1.3
Wisconsin	2,134	243	1,884	3,650	1.6
Wyoming	357	18	178	532	1.1
Total/Average	$116,621	$18,592	$42,459	$146,329	0.6¢

SOURCE: *Highway Statistics 2006* (Washington: Federal Highway Administration, 2007), tables FE-9, LDF, LGF-1, LGF-2, SDF, SF-1, SF-2, and VM-2.

NOTE: Federal, state, and local user fees paid by highway users; diversions from those user fees to nonhighway projects; general taxes spent on highways; and total highway expenditures by state are all in millions of dollars. Subsidy represents the excess of expenditures over user fees in cents per passenger mile. Negative subsidy means highway users paid more than was spent on roads in that state. User fees plus taxes minus diversions will not equal expenses; the difference is interest, bond proceeds, and carry over from previous years. Total taxes include $1.6 billion of federal general funds spent on roads, mostly on federal lands and not broken down by state. Total highway expenditures include $3 billion required to collect gas taxes and other user fees.

money. In fact, state and local governments spend roughly four times as much of their own funds on transportation as the federal government spends. So reforming state and local transportation policies is proportionately more important.

The most important step toward fixing state and local transportation policies is to put transportation on a user-fee basis. This is easier

Table 11.3
2006 TRANSIT DATA FOR 60 MAJOR URBAN AREAS

	Operating Ratio (%)	Transit Trips per Capita	Transit Passenger Miles per Capita	Auto Passenger Miles per Capita	Share of Motorized Passenger Miles (%)
New York	70	195	1,089	9,969	9.8
Los Angeles	25	55	247	13,272	1.8
Chicago	36	72	466	11,832	3.8
Miami	19	31	160	14,767	1.1
Philadelphia	37	66	306	12,061	2.5
Dallas	12	19	111	14,893	0.7
Houston	18	24	139	13,573	1.0
Washington, D.C.	40	110	567	13,414	4.1
Boston	36	95	443	13,486	3.2
Atlanta	31	37	220	18,341	1.2
Detroit	12	13	78	15,506	0.5
Phoenix	19	20	88	14,033	0.6
San Francisco	35	111	630	13,052	4.6
Seattle	18	59	385	14,445	2.6
San Diego	36	35	209	14,638	1.4
Minn.-St. Paul	28	35	166	15,357	1.1
Tampa-St. Pete.	20	11	58	17,106	0.3
Baltimore	27	51	327	14,420	2.2
St. Louis	21	25	133	17,735	0.7
Denver	21	42	230	14,981	1.5
Riverside	18	11	58	13,916	0.4
Portland	23	62	270	11,858	2.2
Cleveland	18	41	172	13,256	1.3
Pittsburgh	22	42	189	13,154	1.4
San Jose	13	26	109	13,697	0.8
Cincinnati	28	19	99	15,555	0.6
Sacramento	18	23	109	13,255	0.8
Las Vegas	41	46	156	13,243	1.2
Norfolk	25	17	76	14,394	0.5
San Antonio	15	30	124	15,528	0.8
Kansas City	13	11	46	18,189	0.3
Milwaukee	31	39	120	15,312	0.8
Indianapolis	19	8	40	13,521	0.3
Orlando	22	20	129	19,052	0.7
Providence	28	18	92	13,208	0.7
Columbus	20	13	53	15,930	0.3

Table 11.3—(Cont'd)
2006 TRANSIT DATA FOR 60 MAJOR URBAN AREAS

	Operating Ratio (%)	Transit Trips per Capita	Transit Passenger Miles per Capita	Auto Passenger Miles per Capita	Share of Motorized Passenger Miles (%)
Austin	4	35	132	12,663	1.0
Memphis	20	12	63	16,286	0.4
Buffalo	24	25	85	13,951	0.6
Salt Lake City	17	22	170	13,699	1.2
Jacksonville	26	12	73	21,617	0.3
Norwalk	30	11	32	13,264	0.2
Charlotte	16	24	119	19,683	0.6
Hartford	26	19	127	14,978	0.8
Louisville	12	17	65	16,557	0.4
Richmond	27	17	58	18,285	0.3
Nashville	25	10	49	24,416	0.2
Oklahoma City	14	4	19	21,407	0.1
Tucson	16	23	85	14,110	0.6
Honolulu	27	97	459	10,400	4.2
El Paso	17	18	86	11,511	0.7
Dayton	17	19	71	16,135	0.4
Rochester	23	18	63	14,497	0.4
New Orleans	4	16	58	13,223	0.4
Albuquerque	11	13	45	13,198	0.3
Birmingham	12	6	29	22,022	0.1
Omaha	21	6	20	12,795	0.2
Raleigh	24	9	28	20,942	0.1
McAllen, Tex.	11	0	1	8,185	0.0
Allentown	16	9	41	12,697	0.3

SOURCES: *2006 National Transit Database* (Washington: Federal Highway Administration, 2007), spreadsheets "operating expenses" and "service"; *Highway Statistics 2006* (Washington: Federal Highway Administration, 2007), table HM-72; *2006 American Community Survey* (Washington: Census Bureau, 2007), table B01003 for urbanized areas.

Operating ratio is the share of operating expenses covered by transit fares. Transit trips per capita is the number of transit trips taken by the average resident of each urbanized area shown. Transit systems in Denver, Los Angeles, Riverside, San Francisco, and Salt Lake City serve multiple urban areas; populations of Boulder, Mission Viejo, Temecula, Concord, Ogden, and Provo-Orem urban areas are included in calculations of per capita trips and passenger miles.

said than done, however, partly because so many interest groups stand to benefit from the current system of subsidies.

Ideally, the institutions managing transportation facilities should be insulated from politics. Many states attempted to achieve this by amending their constitutions to dedicate gas taxes exclusively to highways. Over time, those dedications have eroded, and highway officials who have seen user fees diverted to other programs must beg politicians for other funds.

A few states, including Alaska, New Jersey, Rhode Island, and the District of Columbia, put all gas taxes into the state's general funds, and then the legislature appropriates those funds back to highways. Even if they get back all the funds that highway users paid, this leaves transportation officials as much or more beholden to politicians than to highway users.

The best insulation is to allow transportation officials to collect and keep user fees without requiring them to pass through the legislative process. Most regional toll road authorities and transit agencies, for example, keep 100 percent of the tolls and fares they collect and do not go through state or local appropriations processes to do so.

That works as long as agency goals are narrowly defined. However, the New York Metropolitan Transportation Authority, which manages both interborough bridges and transit, freely uses the revenues collected from bridge tolls to subsidize subways. Similarly, rail transit advocates in Texas recently proposed merging a San Antonio toll road authority with the city's transit agency so that toll revenues could subsidize a light-rail line (though they would explicitly prohibit the merged agency from using transit fares to subsidize a toll road).[9] Such inequitable arrangements reduce the efficiency of our transportation systems and weaken the links between users and providers.

Perhaps the best insulation against political interference would be to privatize transportation facilities. A government toll or transit agency might build up a large reserve fund so that it could rebuild its roads or rail lines when needed, but that fund could well be confiscated by politicians searching for funds for their favorite projects. A private entity that built up a cash reserve would be much less at risk. Privatization would also help promote technological innovations. Although immediate privatization is unlikely, state and local agencies can take the following steps toward improved transportation management.

1. Reform Highway Funding

a. Capitalize existing toll roads. In 2006, a consortium of private companies paid $3.8 billion for a 75-year lease of the Indiana Toll Road. The same consortium of Spanish and Australian companies also paid $1.8 billion for a 99-year lease of the Chicago Skyway. Though sometimes called "privatization," the roads in fact remain in public ownership; a better term would be "capitalization" because Indiana and Chicago received the capital value of the lease up front. The terms of the lease require the private operators to maintain the highways in good condition and add new capacity as needed to relieve congestion.

The governor of Indiana announced that the state was going to use the money it received for leasing the tollway to build new roads elsewhere in the state. As other toll agencies looked at the possibility of capitalizing their roads, however, a backlash grew, largely prompted by people who did not want new roads. One of the more absurd arguments they gave was that we shouldn't "sell" our roads to foreign companies—as if those companies could somehow fold up the roads and take them away.

The reality is that countries in Europe and elsewhere in the world have been franchising roads for many years, while this is still a new concept in the United States. Naturally, the only companies geared up to manage franchised roads are located outside the country. If many more states start capitalizing or franchising transportation facilities, no doubt American investors will become interested. In the meantime, having foreign companies invest in roads is no different from having them invest in shopping malls or other major structures.

One legitimate problem with long-term leases is the question of intergenerational equity. Highway users are likely to be paying tolls to the Chicago Skyway lessee for many decades after whatever the $1.8 billion is spent on is worn out and replaced. Leases of existing toll roads should not be for more than about 30 years, a typical lifespan of transportation projects.

b. Pay for all new capacity with tolls, preferably built by regional toll authorities or franchisees. Even though adding tolls to existing free

224

roads would be a good way to reduce congestion, people are naturally resistant to paying tolls for roads they think they have already
paid for out of gas taxes. Tolling of new capacity is more acceptable,
especially if that new capacity reduces congestion. Regional toll
authorities or private franchisees are likely to build new roads in
the least amount of time for the lowest cost.

c. Pay for major reconstruction with tolls. All transportation facilities
(such as a rail line) need periodic reconstruction or replacement,
and tolling such new construction is another way of phasing in
variable tolls as a replacement for gas taxes. All of these tolls, of
course, should be collected electronically.

d. Transition to vehicle-mile fees to pay for local roads and streets. Not
every highway is congested enough to require variable-priced tolls.
But gas taxes are increasingly ineffective as a way to fund transportation. Vehicle-mile fees would allow state and local governments as
well as private franchisees or highway owners to collect for the
actual use of their roads.

e. Reform highway planning. Proposals 2 and 3 in chapter 10 urge
Congress to make cost-efficiency the ruling criterion for spending
federal funds on transportation and to create a citizen enforcement
process to monitor this. In the event that Congress does not do so,
state legislatures could create a similar goal and process for state
and local spending. This process would especially apply to the use
of federal funds and other funds that are not directly tied to users,
i.e., funds other than tolls and transit fares.

2. Reform the Transit Industry

Our socialized transit model is broken; state and local governments must step up to fix it. Transit agencies, which were originally
created to provide economical mobility to low-income and other
disadvantaged people, have transmogrified into monster bureaucracies with voracious appetites for tax dollars to fund increasingly
costly transit schemes. The solution, as with highways, is a step-by-
step process that relies on user fees, increases private-sector involvement, and creates competition.

One proposal to improve transit has been to use more public-
private partnerships. But transit public-private partnerships are very
different from the partnerships that have successfully built new

highways in many European countries. Under a highway public-private partnership, the government gives a private highway company a franchise to build a road or bridge. The company finances the project completely with its own or borrowed funds and then charges tolls. After a specified number of years, the tolls end, and the highway is turned over to public ownership. This is called a "build-operate-transfer" contract.

Under transit public-private partnerships, a transit agency specifies a project and then asks a private company to build it. The public agency provides most if not all of the construction funds. Once completed, the private company may also operate it, and the public agency continues to provide operating subsidies. This is called a "design-build-maintain-operate" contract.

The difference between the highway and transit models is obvious: In one, the private company provides its own finances and takes the risk that tolls may not cover the costs. In the other, the public agency accepts all the losses and risks, and the private company is guaranteed a profit. Unfortunately, the fading distinction between projects funded out of user fees and those funded out of taxes has allowed transit agencies to claim that highway and transit public-private partnerships are somehow the same. In reality, the transit projects are just one more way to disguise the huge subsidies going to the transit industry.

a. Contract out transit services to private operators. Most transit is directly provided by transit agencies, yet private operators have a proven record of providing transit at a lower cost. Contracting out transit would allow agencies to provide more service at a lower cost.

Colorado law requires Denver's Regional Transportation District to contract out half of its bus operations. In 2007, RTD spent $8.68 per vehicle mile on the buses it operated but paid private operators only $4.60 per vehicle mile for the buses they operated. The contractors lease, operate, and maintain RTD buses; hire the drivers (some of whom are unionized); and pay taxes that RTD is not liable for. Yet they manage to do all this, plus earn a profit, for just 53 percent of RTD's costs.

If contracting out can save so much money, why don't all agencies do it for all their operations? A few, such as in Las Vegas, do, but in 2007, only 8 percent of transit trips and 11 percent of passenger miles nationwide were carried by private contractors. The reason is union pressure: since most contractors are not unionized, the unions prefer to deal with public agencies.

b. Open transit operations to private competitors. Private companies like SuperShuttle and CoachUSA operate thriving airport services. Why can't people take these buses to work or other major urban destinations? The answer in most states, particularly those not in the Sunbelt, is that private bus operators are not allowed to operate scheduled service except to and from airports. Opening service to private competition would spur transit agencies to improve their services.

Companies like SuperShuttle, for example, use a "demand-response" model of transit, picking people up and dropping them off at their doors on a reservation basis. Most transit agencies also offer demand-responsive services, but only to seniors and disabled patrons. Because of the relatively small number of these customers, the cost of public demand-response operations is very high: Taxpayers spent, on average, more than $26 per ride in 2007. Increased patronage would reduce the average cost, and private competition would no doubt lead public agencies to open up their demand-responsive services to everyone.

Private transit operators can do more than provide demand-responsive services. They can offer scheduled services like the Atlantic City jitneys and innovative new services like NY Waterway ferries.

Public transit advocates argue that private operators would "skim the cream" of transit operations, taking the most profitable routes and leaving the dregs to the public agencies. So what if this is true? Under the current model, public agencies lose money on virtually all their operations because their costs are so high. Both transit riders and taxpayers would benefit if private operators cut some of these losses.

c. Consider providing transportation stamps. Many people believe that taxpayers should subsidize transit to provide mobility for those who, due to age, income, or disabilities, are not able to drive. However, proposal 1 in chapter 10 would eliminate federal funding for transit to these groups. The grants that would be eliminated are not actually given to low-income or other disadvantaged people but are given instead to state and local transportation agencies that claim to be helping these people.

Instead of feeding transit bureaucracies, state and local governments that want to provide such subsidies should give them directly to transit users. Such vouchers or "transit stamps" could be applied to any public conveyance, from taxis to airlines. Transit providers would have to compete for this business as well as any other business they can attract.

3. Implement an Advanced Highway Technology Initiative

Twenty-first-century surface transportation will not be dominated by light rail or any form of public transit. Instead, it will improve on the personal transportation that produced such a huge increase in mobility in the 20th century. The next technological step is to turn driver-controlled automobiles into self-driving automobiles.

By greatly increasing average travel speeds, reducing fatalities and accidents, and increasing the amount of traffic that can be carried by existing roads, driverless motor vehicles will have economic and social impacts as revolutionary as the construction of the interstate highway system. The technology for such driverless automobiles already exists, and the only remaining barriers are institutional.

Rapid technological improvements in the telecommunications and computer industries have greatly increased American productivities. These improvements have crucially depended upon the development of standards by equipment manufacturers, communications providers, and software developers. State transportation departments should emulate this process by working with automobile manufacturers to create driverless highway and vehicle standards and implement those standards as rapidly as possible.

Several questions remain: Should all of the hardware and software for driverless vehicles be in the vehicles themselves, or should it be split between the vehicles and the highways? Should some highways be dedicated exclusively for driverless vehicles? Should driverless vehicles be integrated in traffic with driver-operated vehicles? Finding the best answers to these and similar questions could greatly reduce the cost, magnify the benefits, and speed the adaptation of driverless systems.

12. Conclusions

The history of America is the history of mechanized mobility. When America was founded, humans, animals, wind, or water flows powered all transportation. Today, the average American relies on mechanized forms of transportation to travel tens of thousands of miles and ship tens of thousands of ton-miles of goods per year. It has been an amazing transformation, one not replicated anywhere else in the world. Understanding that transformation provides the keys to promoting mobility in the 21st century.

Railroads and waterways have allowed Americans to move vast amounts of freight at low cost. But the only form of transportation that has significantly added to personal mobility is the automobile. The average American today travels 10 times as many miles by car each year as most Americans traveled by rail and urban transit during the golden age of streetcars and intercity passenger rails. The average American travels more than 12 times as many miles by car as the average European travels by bus and train combined.

Automobiles are also the most egalitarian form of mechanized travel. Close to 19 out of 20 American families own or lease at least one automobile, and many who live without a car do so out of choice, not economic hardship. Because time, not cost, is the limiting factor to travel for most Americans, people whose incomes are in the lowest 20 percent probably drive almost as much as those whose incomes are in the highest 20 percent. Unlike streetcars, oceanliners, high-speed rail, and private jets, the automobile provides mobility for the masses, not just an elite.

The automobile's convenience and flexibility in providing door-to-door transport on demand, rather than on someone else's timetable, makes it more valuable than its competitors. This flexibility gives Americans far greater choices about where they live, where they work, where they shop, and whom they visit. Significantly, an important component of the campaign to encourage Americans to drive less and use transit more is built around land-use regulations and subsidies aimed at changing people's housing and shopping choices.

Despite the automobile's greater value, it has a much lower cost than most of its competitors. Including subsidies, the total cost per passenger mile of traveling by auto is less than half as much as Amtrak and less than a third as much as public transit. In addition, a car can carry more than the average number of people used for these cost estimates at little or no extra cost. Families traveling on Amtrak or public transit receive little or no discount, but four or five people can pile into a car that costs, on average, 38 cents per vehicle mile and reduce the cost per passenger mile to 7.5 to 9.5 cents.

Government bureaucracy and ineptitude may account for some of the high cost of Amtrak and transit , but the cost of these modes, including subsidies, will not likely ever drop as low as the cost of driving. Rail transport has always been more expensive than driving. In 1930, the earliest year for which data are available, Americans spent an average of 2.7 cents per passenger mile riding trains and 3.3 cents per vehicle mile driving.[1] Any car with more than one occupant—and in 1930, most of them did have more—cost far less than riding trains.

Building up intercity rail and urban transit service so that they can compete with the automobile's convenience is not a realistic option—it would be prohibitively expensive. In 2007, Americans spent 9.2 percent of their personal incomes on driving and another 0.6 percent on all other forms of passenger transportation. To substitute transit for driving, people would have to devote more than 30 percent of their incomes to transportation.[2]

The specter of high energy prices will not significantly change this calculus. For one thing, intercity rail and urban transit require about as much energy as driving; those who ride these modes to save on energy costs are merely passing their costs onto the taxpayers who subsidize them. For another, the long-term response to high oil prices is not to stop driving but to drive more fuel-efficient cars. When gasoline prices doubled in 2008, people reduced their driving by a mere 4 percent. But if prices had remained high, they would have purchased more economical cars and returned to former levels of driving.

One reason Americans are so much more mobile than people in any other country is that our governments, in general, have not tried to socially engineer people's travel and housing choices through punitive taxation, regulation, and subsidies to favored forms of transportation. That is changing, however, as anti-mobility forces use threats of global warming, obesity, and other alleged crises to justify increasingly intrusive government interference in American lifestyles. Even if the dangers of global warming or energy shortages are real, no evidence supports the anti-mobility ideas that more compact cities and greater transit subsidies will solve those problems, much less that they are the most cost-effective solutions.

Nor can urban redesign substitute accessibility for mobility. Consumers today enjoy low prices because they can reach multiple, competing outlets for the goods they seek. They can choose from a broad selection of products because each retail store serves tens to hundreds of thousands of customers who have a diverse range of tastes. Attempts to put stores within walking distances of residences would lose both of these advantages.

Americans take their mobility for granted, so politicians and planners can easily talk casually about reducing per capita driving and substituting accessibility for mobility. Many people imagine that such proposals will not affect them. As *The Onion* once humorously noted, "98 percent of Americans support the use of mass transit by others."[3] But America's mobility advantage is a major reason why Americans have higher incomes, lower consumer costs, and many other benefits not enjoyed by much of the rest of the world.

At the same time, Americans should understand that existing technologies have just about reached the limits of their abilities to further increase personal mobility. Motor vehicles may contain hundreds of microprocessors underneath their sheet metal skins, but—except for the few that have adaptive cruise control—their ability to operate on highways and interact with other vehicles is no different than it was 50 or 60 years ago. Highways may have a few electronic signs capable of warning about congestion ahead, but fundamentally our roadways are based on designs developed during or prior to the 1950s.

Historically, the key to improving personal mobility has been new technologies offering higher average speeds. Reduced costs are also important, but speed is the most important issue because—given people's travel-time budgets—higher speeds mean access to more resources.

Yet contrary to media hype, high-speed rail is not the next great transport revolution. On a per capita basis, the Japanese and French have spent roughly the same on high-speed trains as the United States spent on interstate highways, yet they produced less than a tenth of the personal mobility and no improvements in freight transport. The fact that high-speed trains require huge subsidies while the interstates were paid for out of user fees further underscores the ineffectiveness of passenger rail as a form of mobility. Aside from its high cost, the flaw of high-speed rail is that, unlike personal transport, it doesn't go where people want to go.

No form of mass transportation, not trains, not planes, and not buses, has ever provided any nation with as much as 2,000 miles of per capita mobility per year—in other words, less than a seventh of the mobility Americans gain from the automobile. Thus, the next transportation revolution will involve personal transportation, meaning a qualitative, not just quantitative, change in automobiles. In short, that means driverless vehicles. The advantages of such vehicles are considerable: four times the capacity of a given area of roadway, higher average speeds, increased safety, and reduced energy costs. Unless the anti-mobility coalition has its way, driverless cars will be commonplace in 2050. The only question is whether they will be commonplace by 2020 or have to wait another decade or two.

If our highway model is obsolete, our public transit model is completely broken. Instead of efficiently serving the public by providing cost-effective transportation for those who cannot or do not want to drive, transit agencies have developed insatiable demands for more tax revenues. Is there an economic boom leading to higher ridership? Then transit agencies demand higher taxes to accommodate the new riders. Is there a recession reducing the tax revenues that support transit? Then transit agencies demand a larger share of taxes to make up the difference. Does a rise in gas prices lead to record ridership? Then transit agencies need more taxes because they, too, must pay higher fuel prices.

Transit systems that depend on taxes to cover three-fourths of their costs are not sustainable. Ironically, transit only seems to work at all because hardly anyone uses it. To operate transit systems carrying a much higher fraction of personal travel would bankrupt the nation.

Consider the problems in the New York urban area. New York's transit system carries more than 40 percent of the nation's transit riders and more than twice the share of regional travel of any other transit system in the nation. Fares cover a third of transit costs, which is higher than the national average. But the region's transit system is in a perpetual fiscal crisis; one reason costs are only three times revenues, instead of four, is that maintenance has been deferred on many of the region's rail lines. Even before the current financial crisis, New York's Metropolitan Transportation Authority projected a $17 billion deficit over the next five years.[4] Recent debates over so-called congestion pricing in Manhattan have really been about finding new sources of money to keep the transit system going.[5]

While it is wonderful to think that we are rich enough to afford expensive but little-used monuments like high-speed trains and urban rail transit systems in cities like Charlotte and Honolulu, the current recession shows we are not. What these things really mean is that a small group of rail contractors and riders get to sponge off the taxes collected from nearly everyone else.

The Obama administration justifies its support of high-speed rail and rail transit on the supposed environmental benefits. But the nation's automobile and airline fleets have historically improved their energy efficiencies by 1 to 3 percent per year, and technologies now under development offer every reason to believe that the trend will continue. Given that record, virtually no passenger rail projects being considered today will save any energy over their lifetimes when compared with driving or flying. Further, rail lines powered by diesel or by electricity generated from burning fossil fuels will typically produce more greenhouse gases per passenger mile than driving or flying. As we develop more sources of renewable electricity, applying that electricity to plug-in hybrids or other electric autos will do more for mobility and reducing emissions than building passenger rail lines.

A major part of the problem here is the mental disconnect between user fees and taxes. When people learn that the government has spent more than $400 billion building interstate highways and only about $200 billion building urban rail transit and intercity high-speed rail, they think it is only fair to spend more on rail. Most will ignore the fact that the highways carry 35 times as many passenger miles as all rail lines put together. The real difference is that the interstates were entirely paid for out of user fees while rail fares have failed to cover the operating costs, much less the capital costs, of any rail line. The glee that high-speed rail advocates feel when subsidized trains put profitable airlines out of business is similarly misplaced.

The distinction between user fees and subsidies is far more important than the difference in costs between different modes of travel. Rail transit's and Amtrak's high costs would not be an issue if passengers found train travel valuable enough to pay those costs, but they don't. To attract passengers, both Amtrak and urban transit agencies set fare prices to be roughly competitive with the cost of driving and expect taxpayers to pick up the difference.

Paying for transportation out of user fees has three advantages over paying out of taxes. First, user fees are fair: the people who get transportation benefits, or at least the vast majority of those benefits, are the ones who pay the costs.

Second, user fees promote efficiency. If people are willing to pay for something out of user fees, it is likely to be efficient, that is, the benefits are greater than the costs. Whether the goal is to improve mobility, reduce air emissions, or save energy, the most efficient ways to achieve that goal are preferable—because a dollar wasted is a dollar no longer available to spend toward that goal.

Third, and perhaps most important, user fees send signals to both users and providers about the value of various kinds of transportation in various places. Fully functioning user fees would let people know that it costs more to provide the capacity to meet peak-period demands than to meet average demand and would let transportation providers know how much people are willing to pay for that added capacity. Funding transportation out of taxes shortcuts such signals—which is, after all, why we have congestion, decrepit bridges, and transportation agencies that insist on high-cost solutions to mobility problems.

Currently, federal transportation programs are not much more than transfers of funds from powerless taxpayers to powerful interest groups. To promote more efficient transportation programs, the best thing Congress can do is to turn over all surface transportation funding and decisionmaking to the states. Short of ending federal control of those programs, Congress should follow the first three recommendations in chapter 10: (1) base the distribution of federal funds on state and local user fees; (2) insist that programs aimed at saving energy and reducing the environmental effects of transportation be cost-efficient; and (3) create a citizen enforcement process to ensure that federal funds are efficiently or cost-efficiently spent.

State and local governments should incrementally privatize transportation facilities and programs, or at least rely more heavily on user fees rather than taxes to pay for transportation. New highways should be paid for with tolls. Public transit should be opened to private competition. Subsidies aimed at providing mobility for low-income and other disadvantaged people should be given directly to those people in the form of transportation stamps rather than to transit bureaucracies.

These ideas will improve the short-term efficiency of America's transportation networks. To smooth the path for the next revolution in transportation technology, states—as the owners of most of the nation's major highways—should work with automakers to develop standards for driverless vehicles and highways and accelerate the implementation of those standards. Given that America's automobile fleet turns over every 18 years, a transition to mostly driverless roads could be complete well before 2030. Without an accelerated program, it could take several decades more.

Chapter 1 examined American transportation in 1800, 1850, 1900, 1950, and 2000. What will 2050 will be like? Anti-mobility forces want to reduce the growth in driving, reduce driving speeds, and encourage people to use other, often slower methods of travel. They hope to achieve these goals by increasing the cost of driving through higher fuel taxes, greater parking fees, and increased traffic congestion. Their objective is to make American travel patterns similar to Europe's—in other words, similar to American travel patterns in around 1950.

Their success would have dire effects on the American economy. Incomes would be lower because average travel speeds would be slower, and employers would have access to a smaller pool of workers. Mobility would be much less egalitarian, as cost rather than time would limit auto travel for far more people than today, and premium-priced high-speed trains would serve mainly a wealthy elite. Housing would cost significantly more—and a stated goal of smart-growth planners is to significantly reduce the share of American families that enjoy the benefits of living in a single-family home. The environmental benefits that would accompany this costly and unfair future are, at best, slight.

A pro-mobility alternative rests on three pillars. First, transportation funding must come from user fees, not general tax dollars. User-fee-driven transportation networks are less likely to become tools for political pork barrel and more likely to focus on the most efficient forms of transport. Second, efforts to reduce the environmental and social costs of transportation must be cost efficient. If the recent recession has taught us anything, it is that we cannot fund every conceivable project just because it feels good.

Finally, mobility advocates must promote new technologies that can increase transportation speeds and personal mobility. Electronic tolling, congestion pricing, and various forms of smart highways and smart vehicles can eliminate congestion, improve fuel efficiency, and increase safety. If they also increase average ground transportation speeds from 34 to 48 miles per hour, these technologies will again double people's access to jobs and resources. Such a doubling contributed to the 160 percent increase in per capita incomes between 1950 and 2000 and could do so again by 2050.

Transportation provides the wheels that turn the American economy. For most of the past two centuries, those wheels turned faster every year. But thanks to poorly designed funding systems, increasingly politicized decisionmaking, and a misguided anti-mobility movement, the wheels have begun to slow.

Americans have a choice. We can spend tens or hundreds of billions of taxpayer dollars on transportation projects that sound good but really serve only a small elite. Or we can restore a user-fee-driven system that will continue to improve personal mobility and reduce transportation costs for generations to come. The former may fit Europe's and Japan's aristocratic heritage. To best serve our way of life, America must choose mobility over image.

Notes

Introduction

1. Eric Wolf, "Transit Authority," *New York Sun*, November 26, 2004, tinyurl.com/84phr7.

2. *Highway Capacity Manual* (Washington: Transportation Research Board, 2000), p. 11-5.

3. With apologies to residents of other countries in the western hemisphere, this book will use the term "America" and "Americans" to refer to the nation and residents of the United States.

4. David Schrank and Tim Lomax, *The 2009 Urban Mobility Report* (College Station, TX: Texas Transportation Institute, 2009), p. 1, tinyurl.com/mk6rvn.

5. Mark Rose, Bruce Seely, and Paul Barrett, *The Best Transportation System in the World: Railroads, Trucks, Airlines, and American Public Policy in the Twentieth Century* (Columbus, OH: Ohio State University Press, 2006), p. 102.

6. Pat S. Hu and Timothy R. Reuscher, *Summary of Travel Trends: 2001 National Household Travel Survey* (Washington: Federal Highway Administration, 2004), p. 45, tinyurl.com/2xsqa6.

Chapter 1

1. *National Transportation Statistics* (Washington: Bureau of Transportation Statistics, 2008), table 1-37.

2. *Panorama of Transport* (Brussels: European Commission, 2007), p. 103; "Summary of Transportation Statistics," Ministry of Land, Infrastructure and Transport, 2008, tinyurl.com/23py4r.

3. *National Transportation Statistics* (2008), table 1-46b.

4. *Panorama of Transport*, p. 68.

5. Rémy Prud'homme and Chang-Woon Lee, "Size, Sprawl, Speed, and the Efficiency of Cities," *Urban Studies* 36, no. 11 (1999): 1849–58.

6. Robert Cervero, "Efficient Urbanization: Economic Performance and the Shape of the Metropolis," *Urban Studies* 38, no. 10 (2001): 1651–71.

7. M. Ishaq Nadiri and Theofanis P. Mamuneas, "Effects of Public Infrastructure and R&D Capital on the Cost Structure and Performance of U.S. Manufacturing Industries," *Review of Economics and Statistics* 76, no. 1 (1994): 22–37.

8. William I. Walsh, *The Rise and Decline of the Great Atlantic & Pacific Tea Company* (Secaucus, NJ: Lyle Stuart, 1986), p. 29.

9. "Happy Birthday, Supermarket!" *Progressive Grocer*, August 2005.

10. Bureau of Economic Analysis, "Personal Incomes Expenditures by Type of Expenditure," in *National Income and Production Accounts* (Washington: Department of Commerce, 2008), table 2.5.5, tinyurl.com/mgxv7d.

11. Warren Brown, "Automobile Played Role on Long Ride to Freedom," *Washington Post*, September 5, 2004, p. G-2.

12. Jane Holtz Kay, *Asphalt Nation: How the Automobile Took over America and How We Can Take It Back* (New York: Crown, 1997), pp. 22–23.

13. A lengthier discussion of the benefits of mobility can be found in Randal O'Toole, *The Best-Laid Plans* (Washington: Cato Institute, 2007), chapter 27, or in Randal O'Toole, *The Greatest Invention: How Automobiles Made America Great* (Bandon, OR: American Dream Coalition, 2006), tinyurl.com/3rzh2p.

14. Per capita gross domestic products for 1800 to the present are adjusted for inflation to 2007 dollars and are from "What Was the U.S. GDP Then?" Measuring Worth, 2009, tinyurl.com/bho8y7.

15. "The Stirrup," *UNESCO Courier*, October 1988, tinyurl.com/8unugd.

16. "Stagecoach Travel Tough but Worth It," Oregon Department of Transportation, 2009, tinyurl.com/d7jolw.

17. *Historical Statistics of the United States: Colonial Times to 1970* (Washington: Census Bureau, 1975), p. 12.

18. Angus Maddison, *The World Economy: Historical Statistics* (Paris: OECD Development Centre, 2001), table 4-1, tinyurl.com/obepqk.

19. *Historical Statistics of the United States: Colonial Times to 1970*, p. 756.

20. Ulysses S. Grant, *Personal Memoirs of U.S. Grant* (New York: Webster, 1885).

21. Norman Bel Geddes, *Magic Motorways* (New York: Random House, 1940), p. 150.

22. *Historical Statistics of the United States: Colonial Times to 1970*, p. 728.

23. Lucius Beebe, *20th Century: The Greatest Train in the World* (Berkeley, CA: Howell North, 1962), p. 14.

24. *Historical Statistics of the United States: Colonial Times to 1970*, p. 730.

25. Michael L. Berger, *The Devil Wagon in God's Country: The Automobile and Social Change in Rural America, 1893–1929* (Hamden, CT: Archon Books, 1979), p. 55.

26. Ibid.

27. "List of town tramway systems in the United States," Wikipedia, tinyurl.com/7za8zb.

28. Paul Barrett, "Chicago's Public Transportation Policy, 1900–1940s," Illinois Periodicals Online, 2001, tinyurl.com/ac7vry.

29. Floyd Clymer, *Treasury of Early American Automobiles 1877–1925* (New York: McGraw-Hill, 1950).

30. *Highway Statistics Summary to 1995* (Washington: Federal Highway Administration, 1996), table MV-200.

31. Paul Barrett, "Chicago's Public Transportation Policy, 1900–1940s."

32. *Historical Statistics of the United States: Colonial Times to 1970*, pp. 711, 729.

33. *Highway Statistics Summary to 1995*, table VM-201.

34. "Motorists Don't Make Socialists, They Say," *New York Times*, March 4, 1906, tinyurl.com/8lgrez.

35. Sylvia Adcock, "The Age of the Auto," *Newsday*, April 12, 1998, tinyurl.com/aywu8n.

36. *Highway Statistics Summary to 1995*, table MV-200.

37. Census Bureau, "Historical Census of Housing Tables—Homeownership," 2004, tinyurl.com/2m5j5j.

38. Peter Geoffrey Hall, *Cities of Tomorrow: An Intellectual History of Urban Planning and Design in the Twentieth Century* (Cambridge, MA: Blackwell, 2002), pp. 79–84.

39. Bureau of Economic Analysis, *National Income and Production Accounts*, tables 2.1 and 2.5.5.

40. *Historical Statistics of the United States: Colonial Times to 1970*, p. 769.

41. M. J. King, "Fear of Flying: Marketing Research and the Jet Crisis," *Journal of American Culture* 7 (1984): 122–27, tinyurl.com/cc2s6o.

42. *Historical Statistics of the United States: Colonial Times to 1970*, pp. 707, 728, 731.

43. Ibid, p. 707.

44. Mark Gillespie, "American Public Has Mixed Feelings on Airline Safety," Gallup, February 2, 2000, tinyurl.com/agzqjr.

45. Note that 34 squared is twice 24 squared.

46. Census Bureau, "Historical Census of Housing Tables," tinyurl.com/2m5j5j.

47. *Historical Statistics of the United States: Colonial Times to 1970*, series J72–J74; *Natural Resources Inventory: 2003 Annual NRI* (Washington: Natural Resources Conservation Service, 2007), p. 5, tinyurl.com/cljsvd.

48. *National Income and Production Accounts*, tables 2.1 and 2.5.5.

49. *National Transportation Statistics* (2008), table 3-16.

50. *National Income and Production Accounts*, table 2.5.5.

51. *2008 Public Transportation Fact Book* (Washington: American Public Transportation Association, 2008), tables 6 and 50.

52. *National Transportation Statistics* (2008), tables 1-37, 3-27a, and 3-29a.

53. *2001 Annual Report* (Washington: Amtrak, 2002), p. 4; *National Transportation Statistics* (2008), table 1-37; *2008 Public Transportation Fact Book*, tables 6, 37, 46, and 50.

54. *National Transportation Statistics* (2008), table 1-46a.

55. Albro Martin, *Railroads Triumphant: The Growth, Rejection, and Rebirth of a Vital American Force* (New York: Oxford, 1992).

56. Albro Martin, *Enterprise Denied: Origins of the Decline of American Railroads, 1897–1917* (New York: Columbia, 1971).

57. *National Transportation Statistics* (2008), table 1-46a.

58. Census Bureau, "Vehicles Available and Household Income in 1999," *Census 2000 Summary File 3* (Washington: Census Bureau, 2000), table QT-H11, geographic area: United States, tinyurl.com/d3o7n.

59. Yacov Zahava and James M. Ryan, "Stabilities in Travel Components over Time," *Transportation Research Record* 750 (1980): 19–26.

60. "Passenger Transportation," in *Transportation in Canada 2001* (Ottawa, ON: Transport Canada, 2001), chapter 12, tinyurl.com/cg8ko8.

61. Per capita GNP from Daniel Workman, "World's Richest Countries," Suite-101.com, 2006, tinyurl.com/amkuhl. Norwegian travel from "New Growth for Public Transport," Statistics Norway, 2006, tinyurl.com/bgzv93. Travel for other European countries from *Panorama of Transport*, pp. 103, 106. *Panorama* presents nation-by-nation numbers for ground travel and EU-25 numbers for air travel; to get per capita totals for individual countries, I added the EU-25 average for air travel to the ground numbers for each nation.

62. *Highway Statistics 2006* (Washington: Federal Highway Administration, 2007), table MF-121T.

63. "Oil and Gas Prices, Taxes, and Consumers," Finance Canada, 2006, tinyurl.com/cun8b4.

64. "Tax Rates on Unleaded Petrol, 2007," CESifo Group, 2007, tinyurl.com/bx2q4d.

65. *Highway Statistics 2005* (Washington: Federal Highway Administration, 2006), table FE-101b.

66. Rémy Prud'homme, "The Current EU Transport Policy in Perspective," paper presented at conference on European Transport Policy, European Parliament, Brussels, July 12, 2005, p. 1, tinyurl.com/b5suom.

67. Prud'homme and Lee, "Size, Sprawl, Speed, and the Efficiency of Cities."

Chapter 2

1. David Schrank and Tim Lomax, *The 2009 Urban Mobility Report* (College Station, TX: Texas Transportation Institute, 2009), p. 1, tinyurl.com/mk6rvn.

2. Ibid.

3. Economic Development Research Group, *The Cost of Congestion to the Economy of the Portland Region* (Portland, OR: Portland Business Alliance, 2005), pp. 13–14.

4. Alan Pisarski, *Commuting in America III* (Washington: Transportation Research Board, 2006), p. 47.

5. Census Bureau, "Journey to Work: 2000," *Census 2000 Brief* (March 2004): p. 5, tinyurl.com/chkjam.

6. Hu and Reuscher, *Summary of Travel Trends: 2001 National Household Travel Survey*, table 26, p. 45, tinyurl.com/2xsqa6.

7. Ibid.

8. *America's Infrastructure Report Card 2009* (Washington: American Society of Civil Engineers, 2009), tinyurl.com/ccgvsr.

9. Kristin Dross, "Battered Bridges," *CBS News*, August 2, 2007, tinyurl.com/dm6x8p.

10. Ea Torriero and Leora Falk, "Lawmaker Seeks Bridge Trust Fund; Plan Raises Gas Tax to Fund Repairs," *Chicago Tribune*, August 9, 2007, tinyurl.com/bgy93c.

11. Peter Cohn, "Oberstar Anticipates $450 Billion Highway Bill in 2009," *National Journal*, April 30, 2008, tinyurl.com/b7uwy3.

12. *Collapse of I-35W Highway Bridge, Minneapolis, Minnesota, August 1, 2007* (Washington: National Transportation Safety Board, 2008), p. xiii, tinyurl.com/cbd7g9.

13. "Deficient Bridges by State and Highway System," Structures, Federal Highway Administration, 2008, tinyurl.com/da9qqm.

14. *2006 Status of the Nation's Highways, Bridges, and Transit: Conditions and Performance* (Washington: Federal Highway Administration, 2007), p. 3-15, tinyurl.com/brvl62.

15. Ibid., p. 3-14.

16. Bureau of Transportation Statistics, "Condition of U.S. Highway Bridges," in *National Transportation Statistics*, 2008, table 1-27, tinyurl.com/at54jv.

17. "Deficient Bridges by State and Highway System," tinyurl.com/da9qqm.

18. "Condition of U.S. Highway Bridges," tinyurl.com/at54jv.

19. Chris LeRose, "The Collapse of the Silver Bridge," *West Virginia Historical Quarterly* 15, no. 4 (October 2001), tinyurl.com/c3ab9t.

20. Theodore V. Galambos, "The Safety of Bridges," *The Bridge* 38, no. 2 (Summer 2008): 21–22, tinyurl.com/ndhr36.

21. "Collapse of a Suspended Span of Route 95 Highway Bridge over the Mianus River," in *Highway Accident Report* (Washington: National Transportation Safety Board, 1984), tinyurl.com/dygnz3.

22. "Collapse of New York Thruway (I-90) Bridge Schoharie Creek," in *Highway Accident Report* (Washington: National Transportation Safety Board, 1988), tinyurl.com/9xbtdc.

23. "Tennessee Is Faulted in Collapse of Bridge," *New York Times*, June 6, 1990, tinyurl.com/9ktwvh.

24. *Transportation for Tomorrow: Report of the National Surface Transportation Policy and Revenue Study Commission* (Washington: Department of Transportation, 2007), pp. 59, 62, tinyurl.com/b7wb5z.

25. *Sellwood Bridge Project Draft Environmental Impact Statement* (Portland, OR: Metro, 2008), p. S-13.

26. "Metro Council Invests Federal Stimulus Money in Regional Transportation Projects," Metro, March 5, 2009, tinyurl.com/ctetxm.

27. "Today, President to Sign Blumenauer Projects for Oregon into Law," Rep. Earl Blumenauer (D-OR), March 11, 2009, tinyurl.com/dcrbsf.

28. Jon Craig, "Stimulus Funds Have Takers," *Cincinnati Enquirer*, February 25, 2009, tinyurl.com/bhb7ex; Larry Sandler, "U.S. Spending Bill Funds Milwaukee Streetcar System," *Milwaukee Journal-Sentinel*, March 13, 2009, tinyurl.com/cr2rwe; Andrea Kelly, "Downtown Streetcar Project Appears on Track," *Arizona Daily Star*, March 2, 2009, tinyurl.com/df2rrm; "Streetcars Headed Back to Washington," UPI, March 15, 2009, tinyurl.com/daxtwm.

29. Dom Nozzi, "Congestion Is Our Friend," *Gainesville Sun*, February 10, 2008, tinyurl.com/cszagx.

30. W. S. Homburger, *Transportation and Traffic Engineering Handbook*, 2nd edition (Englewood Cliffs, NJ: Prentice Hall, 1982).

31. Research Triangle Institute, *National Highway Safety Needs Study* (Chapel Hill, NC: RTI, 1976).

32. Letter from Harold J. McCurry, Retail Merchants Association of Sacramento, to Margaret Woolverton, Quinton Engineers, April 7, 1953.

33. Robert D. Pier, "One-Way Street Experience," *Traffic Engineering* (January 1950): p. 153.

34. City of Denver, *One-Way Street Monitoring Study: Phase 1 Conversion Report* (Denver, CO: City of Denver, January 1990), p. 29.

35. Pflum, Klausmeier & Gehrum Consultants, Inc., *Pennsylvania Street/Delaware Street/Central Avenue Analysis of Impacts Conversion to Two-Way Operation* (Indianapolis, IN: City of Indianapolis, 1999), p. 3.

36. City of Lubbock, "Main & 10th Street Accident Analysis Before/After Study," 1998.

37. David Thomas, "15 MPH Speed Limit to Force People Out of Cars," *London Telegraph*, March 24, 2008, tinyurl.com/c4ag3h.

38. Leslie W. Bunte, Jr., "Traffic Calming Programs & Emergency Response: A Competition of Two Public Goods," report prepared for Master of Public Affairs degree, University of Texas at Austin, 2000.

39. Bohannan Huston, *Albuquerque Downtown Core Street Network Assessment One-Way Conversion Study* (Albuquerque, NM: Bohannan Huston, 2000), p. 2.

40. "Implementing a Transportation Strategy for the 21st Century: Portland Metropolitan Area Federal Transportation Authorization Policy Priorities and Authorization and Appropriations Project Requests," Portland, OR, Metro, 2009, p. 58, Exhibit A to Resolution No. 09-4016, tinyurl.com/cuo2gx.

41. *Regional Transportation Plan* (Portland, OR: Metro, November 1999), p. 1-29.

42. Schrank and Lomax, *The 2007 Urban Mobility Report*, table "Mobility Data for Portland, OR," tinyurl.com/af2rs2.

43. James Mayer, "Wu's Offer of Highway Money Creates a Pileup," *The Oregonian*, July 3, 2006, p. E1.

44. *Portland-Milwaukie Light Rail Project Supplemental Draft Environmental Impact Statement* (Portland, OR: Metro, 2008), p. 5-3.

45. Ben Jacklet, "The Sellwood Solution?" *Portland Tribune*, May 13, 2005, tinyurl.com/br4ery.

46. *Sellwood Bridge Project Draft Environmental Impact Statement*, p. S-13.

47. "A History and Overview of Oregon Transportation Investment Act," Oregon Department of Transportation, 2007, tinyurl.com/cbgttj.

48. Testimony of Henry Hewitt, chair, Oregon Transportation Commission, before the State Senate Natural Resources Committee, April 1, 1998, West Linn, Oregon.

49. Eric Mortenson, "Metro's Wish List for Feds Ranks Desired Transportation Projects," *The Oregonian*, January 20, 2009.

50. Schrank and Lomax, *The 2007 Urban Mobility Report*, table "Mobility Data for Portland, OR"; *Highway Statistics Summary to 1995*, table VM-201; *Highway Statistics 2005*, table VM-1.

51. Census Bureau, "Ranking Tables for Incorporated Places of 100,000 or More: Population in 2000 and Population Change from 1990 to 2000," 2001, tinyurl.com/b57v8m.

52. Schrank and Lomax, *The 2007 Urban Mobility Report*, table "Mobility Data for Salem, OR," tinyurl.com/dgeznx.

53. *1980 Census* (Washington: Department of Commerce, 1982), table 118, "means of transportation to work," for urbanized areas; *1982 National Transit Database* (Washington: Federal Transit Administration, 1983), spreadsheet "417282"; David Schrank and Tim Lomax, *The 2005 Urban Mobility Report* (College Station, TX: Texas Transportation Institute, 2005), table "Mobility Data for Portland, OR."

54. *2007 American Community Survey* (Washington: Census Bureau, 2008), table S0801, "Commuting Characteristics by Sex," Portland, OR-WA Urbanized Area.

55. *2007 National Transit Database* (Washington: Federal Transit Administration, 2008), spreadsheet "service"; *Highway Statistics 2007* (Washington: Federal Highway Administration, 2008), table HM-71.

56. Robert Cervero, "Why Go Anywhere?" in *Fifty Years of City and Regional Planning at UC Berkeley: A Celebratory Anthology of Faculty Essays*, ed. Skip Lowney and John D. Landis (Berkeley, CA: Department of City and Regional Planning, 1998).

57. Dana Tims, "Road to Bigger, Better Damascus Leads to Dead End," *The Oregonian*, January 16, 2009, tinyurl.com/ahwwfa.

58. Sam Adams, "From Here to Portland's Tomorrow," speech to Portland City Club, July 20, 2007.

59. John Charles, *The Mythical World of Transit-Oriented Development* (Portland, OR: Cascade Policy Institute, 2001), tinyurl.com/336pt6.

60. Bruce Podobnik, *Portland Neighborhood Survey Report on Findings from Zone 2: Orenco* (Portland, OR: Lewis & Clark College, 2002), p. 1, tinyurl.com/2hhmwo.

61. Sharon Bernstein and Francisco Vara-Orta, "Near the Rails but Still on the Road," *Los Angeles Times*, June 30, 2007, tinyurl.com/alwpsw.

62. John Holtzclaw et al., "Location Efficiency: Neighborhood and Socioeconomic Characteristics Determine Auto Ownership and Use—Studies in Chicago, Los Angeles, and San Francisco," *Transportation Planning and Technology* 25, no. 1 (2002): 1–27.

63. Clifton Chestnut and Shirley Dang, "Suburbs Drain City Schools," *The Oregonian*, October 12, 2003, p. A1; "U.S. Cities Have Fewer Kids, More Singles," NewsMax.com, June 13, 2001.

64. Prud'homme and Lee, "Size, Sprawl, Speed, and the Efficiency of Cities."

65. Patricia L. Mokhtarian and Cynthia Chen, *TTB or Not TTB, That Is the Question: A Review and Analysis of the Empirical Literature on Travel Time (and Money) Budgets* (Davis, CA: Institute of Transportation Studies, 2002), p. 2.

Chapter 3

1. John W. Frece, "Twenty Lessons from Maryland's Smart Growth Initiative," *Vermont Journal of Environmental Law* 6 (2004–2005), tinyurl.com/8sj28.

2. *Using Income Criteria to Protect Commercial Farmland in the State of Oregon* (Salem, OR: Department of Land Conservation and Development, 1998), p. 2.

3. 1000 Friends of Oregon, *Making the Connections: A Summary of the LUTRAQ Project* (Portland, OR: 1000 Friends of Oregon, 1997), pp. 8–10.

4. *Transportation Partners 1997 Annual Report* (Washington: Environmental Protection Agency, 1998), p. 1.

5. *The Willamette Chronicle* (Eugene, OR: Willamette Valley Livability Forum, 2001), p. 8.

6. Bruce Yandle, "Bootleggers and Baptists in Retrospect," *Regulation* 22, no. 3 (1999): 5–7; tinyurl.com/yo8mzv.

7. IRS form 990s for 2006 for the American Public Transit Association, American Highway Users Alliance, and the Road Information Program, downloaded from guidestar.org.

8. Michael Cunneen and Randal O'Toole, *No Two Ways about It: One-Way Streets Are Better Than Two-Way* (Golden, CO: Independence Institute, 2005), pp. 6, 9.

9. *A Performance Audit of the Utah Transit Authority (UTA)* (Salt Lake City: Legislative Auditor General, 2008), p. 54, tinyurl.com/2aj5bw.

10. If transit is 2 and grows 2 percent per year and driving is 98 and grows 1 percent per year, then in 100 years, transit will be $2 \times 1.02 \char`^100 = 14.5$ while driving will be $98 \times 1.01 \char`^100 = 265.1$. Transit's share at that time will be $14.5/(14.5 + 265.1) = 5.2$ percent.

11. Charles Lave, "The Mass Transit Panacea and Other Fallacies about Energy," *The Atlantic Monthly*, October 1979, tinyurl.com/6c58os.

12. *2030 Metropolitan Transportation Plan for the Albuquerque Metropolitan Planning Area* (Albuquerque, NM: Metropolitan Transportation Board, 2007), p. II-1.

13. Genevieve Giuliano, "The Weakening Transportation-Land Use Connection," *Access* 6 (1995): 3–11.

14. Patricia Mokhtarian and Ilam Salomon, "Travel for the Fun of It," *Access* 15 (Fall 1999): 27.

15. Robert Cervero, "Jobs-Housing Balance Revisited," *Journal of the American Planning Association* 62 (4): 492.

16. William T. Bogart, *Don't Call It Sprawl: Metropolitan Structure in the Twenty-First Century* (New York: Cambridge, 2006), p. 7.

17. *FasTracks Plan* (Denver, CO: Regional Transportation District, 2004), p. ES-11.

18. Giuliano, "The Weakening Transportation-Land Use Connection."

19. Patrick McGreevy and Margot Roosevelt, "Governor Signs Law on Sprawl and Water Supplies but Vetoes Smog-Fighting Port Cargo Fee," *Los Angeles Times*, October 1, 2008, tinyurl.com/c6kgp5.

20. "SB 375 Bill Analysis," Assembly Committee on Local Government, Sacramento, CA, 2008, tinyurl.com/47vay4.

21. Paul Schimek, "Household Motor Vehicle Ownership and Use: How Much Does Residential Density Matter?" *Transportation Research Record* 1552 (1996): 120.

22. Melvyn D. Cheslow and J. Kevin Neels, "Effect of Urban Development Patterns on Transportation Energy Use," *Transportation Research Record* 764 (1980): 70–78.

23. Don Pickrell, "Transportation and Land Use," in *Essays in Transportation Economics and Policy: A Handbook in Honor of John R. Meyer*, ed. Jose A. Gomez-Ibanez, William B. Tye, and Clifford Winston (Washington: Brookings Institute, 1999), p. 425.

24. Giuliano, "The Weakening Transportation-Land Use Connection."

25. Urban populations and densities are from *1990 Census* (Washington: Census Bureau, 1992), table P004, and *2000 Census* (Washington: Census Bureau, 2002), table P2, for urban areas by state. Urban driving is from *Highway Statistics 1990* (Washington: Federal Highway Administration, 1991), table HM-72, and *Highway Statistics 2000* (Washington: Federal Highway Administration, 2001), table HM-72.

26. *2008 Buildings Energy Data Book* (Washington: Department of Energy, 2008), p. 2-7, tinyurl.com/lsndqa.

27. Tracey Kaplan and Sue McAllister, "Cost of Land Drives Home Prices," *San Jose Mercury News*, August 4, 2002.

28. Randal O'Toole, "The Planning Tax: The Case Against Regional Growth-Management Planning," Cato Institute Policy Analysis no. 606, December 6, 2007, p. 10.

29. Ibid., p. 13.

30. *Highway Statistics Summary to 1995*, tables FI200, MF221, and VM201; *Highway Statistics 2006*, tables FI20, MF21, and VM1; *National Air Quality and Emissions Trends Report: 2003 Special Studies Edition* (Washington: Environmental Protection Agency, 2003), table A2.

31. *Highway Statistics Summary to 1995*, table VM201; *Highway Statistics 2006*, table VM1.

32. *Highway Statistics Summary to 1995*, tables HM260 and VM202; *Highway Statistics 2006*, tables HM60 and VM2.

33. *Highway Statistics 2006*, table HF10.

34. Gary Richards, "South Bay Avoids Worst-Commutes List," *Mercury News*, June 19, 2007.

35. Schrank and Lomax, *The 2005 Urban Mobility Report*, table "The Mobility Data for San Jose, CA," tinyurl.com/2ngbg4.

36. Randal O'Toole, "Do You Know the Way to L.A.?" Cato Institute Policy Analysis no. 602, October 17, 2007, pp. 16–17.

37. Gary Richards, "A Sea of Greens for S.J. Drivers: City Tweaks 223 Intersections to Ease Delays," *San Jose Mercury-News*, November 6, 2003.

38. Randal O'Toole, "Does Rail Transit Save Energy or Reduce Greenhouse Gases?" Cato Institute Policy Analysis no. 615, April 14, 2008, pp. 15–20.

Chapter 4

1. Calculations of per capita transit ridership based on urban populations. Transit trips from *2008 Public Transportation Fact Book, Part 2* (Washington: American Public Transportation Association, 2008), p. 2; 1964 and 1980 urban populations from Census Bureau, "Population: 1790–1990, Urban and Rural," in *Population and Housing Unit*

Counts (Washington: Census Bureau, 1992), tinyurl.com/deenfb; 2007 urban population from Census Bureau, *2007 American Community Survey* (Washington: Census Bureau, 2008), geographic component: urban, tinyurl.com/d9x5zd.

2. "COPs and Lease-Backed Bonds," *Innovative Financing Techniques for America's Transit Systems* (Washington: Federal Transit Administration, 1994), chapter 1, tinyurl.com/bwpu73.

3. Lynnley Browning, "Transit Agencies Seek Aid in Avoiding AIG Fees," *New York Times*, November 4, 2008, tinyurl.com/bfdck5.

4. *2007 Public Transportation Fact Book* (Washington: American Public Transportation Association, 2007), p. 6.

5. Ruben N. Lubowski et al., *Major Uses of Land in the United States, 2002* (Washington: Department of Agriculture, 2006), p. 5.

6. *Annual Report on Funding Recommendations: New Starts, Small Starts, Alternative Transportation in Parks and Public Lands* (Washington: Federal Transit Administration, 2008), appendix A.

7. "Dulles Corridor Metrorail Project—Extension to Wiehle Avenue," Federal Transit Administration, 2007, p. 1, tinyurl.com/7b7n6z; Amy Gardner, "Metro to Dulles Gets Formal Federal Backing," *Washington Post*, March 11, 2009, tinyurl.com/dheo95

8. "Wilsonville to Beaverton Commuter Rail," Federal Transit Administration, 2005, p. 1, tinyurl.com/8vt3mb.

9. "Fort Bend Parkway Toll Road," Fort Bend County Toll Road Authority, 2008, tinyurl.com/5t9znq.

10. "Metro Denver's Multi-Modal T-REX Takes Last Step," Metro Denver EDC, 2006, tinyurl.com/3syrll.

11. Passenger miles per track mile calculated from *2007 National Transit Database* (Washington: Federal Transit Administration, 2008), spreadsheets "service" and "fixed guideway"; passenger miles per freeway lane mile from *Highway Statistics 2007*, table HM-72. Freeway passenger miles assumed to be 1.6 times freeway vehicle miles.

12. "FasTracks," Regional Transportation District, 2004, brochure mailed to several hundred thousand Denver-area homes in August 2004.

13. *2007 National Transit Database*, spreadsheet "service"; calculated by dividing vehicle revenue miles into passenger miles. The Federal Transit Administration groups vintage trolleys, such as streetcars in Galveston and Memphis, with light rail; the average of 23 riders per car counts only modern light-rail lines.

14. Bent Flyvbjerg, Mette Skamris Holm, and Søren Buhl, "Underestimating Costs in Public Works Projects: Error or Lie?" *Journal of the American Planning Association* 68, no. 3 (2002): 285.

15. Nasiru A. Dantata, Ali Touran, and Donald C. Schneck, "Trends in U.S. Rail Transit Project Cost Overrun," paper presented to the Transportation Research Board, 2006, table 2, tinyurl.com/mbjv24; *The Predicted and Actual Impacts of New Starts Projects—2007* (Washington: Federal Transit Administration, 2008), p. 11, tinyurl.com/8kpnyr.

16. "Central Phoenix/East Valley Light Rail," Federal Transit Administration, 1998, tinyurl.com/837vda.

17. "Central Phoenix/East Valley Light Rail," Federal Transit Administration, 2004, p. 1, tinyurl.com/9vsa2o.

18. "South Corridor LRT," Federal Transit Administration, 2000, tinyurl.com/7rcxwq.

19. "South Corridor LRT," Federal Transit Administration, 2005, tinyurl.com/8x6dwd.

20. "Dulles Corridor Metrorail Project—Extension to Wiehle Avenue," Federal Transit Administration, 2004, p. 1, tinyurl.com/798bx5.

21. "Dulles Corridor Metrorail Project—Extension to Wiehle Avenue," Federal Transit Administration, 2007, p. 1, tinyurl.com/7b7n6z.

22. "Summary of Changes to FasTracks Program: Attachment 1," Regional Transportation District, 2008, p. 2, tinyurl.com/4kodgc.

23. Flyvbjerg, Holm, and Buhl, "Underestimating Costs in Public Works Projects: Error or Lie?"

24. Parsons Brinckerhoff, *Transportation Alternatives Analysis for the Dane County/Greater Madison Metropolitan Area* (Madison, WI: Transport 2020, 2002), pp. 7-6, 10-2, and 10-22.

25. Transport 2020, *Transport 2020 Oversight Advisory Committee (OAC) Summary Report* (Madison, WI: Transport 2020, 2002), p. 21; *Project Fact Book* (Denver, CO: Regional Transit District, 2006), p. 14.

26. Booz Allen Hamilton, Inc., *Managing Capital Costs of Major Federally Funded Public Transportation Projects* (Washington: Transportation Research Board, 2005), p. 55.

27. *Final Report: Southeast Corridor Major Investment Study* (Denver, CO: Colorado Department of Transportation, 1997), p. 4-24.

28. "A Message from RTD General Manager, Cal Marsella," Regional Transit District, 2005.

29. "America's Transit System Stands at the Precipice of a Fiscal and Service Crisis," Washington Metropolitan Area Transit Authority, 2004, p. 1.

30. Lyndsey Layton and Jo Becker, "Efforts to Repair Aging System Compound Metro's Problems," *Washington Post*, June 5, 2005, tinyurl.com/98e2n; Lena H. Sun and Joe Holley, "Aging Equipment Blamed in Metro Incidents," *Washington Post*, August 28, 2007, tinyurl.com/2sm269.

31. "Chicago Rail System on Verge of Collapse," *Engineering News Record*, November 21, 2007.

32. Denis Cuff, "BART Gets Rusty: Aging System Lacks Billions for Infrastructure," *Contra Costa Times*, September 28, 2007.

33. Mac Daniel, "Group Seeks Debt Relief for the T," *Boston Globe*, January 9, 2007, tinyurl.com/3q7sm3.

34. Em Whitney, "Transportation Advocates Agree: The M.T.A. Is in 'Deep Doo-Doo,'" *The New York Observer*, June 27, 2008, tinyurl.com/4z8omd.

35. *MTA 2007 Adopted Budget* (New York: Metropolitan Transportation Authority, 2007), p. II-2, tinyurl.com/4ud8nb.

36. Eliot Brown, "Paterson Launches Panel to Find M.T.A. Much-Needed Money," *New York Observer*, June 10, 2008, tinyurl.com/3jqlub.

37. "Deficits May Force Cuts in NYC Subway, Bus, Rail," WABC News, September 23, 2008, tinyurl.com/4658gz.

38. "Stage II LRT Reconstruction," Federal Transit Administration, 2004, p. 2, tinyurl.com/8yof2m.

39. Moshe Ben-Akiva and Takayuki Morikawa, "Comparing Ridership Attraction of Rail and Bus," *Transport Policy Journal* 9, no. 2 (2002).

40. All ridership numbers in this section are from *National Transit Database* (Washington: Federal Transit Administration, various years), spreadsheets "service supplied and consumed."

41. Labor/Community Strategy Center, "Bus Riders Union," busridersunion.org.

42. Gary Richards, "VTA backs major cuts," *Mercury News*, May 10, 2003.

43. Randal O'Toole, *Rail Disasters 2005* (Bandon, OR: American Dream Coalition, 2005), p. 6.

44. Randal O'Toole, *Great Rail Disasters* (Golden, CO: Independence Institute, 2004), p. 7.

45. John Charles, "The Mythical World of Transit Oriented Development," Cascade Policy Institute Policy Perspective no. 1019, October 2001, tinyurl.com/336pt6.

46. Robert Cervero, "Transit Oriented Development's Ridership Bonus: A Product of Self-Selection and Public Policies," University of California Transportation Center, Berkeley, 2006, p. 1, tinyurl.com/ayls2a.

47. National Family Opinion, *Consumers Survey Conducted by NAR and NAHB* (Washington: National Association of Realtors, 2002), p. 6.

48. John Landis and Robert Cervero, "BART and Urban Development," *Access* 14 (Spring 1999): 15.

49. "Urban Renewal History Appendix," Portland Development Commission, 2006, p. 3; tinyurl.com/yo2zde.

50. Jennifer Lang, "New Urban Renewal in Colorado's Front Range," Independence Institute, Golden, CO, 2007, p. 7, tinyurl.com/nubsef.

51. John Charles and Michael Barton, *The Mythical World of Transit-Oriented Development: Light Rail and the Orenco Neighborhood* (Portland, OR: Cascade Policy Institute, 2003), tinyurl.com/2kh6s.

52. Podobnik, "Portland Neighborhood Survey Report on Findings from Zone 2: Orenco," p. 1, tinyurl.com/2hhmwo.

53. Sharon Bernstein and Francisco Vara-Orta, "Near the Rails But Still on the Road: Research Casts Doubt on the Region's Strategy of Pushing Transit-Oriented Residential Projects to Get People out of their Cars," *Los Angeles Times*, June 30, 2007.

54. O'Toole, "The Planning Tax: The Case Against Regional Growth-Management Planning," p. 8.

55. Kytja Weir, "Metro May Shut Down Escalators, Will Close Bathrooms for Inaugural," *Washington Examiner*, December 7, 2008, tinyurl.com/9tgsh5.

56. Robert Cervero and Samuel Seskin, *An Evaluation of the Relationship between Transit and Urban Form* (Washington: Transportation Research Board, 1995), p. 3.

57. Joel Garreau, *Edge City: Life on the New Frontier* (New York: Doubleday, 1991), p. 59.

58. Ibid., p. 25.

59. Jim Redden, "Can Goldschmidt Come Back?" *Portland Tribune*, May 21, 2004.

60. Kytja Weir, "Survey: Metrorail Users More Affluent, Better Educated," *Washington Examiner*, May 17, 2009, tinyurl.com/qfd98y.

61. Kytja Weir, "Area Bus Riders Face Service Cuts," *Washington Examiner*, March 31, 2009, tinyurl.com/oabxqt.

62. Metropolitan Transportation Commission, *Final Transportation 2030 Plan* (Oakland, CA: MTC, 2005), p. 35.

63. Bob Egelko, "Inequity in Funding Discriminates against AC Transit Riders, Plaintiffs Claim in Suit," *San Francisco Chronicle*, April 20, 2005, p. B-1.

64. Paul Weyrich, "Can Rail Prevail the First Time Around?" *Railway Age*, June 2000, tinyurl.com/n9ola2.

65. "Summary of Changes to FasTracks Program: Attachment 1," p. 2, tinyurl.com/4kodgc.

66. "FasTracks Annual Program Evaluation Summary: 2008," Regional Transporation District, 2008, p. 3, tinyurl.com/3fwp8z.

67. "Central Subway," Federal Transit Administration, 2006, p. 1, tinyurl.com/9a69eo.

68. "Bayshore Corridor," Federal Transit Administration, 1996, tinyurl.com/8853b5.

69. *Panorama of Transport*, p. 23.

70. Ari Vatanen and Malcolm Harbour, "Strangling or Liberating Europe's Potential?" paper presented at conference on European Transport Policy, European Parliament, Brussels, July 12, 2005, p. 10, tinyurl.com/8pl8rf.

71. *National Transportation Statistics* (2008), table 1-37; *Panorama of Transport*, p. 102.

72. *Key Facts and Figures about the European Union* (Brussels: EU, 2004), p. 52.

73. Lave, "The Mass Transit Panacea and Other Fallacies about Energy."

74. Ibid.

75. "Light Rail Is Defeatable," Independence Institute, 2003, p. 1, tinyurl.com/83r2am.

76. Ben Wear, "Rail Referendum," *Austin American-Statesman*, November 3, 2004.

77. Paul Gessing, "Take Ads Off Taxpayers' Dime," *Albuquerque Journal*, November 20, 2008, tinyurl.com/7v9r2s.

78. "We Keep Atlantic City Moving," Atlantic City Jitney Association, jitneys.net.

79. *2007 National Transit Database*, spreadsheet "service."

80. N. R. Kleinfield, "Trucker Turned Builder: Arthur E. Imperatore; Creating Shangri-La on the Hudson," *New York Times*, January 4, 1987, tinyurl.com/brh73y.

81. Sascha Brodsky, "Many Routes to Ferry King's Success," *Downtown Express*, July 17, 2002, tinyurl.com/b54snr.

82. "NY Waterway Profile," Federal Transit Administration, 2008, tinyurl.com/cp8hco.

Chapter 5

1. David Rogers, "Obama Plots Huge Railroad Expansion," *Politico*, February 17, 2009, tinyurl.com/d2kylj.

2. *A New Era of Responsibility: Renewing America's Promise* (Washington: Office of Management and Budget, 2009), p. 91, tinyurl.com/dyk3l2.

3. *Vision for High-Speed Rail in America* (Washington: Federal Railroad Administration, 2009), p. 6, tinyurl.com/pe4ud2.

4. "High-Speed Rail Corridor Descriptions," Federal Railroad Administration, 2005, tinyurl.com/6s94zd.

5. *Highway Statistics 2007*, table VM-1; *National Transportation Statistics* (Washington: Bureau of Transportation Statistics, 2009 online update), table 1-46a.

6. Jim Scribbins, *The Hiawatha Story* (Milwaukee, WI: Kalmbach, 1970), pp. 70–71.

7. *High Speed Passenger Rail: Future Development Will Depend on Addressing Financial and Other Challenges and Establishing a Clear Federal Role* (Washington: Government Accountability Office, 2009), pp. 64–68, tinyurl.com/phv447.

8. Xin Dingding, "Rapid Beijing-Tianjin Train Link Opens on Friday," *China Daily*, July 31, 2008, tinyurl.com/5qwa23.

9. "Japanese Bullet Trains—40 Years at the Forefront," *Railway Technology*, September 3, 2007, tinyurl.com/5uhxus.

10. Steven Greenhouse, "Europe's Grand Plan for Web of Fast Trains," *New York Times*, January 5, 1989, tinyurl.com/5wnh2v.

11. "Report on the California High-Speed Rail Authority," California Senate Transportation and Housing Committee, Sacramento, CA, 2008, p. 13.

12. Jon Hilkevitch, "Amtrak: True High-Speed Rail Unrealistic, Amtrak Boss Says," *Chicago Tribune*, May 12, 2009, tinyurl.com/q8v7au.

13. "Railroad Land Grants: Paid in Full," Association of American Railroads, 2008, p. 1, tinyurl.com/lesuyr.

14. Elise Hamner, "Railroad Closes Coos Bay Line," *The World*, September 21, 2007, tinyurl.com/2e4b73.

15. *Midwest Regional Rail System Executive Report* (Frederick, MD: Transportation Economics & Management Systems, 2004), pp. 13, 15, tinyurl.com/5mxdrb.

16. Based on a 68 percent increase in the construction costs of Denver passenger rail lines that were projected to cost $4.7 billion in 2004 and $7.9 billion in 2008. See *FasTracks Annual Program Evaluation Summary*, pp. 1–2, tinyurl.com/3fwp8z.

17. *California High-Speed Train Business Plan* (Sacramento, CA: California High-Speed Rail Authority, 2008), p. 19.

18. Wendell Cox and Joseph Vranich, *The California High Speed Rail Proposal: A Due Diligence Report* (Los Angeles, CA: Reason Foundation, 2008), pp. 42–43, tinyurl.com/lbykjh.

19. *California High-Speed Train Business Plan*, p. 21.

20. Katie Worth, "High-Speed Rail Would Benefit from Federal Dollars, but Agencies Need to Finalize Details," *San Francisco Examiner*, March 11, 2009, tinyurl.com/pw8uoy.

21. The California project is projected to cost about $80 million per mile. At this cost, the entire 8,500-mile system would cost $680 billion. The actual cost would probably be lower because other routes have fewer mountains than in California; on the other hand, California's 2004 estimate is probably low considering increases in construction costs since that estimate was made.

22. Mamoru Taniguchi, *High Speed Rail in Japan: A Review and Evaluation of the Shinkansen Train* (Berkeley, CA: University of California Transportation Center, 1992), p. 19, tinyurl.com/c6en4v.

23. Louis D. Hayes, *Introduction to Japanese Politics* (Armonk, NY: M.E. Sharpe, 2004), p. 107.

24. Mitsuhide Imashiro, "Changes in Japan's Transport Market and Privitazation," *Japan Railway and Transport Review* (September 1997): 51–52.

25. All data on Japanese passenger and freight travel by mode are from "Summary of Transportation Statistics," Ministry of Land, Infrastructure, and Transport, 2008, tinyurl.com/mqkjq8.

26. "Company History," East Japan Railway Company, Tokyo, 2005, tinyurl.com/cjxhtd.

27. Chris Isidore, "GM's $35 Billion Albatross," *CNNMoney.com*, January 30, 2009, tinyurl.com/atb2wg.

28. *Best Practices for Private Sector Investment in Railways* (Manila: Asian Development Bank, 2006), p. 13-3, tinyurl.com/cwjehk.

29. Mitsuhide Imashiro, "Changes in Japan's Transport Market and Privatization."

30. Mitsuo Higashi, "JR East's Shinkansen Transport Strategy," presentation to the Forum for Global Cities Conference, December 8, 2008, p. 16, tinyurl.com/dkvlu7.

31. High-speed rail passenger kilometers are from "Traffic Volume and Passenger Revenues," East Japan Railway Company, 2008, tinyurl.com/daqgpx; "Transportation Data," in *Summary of the Company Performance* (Nagoya, Japan: Central Japan Railway Company, 2008), tinyurl.com/d4lko8; and "Results for the Year Ended March 31, 2008," West Japan Railway Company, 2008, p. 29, tinyurl.com/cuxocc.

32. Construction costs of the Shinkansen lines are from the following sources: "Testimony of Hiroki Matsumoto before the House Transportation and Infrastructure Committee," April 19, 2007, p. 2, tinyurl.com/cc7qzf (Tokaido route cost ¥380 billion); Mamoru Taniguchi, *High Speed Rail in Japan: A Review and Evaluation of the Shinkansen Train*, p. 17, tinyurl.com/c6en4v (Sanyo line cost ¥908 billion, Tohoku line cost ¥2.7 trillion, and Joetsu line cost ¥1.7 trillion); "New Shinkansen Route to Serve Olympic Visitors," *Kids Web Japan*, November, 1997, tinyurl.com/coxmvy (Nagano route cost ¥8.4 trillion); and "Kyusho Shinkansen Line," *Trends in Japan* (April 5, 2004): tinyurl.com/csde8f (Kyusho line cost ¥640 billion). "Measuring Worth" (tinyurl.com/cul9zx) was used to adjust yen for inflation, resulting in a total cost of about ¥19.5 trillion yen or (at current conversion rates) about $184 billion. Based on today's populations, this is about $1,450 per capita, compared with a $1,400 per capita cost of the Interstate Highway System.

33. *Panorama of Transport*, pp. 107, 110, tinyurl.com/23py4r.

34. *Key Facts and Figures about the European Union* (Brussels: European Commission, 2004), p. 52.

35. *Panorama of Transport*, p. 102.

36. Ibid., p. 106.

37. Prud'Homme, "The Current EU Transport Policy in Perspective," p. 3.

38. Vatanen and Harbour, "Strangling or Liberating Europe's Potential?" p. 6.

39. "High-Speed Rail Gives Short-Haul Air a Run for the Money in Europe," *Travel Industry Wire*, April 23, 2007, tinyurl.com/6fpys3.

40. *Key Facts and Figures about the European Union*, p. 54.

41. Ibid., p. 53; *National Transportation Statistics* (2008), table 1-46b.

42. Bent Flyvbjerg, *How Optimism Bias and Strategic Misrepresentation Undermine Implementation* (Trondheim, Norway: Norges Teknisk-Naturvitenskapelige Universitet, 2007).

43. *California High-Speed Train Business Plan*, p. 19.

44. Bent Flyvbjerg, *Eliminating Bias through Reference Class Forecasting and Good Governance* (Trondheim, Norway: Norges Teknisk-Naturvitenskapelige Universitet, 2007).

45. *California High-Speed Train Business Plan*, p. 21.

46. "Committee Report: Oversight Hearings of the California High-Speed Rail Authority," California Senate Transportation and Housing Committee, June 2008, p. 18.

47. *California High-Speed Train Business Plan*, p. 18.

48. *Monthly Performance Report for September 2007* (Washington: Amtrak, 2007), p. A-3.3, tinyurl.com/536s4r.

49. Bent Flyvbjerg, Mette K. Skamris Holm, and Søren L. Buhl, "How (In)accurate Are Demand Forecasts for Public Works Projects?" *Journal of the American Planning Association* 71, no. 2 (2005): 131–46.

50. Joseph Vranich, *Supertrains: Solutions to America's Transportation Gridlock* (New York: St. Martins, 1993).

51. Joseph Vranich, "Testimony before the Transportation and Housing Committee, California Senate," October 23, 2008, p. 1, tinyurl.com/cfffxv.

52. *California High-Speed Train Business Plan*, p. 12.

53. *California High-Speed Rail Final Program EIR/EIS* (Sacramento, CA: California High-Speed Rail Authority, 2005), p. 3.1-12.

54. *Highway Statistics 1996* (Washington: Federal Highway Administration, 1997), table VM-2; *Highway Statistics 2006*, table VM-2.

55. *California High-Speed Rail Final Program EIR/EIS*, pp. 3.2-25, 3.2-26.

56. Ibid., pp. 3.5-19–3.5-20.

57. Ibid., p. 3.5-16.

58. Stacy C. Davis and Susan W. Diegel, *Transportation Energy Data Book: Edition 27* (Oak Ridge, TN: Department of Energy, 2008), table 2.14.

59. "787 Dreamliner," Boeing, 2008, tinyurl.com/kouly.

60. "Shifting Gears," *The Economist*, March 5, 2009, tinyurl.com/ctnsas.

61. Steven Polzin, "Energy Crisis Solved!" *Urban Transportation Monitor*, July 11, 2008, pp. 8–9.

62. *California High-Speed Rail Final Program EIR/EIS*, table 3.3-9.

63. "Greenhouse Gas Emissions Detail for California," Energy Information Agency, 2008, tinyurl.com/qvg9rb.

64. *Final Environmental Impact Statement Florida High Speed Rail Tampa to Orlando* (Washington: Federal Railroad Administration, 2005), p. 4-119, tinyurl.com/6ysffl.

65. Ibid., p. 4-117.

66. Ibid., p. 4-119.

67. Ibid., p. 4-48.

68. Ibid., p. 4-111.

69. Ibid., p. 2-38.

70. "Bullet Train News," 2008, floridabullettrain.com.

71. *Midwest Regional Rail System Executive Report* (Frederick, MD: Transportation Economics & Management Systems, 2004), p. 6, tinyurl.com/5mxdrb.

72. *Midwest Regional Rail System Executive Report*, pp. 13, 15, tinyurl.com/5mxdrb.

73. Based on a 68 percent increase in the construction costs of Denver passenger rail lines that were projected to cost $4.7 billion in 2004 and $7.9 billion in 2008. See *FasTracks Annual Program Evaluation Summary*, pp. 1–2, tinyurl.com/3fwp8z.

74. *Midwest Regional Rail System Executive Report*, p. 11, tinyurl.com/5mxdrb.

75. Ibid., p. 10.

76. *Monthly Performance Report for September 2007*, p. A-3.5.

77. Traffic Monitoring Information System, "Annual Average Daily Traffic Report," Michigan Department of Transportation, 2008, apps.michigan.gov/tmis.

78. *Midwest Regional Rail System Executive Report*, pp. 9, 12, tinyurl.com/5mxdrb.

79. Ibid., p. 17, tinyurl.com/5mxdrb.

80. "Committee Report: Oversight Hearings of the California High-Speed Rail Authority," pp. 24–27.

81. William T. Bogart, *Don't Call It Sprawl: Metropolitan Structure in the Twenty-First Century* (New York: Cambridge University Press, 2006), p. 7.

82. Howard French, "Shanghai Journal; All Aboard! But Don't Relax. Your Trip Is Already Over," *New York Times*, April 22, 2004, tinyurl.com/6g3deq.

83. "Committee Report: Oversight Hearings of the California High-Speed Rail Authority," pp. 24–25.

84. Letter from Jerry Wilmoth, Union Pacific Railroad, to Mehdi Morshed, California High-Speed Rail Authority, May 13, 2008.

85. "Scores Killed in High-Speed Train Crash in Germany," CNN, June 4, 1998.

86. "Committee Report: Oversight Hearings of the California High-Speed Rail Authority," p. 25.

87. "California High Speed Rail Authority Image Gallery," California High Speed Rail Authority, 2008, cahighspeedrail.ca.gov/gallery.aspx.

Chapter 6

1. Randal O'Toole, *Achievement of Improved Air Quality through Transportation Control Strategies: A Plan for Portland, Oregon* (Portland, OR: OSPIRG, 1972).

2. *Highway Statistics Summary to 1995*, table VM-201; *Highway Statistics 2006*, table VM-1.

3. Davis and Diegel, *Transportation Energy Data Book: Edition 27*, tables 12.2, 12.4, 12.6, and 12.8.

4. "Optimizing Traffic Signal Timing Significantly Reduces the Consumption of Fuel," Clinton Climate Initiative, 2008, tinyurl.com/b494vt.

5. "Governor Schwarzenegger Signs Sweeping Legislation to Reduce Greenhouse Gas Emissions through Land Use," press release, California Office of the Governor, Sacramento, CA, September 30, 2008, tinyurl.com/dxcoa3.

6. *2000 Census* (Washington: Census Bureau, 2002), table P30; *2007 American Community Survey*, table C08006, urbanized areas.

7. *2006 National Transit Database* (Washington: Federal Transit Administration, 2007), spreadsheet "energy consumption."

8. Davis and Diegel, *Transportation Energy Data Book: Edition 27*, tables 2.13 and 2.14.

9. Environmental Protection Agency, *Model Year 2008 Fuel Economy Guide* (Washington: EPA, 2007), tinyurl.com/25y3ce.

10. Energy Information Administration, "Fuel and Energy Emission Coefficients," Department of Energy, tinyurl.com/pqubq.

11. Energy Information Administration, *State Electricity Profiles 2006* (Washington: Department of Energy, 2007), table 5.

12. Vehicle Technologies Program, "Vehicle Occupancy by Type of Vehicle," Department of Energy, 2003, tinyurl.com/2ttp7h. Calculation of average occupancy of light trucks based on vans, SUVs, and pickups weighted by vehicle numbers shown in Hu and Reuscher, *Summary of Travel Trends: 2001 National Household Travel Survey*, table 20.

13. *2006 National Transit Database*, spreadsheet "service"; calculated by dividing passenger miles by vehicle revenue miles.

14. "Intercensal Estimates of Total Households by State," Census Bureau, 2002; Hu and Reuscher, *Summary of Travel Trends: 2001 National Household Travel Survey*, table 15.

15. *2007 National Transit Database*, spreadsheets "service" and "revenue-vehicle inventory."

16. Davis and Diegel, *Transportation Energy Data Book: Edition 27*, table 2.13.

17. Ibid., table 2.14.

18. Brandon Loomis, "New TRAX Passenger Tracking System Shows Ridership Lower Than Thought," *Salt Lake Tribune*, December 20, 2007.

19. *2006 National Transit Database* (Washington: Department of Transportation, 2007), spreadsheets "revenue-vehicle inventory" and "service."

20. Stacy C. Davis and Susan W. Diegel, *Transportation Energy Data Book: Edition 26* (Oak Ridge, TN: Department of Energy, 2007), table B.6.

21. *2006 Provisional National Transit Database*, spreadsheet "energy consumption."

22. Nicholas Lutsey and Daniel Sperling, "Energy Efficiency, Fuel Economy, and Policy Implications," *Transportation Research Record* 1941 (2005): 8–17.

23. "Automakers Support President in Development of National Program for Autos," *PRNewswire*, May 18, 2009, tinyurl.com/pzaokn.

24. "Fact Sheet: Energy Independence and Security Act of 2007," The White House, December 19, 2007, tinyurl.com/mdurvu.

25. Bureau of Transportation Statistics, "Median Age of Automobiles and Trucks in Operation in the United States," Research and Innovative Technology Administration, 2003, table 1-25, tinyurl.com/5oszkn.

26. Calculations assume a straight-line increase in new-car fuel economy between now and 2020, no change in new-car fuel economy after 2020, and replacement of the existing auto fleet at the rate of 6.25 percent per year.

27. Andrew N. Kleit, "CAFE Changes, By the Numbers," *Regulation* 26, no. 3 (2002): 32–35, tinyurl.com/q4y92e.

28. *1991 National Transit Database* (Washington: Department of Transportation, 1992), table 19; *1995 National Transit Database* (Washington: DOT, 1996), table 26.

29. *1985 National Transit Database* (Washington: DOT, 1986), table 3161; *1991 National Transit Database*, table 19.

30. *2004 National Transit Database* (Washington: DOT, 2005), table 19.

31. *2001 National Transit Database* (Washington: DOT, 2002), table 28; *2005 National Transit Database* (Washington: DOT, 2006), table 19.

32. *1982 National Transit Database*, table 417812; *1987 National Transit Database* (Washington: DOT, 1988), table 16.

33. *1997 National Transit Database* (Washington: DOT, 1998), table 26; *1999 National Transit Database* (Washington: DOT, 2000), table 28.

34. *2001 National Transit Database*, table 28; *2005 National Transit Database*, table 19.

35. *North Corridor Interstate MAX Final Environmental Impact Statement* (Portland, OR: Metro, 1999), p. 4-104.

36. *North Link Light Rail Transit Project Final Supplemental Environmental Impact Statement* (Seattle, WA: Sound Transit, 2006), p. 4-112, tinyurl.com/2q48do.

37. *North Link Light Rail Transit Project Final Supplemental Environmental Impact Statement*, p. 4-216, tinyurl.com/3cj5pd.

38. "Record of Decision for Central Puget Sound Regional Transit Authority's (Sound Transit) North Link Segment of the Central Link Light Rail Transit Project: Response to CETA May 2, 2006 Letter," Federal Transit Administration, June 7, 2006, tinyurl.com/2we4ur.

39. "Environmental Consequences," in *Southeast Corridor Light Rail Transit in Dallas County, Texas, Final Environmental Impact Statement* (Dallas, TX: Dallas Area Rapid Transit, 2003), chapter 5, tinyurl.com/2da5c3.

40. Calculated by comparing passenger miles per directional route mile from tables 19 and 23 of the 2005 *National Transit Database* with vehicle miles (multiplied by 1.6 to get passenger miles) per freeway lane mile from table HM72 of the 2005 *Highway Statistics*.

253

41. *Reducing U.S. Greenhouse Gas Emissions: How Much at What Cost?* (Washington: McKinsey & Company, 2008), pp. ix, xiii.

42. Peter Bell, "Message from the Council Chair" (St. Paul, MN: Metropolitan Council, 2007), tinyurl.com/2hvfnl.

43. Nasiru A. Dantata, Ali Touran, and Donald C. Schneck, "Trends in U.S. Rail Transit Project Cost Overrun," paper presented to the Transportation Research Board 2006 Annual Meeting, January 2006, table 3, tinyurl.com/mbjv24.

44. *2006 Provisional National Transit Database*, spreadsheet "operating expenses."

45. Jim Foti, "Hybrid Buses Thunder Down Nicollet Mall—Quietly," *Minneapolis Star-Tribune*, November 15, 2007, tinyurl.com/2c33mj.

46. Calculation based on *2006 Provisional National Transit Database*, spreadsheet "fuel consumption"; and Davis and Diegel, *Transportation Energy Data Book: Edition 26*, table A.3.

47. Gargi Chakrabarty, "Denver Public Schools Opt for Biodiesel," *Rocky Mountain News*, October 12, 2005.

48. *2006 Provisional National Transit Database*, spreadsheets "fuel consumption" and "service."

49. Todd W. Bressi, "From Bus Route to Urban Form: L.A.'s Electric Trolley Bus Plan," *Places* 9, no. 1 (1994): 66, tinyurl.com/djclja.

50. "New Shuttle Bus Inventory for Sale," TESCO, Oregon, Ohio, 2007, tinyurl. com/2zuscj.

51. Schrank and Lomax, *The 2007 Urban Mobility Report*, p. 1.

52. Robert Cervero, "Are Induced Travel Studies Inducing Bad Investments?" *Access* 22 (Spring 2003): 27; tinyurl.com/34nesx.

53. *Highway Statistics 2005*, table HF10.

54. Jack Tone, "Denver's I-25 HOT Lanes," *The Westernite*, July–August 2007, pp. 1–5, tinyurl.com/3at5cc.

55. Gary Richards, "A Sea of Greens for S.J. Drivers: City Tweaks 223 Intersections to Ease Delays."

56. Federal Highway Administration, *Traffic Signal Timing* (Washington: Department of Transportation, 2005), ops.fhwa.dot.gov/traffic_sig_timing/index.htm.

57. *National Traffic Signal Report Card* (Washington: National Transportation Operations Coalition, 2007), p. 4.

58. *Public Transportation Fact Book 58th Edition* (Washington: American Public Transportation Association, 2007), table 37; *Public Transportation Fact Book 57th Edition* (Washington: American Public Transportation Association, 2006), table 37.

59. "Shares of urban travel" calculated by comparing transit passenger miles from the *National Transit Database* (ntdprogram.gov) with highway vehicle miles (multiplied by 1.6 to account for occupancy rates) from the Federal Highway Administration's *Highway Statistics* series (tinyurl.com/mnpuyk).

60. Transit's share of commuting in 1990 is from the *1990 Census*, table P049, "means of transportation to work," for urbanized areas; transit's share in 2005 is from the *2005 American Community Survey*, table S0802, "means of transportation to work by selected characteristics," for urbanized areas. Both tables are accessible from the Census Bureau's American Factfinder web page, tinyurl.com/ufd9.

Chapter 7

1. See, for example, "Debunking Common Myths about AMTRAK," National Association of Railroad Passengers, 2003, tinyurl.com/muwao3.

2. Daniel Klein and John Majewski, "America's Toll Road Heritage: The Achievements of Private Initiative in the Nineteenth Century," in *Street Smart: Competition, Entrepreneurship, and the Future of Roads*, ed. Gabriel Roth (Oakland, CA: Independent Institute, 2006), pp. 280–81.

3. Ibid., p. 288.

4. Ibid., pp. 290–291.

5. *Historical Statistics of the United States: Colonial Times to 1970*, series Q289, p. 728.

6. "Railroad Land Grants: Paid in Full," Association of American Railroads, 2008, p. 1, tinyurl.com/9kz4g5.

7. All dates in this and the next nine paragraphs are from *2007 Public Transportation Fact Book*, pp. 6–7.

8. "List of Interurban Railways," Wikipedia, tinyurl.com/7j3ush.

9. "List of town tramway systems—United States," Wikipedia, tinyurl.com/7za8zb.

10. For refutations of this myth, see Scott Bottles, *Los Angeles and the Automobile: The Making of the Modern City* (Berkeley, CA: University of California Press, 1987), pp. 3–4; Christine Cosgrove, "*Roger Rabbit* Unframed: Revising the GM Conspiracy Theory," *ITS Review Online* 3, no. 1 (Winter 2004–Spring 2005), tinyurl.com/2bcg2t; Martha J. Bianco, "Kennedy, 60 Minutes, and Roger Rabbit: Understanding Conspiracy-Theory Explanations of the Decline of Urban Mass Transit," Portland State University Center for Urban Studies Discussion Paper 98-11, November 1998; and Cliff Slater, "General Motors and the Demise of Streetcars," *Transportation Quarterly* 51, no. 3 (Summer 1997): 45–66, tinyurl.com/yuth5m.

11. Bill Vandervoort, "Cities Served by National City Lines," 2005, tinyurl.com/9tuzb7.

12. "Physical Growth of the City of St. Louis," St. Louis City Planning Commission, 1969, tinyurl.com/ckwand.

13. George M. Smerk, *The Federal Role in Urban Mass Transportation* (Bloomington, IN: Indiana University, 1991), pp. 60–61.

14. "Long Island (Vanderbilt) Motor Parkway: Historic Overview," Eastern Roads, tinyurl.com/9mk2lu.

15. *Highway Statistics Summary to 1995*, table HF-210.

16. Ibid.

17. Mark Rose, *Interstate: Express Highway Politics, 1939–1989* (Knoxville, TN: University of Tennessee Press, 1990), p. 5.

18. *Highway Statistics Summary to 1995*, table HF-210.

19. Thomas MacDonald, letter to *Manchester Sunday News*, April 22, 1947, tinyurl.com/9y52e9.

20. Ibid.

21. Peter Samuel, "Morale: The Importance of History," *Tollroads Newsletter* 40 (February 2000): 20, tinyurl.com/8r554n.

22. *The Interstate and National Highway System: A Brief History and Lessons Learned* (Washington: National Cooperative Highway Research Program, 2006), p. 21, tinyurl.com/9jc6k6.

23. *Toll Roads and Free Roads* (Washington: Bureau of Public Roads, 1939).

24. Richard Weingroff, "Creating the Interstate Highway System," *Public Roads* 60, no. 1 (Summer 1996), tinyurl.com/9zgyg.

25. Dan McNichol, *The Roads That Built America: The Incredible Story of the U.S. Interstate System* (New York: Sterling, 2006), p. 100.

26. Rose, *Interstate: Express Highway Politics, 1939–1989*, pp. 7, 20.

27. Richard Weingroff, "Why Does I-70 End in Cove Fort, Utah?" in Ask the Rambler, Federal Highway Administration, 2008, tinyurl.com/9vuadb.

28. McNichol, *The Roads That Built America: The Incredible Story of the U.S. Interstate System*, p. 105.

29. *General Location of National System of Interstate Highways Including All Additional Routes at Urban Areas Designated in September, 1955* (Washington: Bureau of Public Roads, 1955).

30. Rose, *Interstate: Express Highway Politics, 1939–1989*, p. 89.

31. McNichol, *The Roads That Built America: The Incredible Story of the U.S. Interstate System*, pp. 106, 140.

32. Richard Weingroff, "Why Does The Interstate System Include Toll Facilities?" in Ask the Rambler, Federal Highway Administration, 2008, tinyurl.com/9mgejw.

33. "Interstate FAQ: Why Did It Cost So Much More Than Expected?" Federal Highway Administration, 2006, tinyurl.com/4u7xbb.

34. *Highway Statistics 2005*, table FE-101A, tinyurl.com/3rzwpm.

35. "Interstate FAQ: What Did It Cost?" Federal Highway Administration, 2006, tinyurl.com/3qnnwk.

36. "An $850 Billion Challenge," *Washington Post*, December 22, 2008, page A1, tinyurl.com/74t9ey.

37. McNichol, *The Roads That Built America: The Incredible Story of the U.S. Interstate System*, p. 139.

38. Jane Jacobs, *The Death and Life of Great American Cities* (New York: Vintage, 1963), p. 7.

39. Chris Niles, "Interview with a Freeway Fighter," *Intersect*, May 5, 1997, tinyurl.com/9vnycs.

40. Quoted in Stephen Goldsmith, *The Twenty-First Century City: Resurrecting Urban America* (Washington: Regnery, 1997), p. 90.

41. Kenneth T. Jackson, *Crabgrass Frontier: The Suburbanization of the United States*, (New York: Oxford University Press, 1985), p. 238.

42. Darwin Stolzenbach, *Interview with Professor Alan Altshuler, Former Secretary of Transportation, Massachusetts* (Washington: American Association of State Highway and Transportation Officials, 1981), pp. 3–4.

43. Ralph Nader, *Unsafe At Any Speed: The Designed-In Dangers of the American Automobile* (New York: Grossman, 1965).

44. A. Q. Mowbry, *Road to Ruin* (Philadelphia: J. B. Lippincott, 1969); John Jerome, *The Death of the Automobile: The Fatal Effect of the Golden Era, 1955–1970* (New York: W. W. Norton, 1972); Kenneth R. Schneider, *Autokind vs. Mankind: An Analysis of Tyranny, A Proposal for Rebellion, A Plan for Reconstruction* (New York: W. W. Norton, 1971); Richard Hébert, *Highways to Nowhere: The Politics of City Transportation* (Indianapolis, IN: Bobbs-Merrill, 1972).

45. Rose, *Interstate: Express Highway Politics, 1939–1989*, p. xi.

46. Karen Stufflebeam Row, Eva LaDow, and Steve Moler, "Glenwood Canyon, 12 Years Later," *Public Roads* 67, no. 5 (March/April 2004), tinyurl.com/8lhrn8.

47. Stolzenbach, *Interview with Professor Alan Altshuler, Former Secretary of Transportation, Massachusetts*, p. 36.

48. Ronald Utt, "A Primer on Lobbyists, Earmarks, and Congressional Reform," The Heritage Foundation Backgrounder no. 1924, April 27, 2006, table 1, tinyurl.com/2jfkhu.

49. Jim Abrams, "House Members Seek $136.3 Billion in Road Projects," Associated Press, May 21, 2009, tinyurl.com/ljyndc.

50. *Highway Statistics 2006*, table FA-4.

51. Ibid., table FA-4a.

52. "FY 2009 Apportionments, Allocations, and Program Information," Federal Transit Administration, 2008, table 4, tinyurl.com/7k7f8v.

53. *2007 National Transit Database*, spreadsheets "operating expenses," "capital use," and "fare revenues."

54. *2006 National Transit Database*, spreadsheets "operating expenses," "capital use," and "fare revenues"; *Highway Statistics 2006*, table HF-10.

55. *2006 National Transit Database*, tables 3 through 10.

56. *2006 Annual Report* (Washington: Amtrak, 2007), p. 6.

57. Ibid., pp. 33, 35.

58. *Highway Statistics Summary to 1995*, tables MF-201, and VM-201; *Highway Statistics 2007*, tables FE-101a, MF-121T, and VM-1; "Current Dollar and 'Real' Gross Domestic Product," Bureau of Economic Analysis, 2009, tinyurl.com/ad629c.

59. Peter Samuel, "Toll Collection Costs," unpublished paper by the editor of *Tollroad News*.

60. James M. Whitty, *Oregon's Mileage Fee Concept and Road User Fee Pilot Program* (Salem, OR: Oregon Department of Transportation, 2007), p. 8, tinyurl.com/c8ownh.

61. Ibid., p. 10.

62. Ibid., p. 32.

63. Ibid., p. 33.

64. Ibid., p. 11.

65. "Governor Kulongoski Submits Legislation for 2009 Session," Gov. Ted Kulongoski, Oregon, press release, December 18, 2008, tinyurl.com/b352al.

66. Larry Copeland, "Drivers Test Paying by Mile Instead of Gas Tax," *USA Today*, September 21, 2007, tinyurl.com/2gfx5o; Ed Sealover, "Mileage Fee, Tolls Become Tough Sells in Road-Funding Bill," *Rocky Mountain News*, January 22, 2009, tinyurl.com/dh4m2u.

67. "Welcome to MTA Bridges and Tolls," Metropolitan Transportation Authority, tinyurl.com/aq6pyg.

68. Amy Gardner, "Control of Dulles Toll Road in New Hands," *Washington Post*, November 4, 2008, tinyurl.com/c493j5.

69. Patrick Driscoll, "Details Offered on Bus, Toll Agency," *San Antonio Express-News*, February 6, 2009, tinyurl.com/bdv2j8.

Chapter 8

1. *2006 Metropolitan Transportation Plan* (Sacramento, CA: SACOG, 2006), p. 3.

2. Ibid.

3. Ibid., p. 4.

4. Ibid., p. 49.

5. Ibid., p. 23.

6. Ibid., p. 29.

7. Ibid., p. 5.

8. Rita Mae Brown, *Sudden Death* (New York: Bantam Books, 1983), p. 68.

9. U.S. Code 23, § 134(i)(1).

10. Dom Nozzi, "Congestion Is Our Friend," *Gainesvile Sun*, February 9, 2008, tinyurl.com/cszagx.

11. *Regional Transportation Plan Update* (Portland, OR: Metro, 1996), p. 1-20.

12. *1999 Regional Transportation Plan* (Portland, OR: Metro, 1999), p. 6-38.

13. *Transportation Policy Plan* (St. Paul, MN: Metropolitan Council, 1996), pp. 17, 54, 72, 76.

14. *2006 Metropolitan Transportation Plan* (Sacramento), p. 3.

15. Michael Penic, "Addressing Congestion and Air Quality Issues through Highway Planning," paper presented to the Preserving the American Dream Conference, Washington, DC, February 24, 2003.

16. O'Toole, *The Best-Laid Plans*, pp. 163–66.

17. Edward Weiner, *Urban Transportation Planning in the United States: An Historical Overview* (Washington: U.S. Department of Transportation, 1997), p. 24.

18. Ibid., pp. 25–26.

19. Ibid., pp. 30, 59.

20. Ibid., pp. 71–73.

21. Robert Cervero et al., "BART@20: Land Use and Development Impacts," Working Paper no. 308, University of California Transportation Center, 1995, p. 1, tinyurl.com/2w2t33.

22. Ibid., p. 8.

23. Weiner, *Urban Transportation Planning in the United States: An Historical Overview*, p. 91.

24. Shorey Peterson, "The Highway from the Point of View of the Economist," in *Highways in Our National Life: A Symposium*, ed. Jean Labatut and Wheaton J. Lane (Princeton, NJ: Princeton University Press, 1950), p. 194.

25. Ronald Utt, "A Primer on Lobbyists, Earmarks, and Congressional Reform," The Heritage Foundation Backgrounder no. 1924, April 27, 2006, table 1, tinyurl.com/2jfkhu.

26. Bonnie E. Browne, "Rational Planning and Responsiveness: The Case of the HSAs," *Public Administration Review* 41, no. 4 (July–August 1981): 437.

27. *2030 San Diego Regional Transportation Plan: Final* (San Diego, CA: San Diego Association of Governments, 2007), p. 2-2.

28. *2030 Regional Transportation Plan* (Portland, OR: Metro, 2004), p. 3-1.

29. *New Visions 2030: The Plan for a Quality Region: Summary Document* (Albany, NY: Capital District Transportation Committee, 2007), p. 15.

30. *2030 San Diego Regional Transportation Plan: Final*, p. 5-28.

31. *2030 Long Range Transportation Plan* (Nashville, TN: Nashville Area MPO, 2006), p. 76

32. *Envision6: 2030 Regional Transportation* Plan (Atlanta, GA: Atlanta Regional Commission, 2007), p. 36.

33. *Regional Transportation Plan 2007–2030* (Salt Lake City, UT: Wasatch Front Regional Council, 2007), p. 106.

34. *2030 Long Range Transportation Plan* (Savannah, GA: Chatham County-Savannah MPO, 2004), p. 11.

35. *New Visions 2030: The Plan for a Quality Region: Summary Document* (Albany), p. 15.

36. *2030 San Diego Regional Transportation Plan: Final*, p. 2-3.

37. *Regional Transportation Plan 2007–2030* (Salt Lake City), p. 43.

38. *MAPA 2030 Long Range Transportation Plan* (Omaha, NE: Metropolitan Area Planning Agency, 2006), p. 14.

39. *2030 Long-Range Transportation Plan for the Erie and Niagara Counties Region* (Buffalo, NY: Greater Buffalo-Niagara Region, 2007), p. 27.

40. *Access and Mobility 2030: Regional Transportation Plan* (Newark, NJ: North Jersey Transportation Planning Authority, 2005), p. 34, tinyurl.com/2y2orv.

41. U.S. Code 23, § 134(h)(1).

42. *2030 Long Range Transportation Plan* (Nashville), pp. 87–88.

43. *2006 American Community Survey* (Washington: Census Bureau, 2007), table S0801, "Commuting Characteristics by Sex," Nashville-Davidson, TN, Urbanized Area, tinyurl.com/3xcubv.

44. *2030 Long Range Transportation Plan* (Nashville), p. 88.

45. *2030 Long Range Transportation Plan: Summary* (Jacksonville, FL: First Coast MPO, 2005), p. 5, tinyurl.com/3deeml.

46. *The North Front Range 2030 Regional Transportation Plan* (Ft. Collins, CO: North Front Range MPO, 2004), p. 168.

47. Metropolitan Transportation Commission, *Bay Area Transportation Blueprint for the 21st Century: Evaluation Report* (Oakland, CA: MTC, 2000), figure 11.

48. *MTC, Where Are Our Buses? Challenging the Bay Area's Separate and Unequal Transit System* (Oakland, CA: Communities for a Better Environment, 2006), tinyurl. com/3b9shj.

49. *CAMPO Mobility 2030 Plan* (Austin, TX: Capital Area Metropolitan Planning Organization, 2005), p. 36, tinyurl.com/ywwo2s.

50. *2025 Long-Range Plan for Erie and Niagara Counties* (Buffalo: Greater Buffalo-Niagara Regional Planning Council, 2001), pp. 9-1, 11-2.

51. *2030 Long Range Transportation Plan: Needs Plan* (Jacksonville, FL: First Coast Metropolitan Planning Organization, 2005), pp. 7-3–7-4, tinyurl.com/35op2s.

52. *Wasatch Front Urban Area Long Range Transportation Plan* (Salt Lake City, UT: Wasatch Front Regional Council, 2007), pp. 50–52, tinyurl.com/ksmpag.

53. *2025 Long-Range Plan for Erie and Niagara Counties* (Buffalo), pp. 9-1, 11-2.

54. *2030 Long-Range Transportation Plan for the Erie and Niagara Counties Region* (Buffalo: Greater Buffalo-Niagara Regional Planning Council, 2007), tinyurl.com/ 27594s.

55. *2030 Lang Range Transportation Plan: Needs Plan* (Jacksonville), pp. 7-3–7-4.

56. *Wasatch Front Urban Area Long Range Transportation Plan* (Salt Lake City, UT: Wasatch Front Regional Council, 2007), p. 107, tinyurl.com/yp63pr.

57. *Wasatch Front Urban Area Long Range Transportation Plan* (Salt Lake City, UT: Wasatch Front Regional Council, 2007), pp. 209–73, tinyurl.com/ys87xb. The transportation effects are described in four paragraphs on page 230.

58. *Draft 2008 Regional Transportation Plan* (Los Angeles, CA: Southern California Association of Governments, 2008), p. 172.

59. David Cox, "FHwA Comments on Draft 1.0 Regional Transportation Vision," Federal Highway Administration letter to Metro, Portland, OR, January 2007, tinyurl.com/lmd8qv.

60. "More Than One-Third Say Traffic Congestion Is a Serious Problem in Their Community," *The Harris Poll* 16 (February 22, 2007), tinyurl.com/2veece.

61. Schrank and Lomax, *The 2007 Urban Mobility Report*, p. 1.

62. *Legacy 2035* (St. Louis, MO: East-West Gateway Coordinating Council, 2007), p. 102, tinyurl.com/yqk8ma.

63. *2005 National Transit Database*, tables 1, "operating funds and fares," and 5, "capital funds"; *Highway Statistics 2006*, table HF10. Highway subsidies are calculated by subtracting diversions of highway user fees to transit and nonhighway purposes from property, income, and other taxes and dividing the remainder by the total expenditure on highways.

64. *A Review of the Transportation Prioritization Process* (Salt Lake City, UT: Legislative Auditor General, 2007), pp. 5–6, tinyurl.com/35uw36.

65. Ibid., p. 7.

66. Ibid., p. 1.

67. Salt Lake County Council of Governments, "Minutes," November 26, 2007, meeting of the Expanded COG, Salt Lake County Council of Governments, p. 4, tinyurl.com/2jyfax.

68. *A Performance Audit of the Utah Transit Authority* (Salt Lake City, UT: Legislative Auditor General, 2008), p. 54, tinyurl.com/2aj5bw.

69. Brandon Loomis, "New TRAX Passenger Tracking System Shows Ridership Lower Than Thought," *Salt Lake Tribune*, December 19, 2007.

70. Lave, "The Mass Transit Panacea and Other Fallacies about Energy."

71. O'Toole, *Does Rail Transit Save Energy or Reduce Greenhouse Gas Emissions?*, tables 1 and 5.

72. *2004 Regional Transportation Plan* (Portland, OR: Metro, 2004), p. 5-6.

73. Transit's current share of passenger miles is calculated from *Highway Statistics 2005*, table HM72 (with vehicle miles multiplied by 1.6 to get passenger miles), and *2005 National Transit Database*, table 19. The increase in transit's share of passenger miles is assumed to be proportional to the increase in transit's share of trips.

74. *2030 Metro Vision Regional Transportation Plan* (Denver, CO: DRCOG, 2005), p. 113, tinyurl.com/yvqzte.

75. *OKI 2030 Regional Transportation Plan* (Cincinnati, OH: Ohio-Kentucky-Indiana Regional Council, 2001), p. 7-6.

76. *OKI 2030 Regional Transportation Plan 2004 Update* (Cincinnati, OH: Ohio-Kentucky-Indiana Regional Council, 2004), p. 8-6.

77. Ibid., p. 8-8.

78. *Transportation Redefined II* (St. Louis, MO: East-West Gateway Coordinating Council, 2000), pp. 13, 19; *Legacy 2035* (St. Louis), p. 90.

79. *2006 Metropolitan Transportation Plan* (Sacramento, CA: SACOG, 2006), p. 17.

80. Ibid., pp. 22–23.

81. *Transportation 2030 Plan for the San Francisco Bay Area* (Oakland, CA: Metropolitan Transportation Commission, 2005), p. 64, www.mtc.ca.gov/planning/2030_plan/downloads/final_2030_plan/5-Investments_T2030Plan.pdf.

82. Ibid., p. 65.

83. *2035 Metro Vision Regional Transportation Plan* (Denver, CO: DRCOG, 2007), pp. 20–23.

84. *2004 Regional Transportation Plan* (Portland, OR: Metro, 2004), p. 1-1.

85. *Regional Framework Plan* (Portland, OR: Metro, 1997), p. 23.

86. *Southern California Compass Growth Vision Report* (Los Angeles, CA: Southern California Association of Governments, 2004), pp. 81, 88, 91.

87. *2035 Metro Vision Regional Transportation Plan* (Denver), p. 123; *2004 Regional Transportation Plan* (Portland, OR), p. 5-4.

88. *The Relationship between Air Quality and Urban Development Patterns: Analysis and Prospectus for Sensitivity Testing* (Denver, CO: DRCOG, 1977), pp. 24, 26.

89. Ibid., p. 16.

90. Ibid., p. 14.

91. *TSM Sensitivity Report: An Analysis of the Potential for Transportation System Management Strategies in the Denver Area* (Denver, CO: DRCOG, 1979), p. ii.

92. *An Evaluation of Designated Regional Activity Centers in the Denver Metropolitan Area* (Denver, CO: DRCOG, 1981), p. 1.

93. *2035 Metro Vision Regional Transportation Plan* (Denver), p. 36.

94. Peter Drucker, *The New Realities* (New York: Harper & Row, 1989), p. 64.

Chapter 9

1. E. L. Doctorow, *World's Fair* (New York: Random House, 1985).

2. Roland Marchand, "The Designers Go to the Fair, II: Norman Bel Geddes, The General Motors 'Futurama,' and the Visit to the Factory Transformed," in *Design History: An Anthology*, ed. Dennis P. Doordan (Cambridge, MA: MIT Press, 1995), p. 111.

3. Norman Bel Geddes, *Horizons* (Boston: Little, Brown, 1932), p. 5.

4. Marchand, "The Designers Go to the Fair, II," pp. 107–8.

5. Ibid., p. 109.

6. Norman Bel Geddes, *Magic Motorways* (New York: Random House, 1940), p. ii.

7. Ibid., p. 288.

8. Ibid., pp. 73–75.

9. Ibid., cover.

10. Ibid., p. 10.

11. *Performance Audit Report: Managing and Reducing Congestion in Puget Sound* (Olympia, WA: Washington State Auditor, 2007), p. 10.

12. *Addressing the Safety Issues Related to Younger and Older Drivers* (Washington: National Highway Traffic Safety Administration, 1993), figure 16, tinyurl.com/9dngro.

13. Robert N. Charette, "This Car Runs on Code," *IEEE Spectrum*, February 2009, tinyurl.com/apd5lq.

14. "25 Years of 'Eureka' Moments," *USA Today*, May 20, 2007, tinyurl.com/8zedm5.

15. "Congestion Pricing/Variable Tolls," *Tollroads News*, January 30, 2009, tinyurl.com/de6yv3.

16. Xi Zou, "Simulation and Analysis of Mixed Adaptive Cruise Control/Manual Traffic," thesis submitted to the University of Minnesota, Minneapolis, MN, March 2001, rational.ce.umn.edu/Theses/XiZou_Thesis.pdf.

17. "Nissan Demos New Lane Keeping Products," *IVSource*, February 12, 2001, tinyurl.com/os335p.

18. Mark Arnold, "Ford Introduces New Blind-Spot System," *Jalopnik*, April 9, 2008, tinyurl.com/dbwxx6; "Collision Free Cars Are Coming," *The Future of Things*, October 15, 2008, tinyurl.com/dkogj2.

19. Terri O'Connor, "Lane Change Aid," *ITS Decision*, April 19, 2004, tinyurl.com/qd8rnn.

20. Mike Schagrin, *Cooperative Intersection Vehicle Avoidance System Initiative* (Washington: Department of Transportation, 2004), tinyurl.com/73n8ov.

21. Lee Armstrong, "IEEE P802.11 Task Group P Meeting Update," IEEE, 2008, tinyurl.com/az2agc.

22. "1. Demo '97 in San Diego, California," *Vehicle Demonstrations*, PATH, 2004, tinyurl.com/caj3wo.

23. Han-Shue Tan, "Automated Rotary Plow Demonstration," in *California PATH Annual Report 2003* (Richmond, CA: PATH, 2004), p. 18.

24. Denis Cuff, "Bus of Future Rolled Out for First Test Drive," *Oakland Tribune*, September 5, 2008, tinyurl.com/ld8u2f.

25. Sarah Yang, "Researchers Showcase Automated Bus That Uses Magnets to Steer through City Streets," *UC Berkeley News*, September 5, 2008, tinyurl.com/7jf54u.

26. Stefanie Olsen, "Stanford Wins $2 Million in Robotic Car Race," CNET News, October 9, 2005, tinyurl.com/n8mt43.

27. "Carnegie Mellon Tartan Racing Wins $2 Million DARPA Urban Challenge," Carnegie Mellon, 2007, tinyurl.com/bubjdg.

28. "Technology," Carnegie Mellon Tartan Racing, 2007, tinyurl.com/bcgz92.

29. Bel Geddes, *Magic Motorways*, pp. 75–76.

30. Chuck Squatriglia, "GM Says Driverless Cars Could Be on the Road by 2018," Associated Press, January 7, 2008, tinyurl.com/7njotq.

31. Ibid.

32. *National Transportation Statistics* (Washington: Bureau of Transportation Statistics, 2009 online update), table 1-25, tinyurl.com/5oszkn.

33. "You Can See the Blood on Color Video," *Washington Post*, January 15, 1950, p. L1.

34. "Wired, Zapped, and Beamed, 1960s through 1980s," in *Communications History* (Washington: Federal Communications Commission, 2005), tinyurl.com/dbwox4.

35. Salvador Alvarez et al., *HDTV: The Engineering History* (Cambridge, MA: MIT, 1999), p. 11, tinyurl.com/aysf6k.

36. Charles Platt, "The Great HDTV Swindle," *Wired*, February 1997, tinyurl.com/cky9t5.

37. Adam D. Thierer, "The HDTV Transition: What Went Wrong?" Cato Institute, May 1, 2002, tinyurl.com/c8vos5.

38. "Towards Smarter, Safer and Cleaner Cars," i2010 Intelligent Car Initiative, European Commission, 2007, tinyurl.com/73lny9.

39. "Cars That Talk: Commission Earmarks Single Radio Frequency for Road Safety and Traffic Management," *Europa* (Brussels: European Commission, 2008), tinyurl.com/9hd6or.

Chapter 10

1. Brian Reidl, fellow in federal budgetary affairs, The Heritage Foundation, "Discretionary Spending Trends: Past, Present, and Future," testimony before the House Budget Committee, February 16, 2006, p. 6, tinyurl.com/p2wr3v.

2. *Fiscal Year 2009 Budget in Brief* (Washington: Department of Transportation, 2008), p. 74.

3. *Budget in Brief Fiscal Year 2009* (Washington: Federal Aviation Administration, 2008), p. 11.

4. *Fiscal Year 2009 Budget in Brief*, p. 74.

5. Ibid.

6. "Federal Economic Stimulus—Information by Transportation Mode," Florida Department of Transportation, 2009, tinyurl.com/p5j2hk.

7. Eamonn Butler and Keith Boyfield, *Around the World in 80 Ideas* (London: Adam Smith Institute, 2001), chapter 23, tinyurl.com/bt5m63.

8. Ronald Utt, "Proposal to Turn the Federal Highway Program Back to the States Would Relieve Traffic Congestion," The Heritage Foundation Backgrounder no. 1709, November 21, 2003, tinyurl.com/alcyxw.

9. Ira Carnahan, "Let States Keep Their Gas Taxes," *Forbes*, August 3, 2005, tinyurl.com/d25jen.

10. *Highway Statistics 2006*, table MF-121T.

11. Ibid., tables DF, FE-9, and LGF-21.

12. U.S. Code 23 § 134(i), U.S. Code 23 § 135(f), U.S. Code 49 § 5304(f), U.S. Code 49 § 5303(i).

13. *Review of FasTracks Options and Additional Analysis* (Denver, CO: RTD, 2008), p. 7, tinyurl.com/63aj2j.

14. Joel Schwartz, "Clearing the Air," *PERC Reports* 26, no. 1 (Spring 2008): 12–15, tinyurl.com/669ngv.

15. Arnold M. Howitt and Alan Altschuler, "The Politics of Controlling Auto Air Pollution," in *Essays in Transportation Economics and Policy: A Handbook in Honor of John R. Meyer*, ed. J. Gomez-Ibanez, W. B. Tye, and C. Winston (Washington: National Academy Press, 1999), p. 225.

16. Ibid., p. 241.

17. Utt, *A Primer on Lobbyists, Earmarks, and Congressional Reform*.

18. Charles Lave, "It Wasn't Supposed to Turn out Like This: Federal Subsidies and Declining Transit Productivity," *Access* 5 (Fall 1994): 21.

19. *2008 Public Transportation Fact Book*, tables 5 and 46.

20. *National Transportation Statistics* (2008), tables 1-37, 3-07, and 3-16; *2006 National Transit Database*, spreadsheets "capital use" and "operating expenses"; *National Economic Accounts* (Washington: Bureau of Economic Analysis, 2008), table 2.5.5; *2006 Annual Report* (Washington: Amtrak, 2007), p. 20.

21. U.S. Code 49 § 5333(b).

22. *2007 National Transit Database*, spreadsheets "operating expenses" and "service."

23. Ibid., spreadsheet "service."

24. Kevin Flynn, "Union Aims to Nix Mandated Level of RTD Contractors," *Rocky Mountain News*, February 7, 2007, tinyurl.com/8aohrq.

25. *2006 Public Transportation Fact Book* (Washington: American Public Transportation Association, 2006), tables 7 and 23; *2008 Public Transportation Fact Book*, tables 5 and 23.

Chapter 11

1. *Highway Statistics 2006*, table SDF.

2. Ibid.

3. Ibid.

4. Ibid.

5. Ibid., table SF-1.

6. Ibid., table LGF-4B.

7. *2006 National Transit Database*, tables 5 & 9.

8. "The United States of Transit Cutbacks," Transportation for America, 2009, tinyurl.com/cr8yfp.

9. Patrick Driscoll, "Details Offered on Bus, Toll Agency," *San Antonio Express-News*, February 6, 2009, tinyurl.com/bdv2j8.

Chapter 12

1. *Historical Statistics of the United States: Colonial Times to 1970*, p. 728; *Highway Statistics Summary to 1995*, table VM-201; Bureau of Economic Analysis, "Personal Incomes Expenditures by Type of Expenditure," table 2.5.5, bea.gov.

2. Based on transit's average cost of 81 cents a mile and driving's average cost of 24 cents a mile, both numbers including capital, maintenance, and operating costs. See Bureau of Economic Analysis, "Personal Incomes Expenditures by Type of Expenditure," table 2.5.5, bea.gov.

3. "Report: 98 Percent of U.S. Commuters Favor Public Transportation for Others," *The Onion*, November 29, 2000, tinyurl.com/4wvsx3.

4. Eliot Brown, "Paterson Launches Panel to Find M.T.A. Much-Needed Money," *New York Observer*, June 10, 2008, tinyurl.com/3jqlub.

5. Paige Kollock, "New Yorkers Mostly Hostile to Suggested Congestion Charge," *City Mayors*, June 11, 2007, tinyurl.com/a82et3.

Index

Page references followed by t refer to tables.

265

About the Author

Randal O'Toole is a senior fellow at the Cato Institute who has written three previous books and numerous papers on transportation, urban growth, and public land issues, including his most recent book, *The Best-Laid Plans: How Government Planning Harms Your Quality of Life, Your Pocketbook, and Your Future*. Described by *U.S. News and World Report* as a researcher who "has earned a reputation for dogged legwork and sophisticated number crunching," he has been a leader in innovative thinking on environmentalism, natural resources, and urban land use. From 1975 through 1995, O'Toole helped the nation's leading environmental groups eliminate government subsidies that were harmful to the environment. In 1998, Yale University named O'Toole its McCluskey Conservation Fellow. He was the Scaife Visiting Scholar at UC Berkeley in 1999 and 2001 and the Merrill Visiting Professor at Utah State University in 2000. In 2003, he helped form the American Dream Coalition, which is a grassroots group that promotes free-market solutions to urban problems. An Oregon native, O'Toole currently resides in Camp Sherman, Oregon.

Cato Institute

Founded in 1977, the Cato Institute is a public policy research foundation dedicated to broadening the parameters of policy debate to allow consideration of more options that are consistent with the traditional American principles of limited government, individual liberty, and peace. To that end, the Institute strives to achieve greater involvement of the intelligent, concerned lay public in questions of policy and the proper role of government.

The Institute is named for *Cato's Letters*, libertarian pamphlets that were widely read in the American Colonies in the early 18th century and played a major role in laying the philosophical foundation for the American Revolution.

Despite the achievement of the nation's Founders, today virtually no aspect of life is free from government encroachment. A pervasive intolerance for individual rights is shown by government's arbitrary intrusions into private economic transactions and its disregard for civil liberties.

To counter that trend, the Cato Institute undertakes an extensive publications program that addresses the complete spectrum of policy issues. Books, monographs, and shorter studies are commissioned to examine the federal budget, Social Security, regulation, military spending, international trade, and myriad other issues. Major policy conferences are held throughout the year, from which papers are published thrice yearly in the *Cato Journal*. The Institute also publishes the quarterly magazine *Regulation*.

In order to maintain its independence, the Cato Institute accepts no government funding. Contributions are received from foundations, corporations, and individuals, and other revenue is generated from the sale of publications. The Institute is a nonprofit, tax-exempt, educational foundation under Section 501(c)3 of the Internal Revenue Code.

CATO INSTITUTE
1000 Massachusetts Ave., N.W.
Washington, D.C. 20001
www.cato.org